An Index to
Biographical Fragments
in Unspecialized
Scientific Journals

by

E. SCOTT BARR

The University of Alabama Press
UNIVERSITY, ALABAMA

To my wife

Phoebe

for encouragement, enthusiasm,

and endurance

Contents

This index has two functions. It provides a means for readily locating biographical information and contemporary comment, both fragmentary and extensive, concerning distinguished persons who, prior to about 1920, were active in the sciences (most commonly, but not exclusively). Such biographical fragments are often difficult to find, for they are frequently not indexed. The other function of this work is to make possible the location of information concerning another larger group of individuals—people who were admired and respected by their contemporaries but are now generally unknown. For many in this second group it is almost impossible to find anything at all in commonly available sources to supplement the ephemeral notices cited here.

For persons fortunate enough to have access to libraries having extensive holdings of scientific journals, this list serves as a comprehensive composite index for material scattered through many volumes of different journals. On the other hand, where local journal holdings are incomplete or inadequate, the citations given here provide an efficient means for arranging for photocopying or interlibrary loans.

The preparation of this index came as a consequence of finding that I needed such a reference work when I was collecting information of a biographical nature about early workers in the field of physics, especially those men who were, as now seen in perspective, of second-order importance. It began with a search through the volumes of NATURE to find the "Scientific Worthies" sketches scattered through its volumes. This grew into a spare-time activity and involved the page-by-page scanning of many volumes of bound journals, during a number of years while I was on the staff of the Physics Department of The University of Alabama. I limited my survey to English language journals, and to those concerned with the whole spectrum of the sciences, not just one science. Each journal was scanned from its first issue up to about 1920 (with some exceptions), on the assumption that since then biographical material is relatively readily available. Citations were made only of information about individuals, not of items by them, and were made for all persons—scientists and nonscientists—found mentioned by name. Notations were also made of the locations of the many portraits found.

This index covers about 7700 individuals, providing about 15,000 citations and about 1500 portrait locations which were found in the following:

A AMERICAN JOURNAL OF SCIENCE, 200 volumes, the first four series, covering the period 1819 to 1920.

E PROCEEDINGS OF THE EDINBURGH ROYAL SOCIETY, 40 volumes, covering the period 1832 to 1920.

L PROCEEDINGS OF THE ROYAL SOCIETY (of London), 172 volumes, covering the period 1800 to 1905 in its first series (75 volumes), the subsequent series A from 1905 to 1931-1932 (60 volumes) and series

B   from 1905 to 1932-1933 (37 volumes). For this particular jour-
     nal my scanning was extended to cover all volumes up to the time
     when the Society began publishing its obituary notices of members
     separately from its journal.
N   NATURE, 100 volumes, covering the period 1869 to 1918. This was
     the first journal scanned, and the termination with volume 100 was
     arbitrary.
P   POPULAR SCIENCE MONTHLY, 87 volumes, covering the period 1872 to
     1915, at which time the nature of the publication was radically
     altered and biographical information was no longer included.
PM   PHILOSOPHICAL MAGAZINE, 210 volumes (the first five series), cover-
     ing the period 1798 to 1902, when publication of biographical ma-
     terial stopped.
S1   SCIENCE, First Series, 24 volumes, covering the period from 1883
     to 1894. This prefix is used to distinguish volumes in this series
     from similarly numbered volumes in the "New Series."
S   SCIENCE, New Series, 50 volumes, covering the period 1895 to 1919.

The fragments as found in the journals were frequently incomplete,
imprecise, or inaccurate, so it was felt advisable to add information
which would help to identify clearly the person being cited. Most entries, therefore, give the full name of the person, his specialty (if
determinable), and his nationality. This necessitated for each person
a comparison of the citation information with that available from the
Catalogue of Scientific Papers of the Royal Society of London, Poggen-
dorff's Biographische- und Literarische Handworterbuch, American Men of
Science, the Index Biographique of the Academy of France, and other
standard reference works. For the many people for whom complete reference biographical information is missing or not available, it is
hoped that the additional descriptive material here will provide some
useful ready data.
     It is appropriate here for me to ask the user's indulgence for the
errors which surely have been made—or perpetuated—here. Different
"standard" sources often disagree concerning the spelling of a man's
name or his dates. Birth and death dates were often troublesome because of journal imprecision. Frequently the January issue of a journal reports that so-and-so died "recently," thus making the year of
death uncertain, being possibly either of two years. Many times the
birth date had to be inferred from the statement that so-and-so "died
at the age of...," with no indication as to whether his death came just
before or just after his birthday. Consequently, for many of the death
dates followed by ?, the correct date is probably that given or the
preceding year. The designations of a man's specialty and his native
land often had to be determined by inference from internal evidence;
hence these can be unreliable. They are included as a help in discrim-
inating between persons, especially contemporaries, of very similar
names.
     The arrangement of the entries in alphabetical order by family
name involved some arbitrary decisions. In general, prefixes such as
de, della, d', von, etc., have been ignored in alphabetizing: for in-
stance von Helmholtz is entered under H. However, in some cases names
of this kind have become almost inseparable by custom and are treated
accordingly (for example, Dutch names such as Van der Waals, which is

under V, and American families of European origin). Cross-references have been given in a few cases, but it was felt that ordinarily the name can be found with but little trouble under another probable letter when not located where first sought. All in all, alphabetization proved to be a difficult and frustrating matter, particularly with regard to transliterated Russian names.

In preparing this index, a series of checks and verifications was employed, and proof was read carefully at each stage. Despite such precautions, it seems likely that errors are still present here, especially in the spelling of unusual names and possibly in the transposition of numerals. At the end of this index are tables giving volume number and publication date for the runs covered here. These tables are provided for possible help when a citation is not found at the indicated place because of an undetected error in either the volume or its date.

In carrying out this compilation—which I would never have undertaken had I known what the compilation would involve—I have been helped by many able and generous people. Members of the staff of the Library of The University of Alabama, particularly those in the Science Library and in the Interlibrary Loan Office, have given invaluable aid. The completion of this index was possible only because of the admirable journal collection of the Library and the generous loans of a few missing volumes by other libraries.

I am grateful for the sponsorship of parts of my project by The University of Alabama Research Grants Committee, under their project numbers 475 and 626, through provision of grants to cover released time for me during several summers, and for funds for supplies and typing costs. In this connection I want to thank also Mrs. Amanda K. Rice for her excellent typing of most of the final draft of my manuscript.

I am most thankful to The University of Alabama Financial Aids Office, which supervises the students' work-study program, for providing me with help by Phyllis Burnett, Donna Breedlove, and James Brasher. The intelligent, reliable, and concerned assistance of these young people was invaluable; their help in verifying citations and checking names and dates saved me many hours of labor.

In addition to all those mentioned above and to those who gave encouragement when it was most appropriate, and who jointly made the completion of my project possible, I am indebted to the staff of The University of Alabama Press, who so ably and cooperatively converted my manuscript into this volume.

Tuscaloosa, Alabama   E. Scott Barr

- - - - - - - - - - - - - - - - - - - -

ABBREVIATIONS USED (in addition to the letters identifying the journals indicated in the foreword): P = portrait, f = frontispiece, fp = facing page.

An Index to
Biographical Fragments
in Unspecialized
Scientific Journals

ADAMS, CHARLES F., physics,
1854?-1914, U.S.A.
S 40 (1914) 780
S 42 (1915) 826
ADAMS, CHARLES KENDALL,
education, 1835-1902, U.S.A.
S 16 (1902) 158, 197
ADAMS, CHARLES LADAN, drawing,
-1914, U.S.A.
S 40 (1914) 479
ADAMS, HERBERT BAXTER,
history, 1850-1901, U.S.A.
S 14 (1901) 228
ADAMS, ISAAC, chemistry,
1836-   , U.S.A.
S 21 (1905) 875-876
ADAMS, JOHN COUCH, astronomy,
1819-1892, England
A 143 (1892) 248
E 20 (1892-1895) 12, i-v
L 5 (1843-1850) 773
N 34 (1886) P 565-566
N 45 (1892) 301-302
N 49 (1893) 67
N 56 (1897) 73-75
N 64 (1901) 576
P 41 (1892) P fp 433,
545-550
PM V 43 (1897) 71-72
PM V 50 (1900) 617-618
S 1 (1895) 640
ADAMS, WILLIAM GRYLLS,
astronomy-physics, 1836-
1915, England
A 189 (1915) 686
L A91 (1914-1915) lxiii-
lxiv
N 95 (1915) 211-212
S 41 (1915) 641
ADAMSON, DANIEL, engineering,
1818-1890, England
N 41 (1890) 281
ADAMSON, ROBERT, philosophy,
1852-1902, Scotland
N 15 (1902) 318
ADEMELLO, ALFONSO, medicine,
-1896?, Italy
S 3 (1896) 98
ADENSAMER, THEODOR, biology,
-1900, Austria
S 12 (1900) 1014
ADERHOLD, RUDOLF FERDINAND
THEODOR, biology, 1865-
1907, Germany
S 25 (1907) 599, 798

ADIE, ALEXANDER JAMES,
engineering-optics, 1808-
1878, Scotland
E 4 (1857-1862) 225-227
E 10 (1878-1880) 329
AFANASIEV, VASSILI A.,
anatomy, 1849?-1904, Russia
S 19 (1904) 398-399
AFSCHULTEN, BENJAMIN AUGUST,
chemistry, 1856?-1912,
Denmark
S 36 (1912) 628
AFZELIUS, ADAM, biology,
1750-1836, Sweden
A 33 (1837-1838) 211
L 4 (1837-1843) 18
AGARDH, KARL ADOLF, botany,
1785-1859, Sweden
A 79 (1860) 441
AGARDH, JAKOB GEORG,
phycology, 1813-1901,
Sweden
A 161 (1901) 332
N 63 (1901) 377-378
S 13 (1901) 356
AGASSIZ, ALEXANDRE EMMANUEL
RODOLPH, geology-zoology,
1835-1910, Switzerland
A 179 (1910) 464
N 83 (1910) 163
N 92 (1914) 601-604
P 71 (1907) P 378-379
P 76 (1910) 514-517
P 77 (1910) P 418-446,
515
P 82 (1913) P 618
Sl 5 (1885) 140, 472
Sl 6 (1885) 258
S 31 (1910) 497, 574, 614
S 33 (1911) 873-887
AGASSIZ, ELIZABETH CABOT CARY
(MRS. LOUIS), biology-
education, 1822-1907,
U.S.A.
N 26 (1907) 30
S 16 (1902) 1039
AGASSIZ, JEAN LOUIS RODOLPHE,
geology-zoology, 1807-1873,
Switzerland
A 107 (1874) 77-80, 446-
448
A 110 (1875) 485-487
A 118 (1879) 346
L 25 (1877) xxii-xxx
N 19 (1879) P 573-576

AGASSIZ (continued)
  N 33 (1886) 289-291
  N 48 (1893) 52-53
  N 53 (1896) 529-530
  P   4 (1873-1874) P fr,
      495-499, 608-618, 633,
      637
  P 32 (1887-1888) 17-26
  P 62 (1902-1903) P 332
  P 70 (1907) 304-306, P 566-
      569
  P 71 (1907) 5-20, 542-549
  Sl 6 (1885) 258, 330-332,
      P fp 344, 360, 421-424
  Sl 12 (1888) P 298
  S   3 (1896) 745-746
  S   5 (1897) 285-289
  S 10 (1899) 630-632
  S 14 (1901) 177
  S 37 (1913) 783
AGNESI, MARIA GAETANA,
  mathematics, 1718-1799,
  Italy
  P 53 (1898) P fp 289,
      403-409
AGNEW, CORNELIUS REA,
  education-ophthalmology,
  1830-1888, U.S.A.
  Sl 11 (1888) 195
AGNEW, SIR STAIR, law,
  1831-1916, Scotland
  E 37 (1916-1917) 11
AGRAMONTE, ARISTIDES,
  bacteriology, 1869-1931,
  Cuba
  P 87 (1915) P 174
AGRICOLA, GEORGIUS (GEORG
  BAUER), mineralogy, 1490?-
  1555, Germany
  A 118 (1879) 327
  S 27 (1908) 54
AHRENS, FELIX BENJAMIN,
  chemistry, 1863-1910,
  Poland
  S 32 (1910) 915
AIKIN, ARTHUR, geology,
  1773-1854, England
  A 70 (1855) 391-392
AIMÉ, GEORGES, astronomy-
  physics, 1810-1846,
  France
  A 53 (1847) 143-144

AIRY, SIR GEORGE BIDDELL,
  astronomy, 1801-1892,
  England
  A 143 (1892) 248
  E 19 (1891-1892) i-viii
  E 20 (1892-1895) 12
  L   3 (1830-1837) 89-90
  L   5 (1843-1850) 575
  L 51 (1892) i-xxi
  N 18 (1878) P 689-691
  N 45 (1892) 232-233
  N 55 (1896) 145-146
  P   3 (1873) P fr, 101-104
  Sl 19 (1892) 64-65
  S 10 (1899) 963
AITCHISON, JAMES EDWARD
  TIERNEY, botany, 1835-1898,
  India
  E 22 (1897-1899) 717-718
  L 64 (1899) xi-xiii
  N 58 (1898) 578
AITKEN, ANDREW PEEBLES,
  chemistry,   -1904,
  Scotland
  S 19 (1904) 743
AITKEN, DAVID, theology,
  c. 1800-1875, Scotland
  E   9 (1875-1878) 14-15
AITKEN, JOHN, meteorology,
  1839-1919, Scotland
  A 199 (1920) 86
  E 22 (1897-1899) 707-708
  N 100 (1917) 276
AITKEN, SIR WILLIAM, medicine,
  1825-1892, England
  L 55 (1894) xiv-xvi
ALBANESE, MANFREDI,
  pharmacology,   -1913,
  Italy
  S 37 (1913) 516
ALBERDARE, SIR HENRY AUSTIN
  BRUCE, government, 1815-
  1895, England
  L 59 (1896) xiv-xv
ALBERTSON, MRS. MARY A.,
  botany,   -1914, U.S.A.
  S 40 (1914) 341
ALBERTUS MAGNUS (ALBERT OF
  COLOGNE: COUNT von
  BOLLSTÄDT), science,
  c. 1200-1280, Germany
  P 71 (1907) P 87

AL-BÎRÛNÎ (Abu Rayhan Muhammad
Ibm Ahmad), science, 973-
1050?, Persia
N 38 (1888) 97-98
ALBRECHT, CARL THEODOR,
geodesy, 1843-1915,
Germany
A 190 (1915) 670
N 96 (1915) 150
S 42 (1915) 524
ALCOCK, ALFRED WILLIAM,
zoology, 1859-1935, Scot-
land
N 64 (1901) 36
ALCOCK, NATHANIEL HENRY,
physiology, 1871-1913,
Canada
S 38 (1913) 22
ALCOCK, SIR RUTHERFORD,
geography, 1809-1897,
England
S 6 (1897) 732
ALDERMAN, EDWIN ANDERSON, edu-
cation, 1861-1931, U.S.A.
P 67 (1905) P 281-285
ALDERSON, SIR JAMES, medicine,
1794-1833?, England
L 34 (1883) vi-vii
ALDINI, GIOVANNI, physics,
1762-1834, Italy
A 27 (1834-1835) 405
ALDRICH, CHARLES, history-
ornithology, 1828-1909,
U.S.A.
S 29 (1909) 610
ALDROVANDI, ULISSE, biology,
1522-1605, Italy
N 76 (1907) 282-283
S 26 (1907) 159
d'ALEMBERT, JEAN LeROND,
mathematics-physics,
1717-1783, France
S 1 (1895) 141-157
ALEXANDER, A.B., statistics,
-1916, U.S.A.
S 44 (1916) 707
ALEXANDER, BÉLA, radiology,
1859?-1916, Hungary
S 43 (1916) 492
ALEXANDER, BOYD, exploration-
zoology, 1873-1910, England
S 31 (1910) 901
ALEXANDER, SIR JAMES EDWARD,
archeology-exploration,
1803-1885, Scotland
E 13 (1884-1886) 357-358
E 14 (1886-1887) 170-174

ALEXANDER, JOHN HENRY, geodesy,
1812-1867, U.S.A.
Sl 21 (1893) 291
ALEXANDER, ROBERT, law, 1795-
1843, England
L 5 (1843-1850) 488
ALEXANDER, SAMUEL, botany,
1837?-1917, U.S.A.
S 45 (1917) 498-499
ALEXANDER, STEPHEN, astro-
physics, 1806-1883, U.S.A.
Sl 2 (1883) 27
S 10 (1899) 675
ALEXANDER, WILLIAM LINDSAY,
theology, 1808-1884,
Scotland
E 13 (1884-1886) 354-355
E 14 (1886-1887) 138-143
ALGER, FRANCIS, mineralogy,
1807-1863, U.S.A.
A 88 (1864) 302, 449
ALISON, ARCHIBALD, history-
law, 1792-1867, England
E 6 (1866-1869) 185-187
ALISON, ARCHIBALD, theology,
1757-1839,
L 4 (1837-1843) 177
ALISON, WILLIAM PULTENEY,
medicine, 1789-1859,
Scotland
E 4 (1857-1862) 217-222
AL-KHWARIZMI, mathematics,
fl. c.823, Persia
S 43 (1916) 389-391
ALLAN, ROBERT, mineralogy,
1806-1863,
E 5 (1862-1866) 130-131
ALLAN, THOMAS, mineralogy,
1777-1833, Scotland
L 3 (1830-1837) 227
PM 3 (1833) 317-318
ALLARDYCE, CONSTANCE (MRS.
WILLIAM), geology,
-1919, England
S 50 (1919) 585
ALLBUTT, SIR THOMAS CLIFFORD,
medicine, 1836-1925,
England
L B101 (1927) P xx-xxii
S 44 (1916) 304
ALLCHIN, WILLIAM HENRY, medi-
cine, 1846-1911, England
N 88 (1912) 521
ALLEN, ALFRED HENRY, chemistry,
1847-1904, England
S 20 (1904) 189

ALLEN, ALFRED REGINALD,
neurology, 1876?-1918,
U.S.A.
S 48 (1918) 467
ALLEN, ALFRED V., microscopy,
1834?-1898, England
S 7 (1898) 674
ALLEN, DUDLEY PETER, surgery,
1852-1915, U.S.A.
S 41 (1915) 163
ALLEN, (CHARLES) GRANT,
writer, 1848-1899, Canada
S 10 (1899) 662
ALLEN, HARRISON, medicine,
1841-1897, U.S.A.
S 6 (1897) 764
S 7 (1898) P fp 253, 262-
265
ALLEN, OSCAR DANA, chemistry,
1836-1913, U.S.A.
A 185 (1913) 560
S 37 (1913) 408, 598
ALLEN, RICHARD HINCKLEY,
astronomy,   -1908,
U.S.A.
S 27 (1908) 276
ALLEN, WALTER MORRISON, optics,
1867?-1909, U.S.A.
S 29 (1909) 294
ALLEN, WILLIAM, chemistry,
1770-1843, England
L 5 (1850-1854) 532-533
ALLEN, WILLIAM, exploration,
1793?-1864, England
L 14 (1865) i
ALLEYNE, SIR JOHN GAY NEWTON,
engineering, 1820-1912,
England
S 35 (1912) 415
ALLIN, ARTHUR, psychology,
1869-1903, Canada
S 18 (1903) 703
ALLMAN, GEORGE JAMES, biology,
1812-1898, Ireland
E 23 (1899-1901) 5-6
L 75 (1905) 25-27
N 59 (1898) 203-204, 269-
270
S 8 (1898) 834, 867
ALLMAN, GEORGE JOHNSTON, mathe-
matics, 1824-1904, Ireland
L A78 (1907) xii-xiii
N 59 (1898) 269
N 70 (1904) 83, 372
S 19 (1904) 838

d'ALMEDIA, JOSEPH CHARLES,
physics, 1822-1880, France
A 121 (1881) 86
ALSBERG, CARL LUCAS, pharma-
cology, 1877-1940, U.S.A.
P 84 (1914) P 201
ALSTON, EDWARD RICHARD,
zoology, 1845-1881, Scot-
land
N 23 (1881) 485
ALTHAUS, JULIUS, medicine,
1833-1900, Germany
S 11 (1900) 1038
ALTHOFF, ..., education,
1839?-1908, Germany
S 28 (1908) 679
ALTMANN, RICHARD, histology,
1852-1900, Germany
S 13 (1901) 79
ALVAREZ, J.M., hygiene,
1860?-1917, Argentina
S 45 (1917) 212
ALVORD, HENRY ELIJAH, agri-
culture, 1844-1904, U.S.A.
S 20 (1904) 509
ALZHEIMER, ALOIS, psychiatry,
1864-1915, Germany.
S 43 (1916) 236
AMAGAT, ÉMILE HILAIRE, physics,
1841-1915, France
A 189 (1915) 686
E 36 (1915-1916) 26
L A91 (1914-1915) lxv-
lxviii
N 95 (1915) 41
AMALIZKI, VLADIMIR PROCHORO-
VICH, geology-paleontology,
-1905, Poland
S 22 (1905) 726
AMATI, AMATO, geography,
-1904, Italy
S 19 (1904) 933
AMBROSETTI, JUAN D., ethnog-
raphy,   -1917,
Argentina
S 45 (1917) 588
AMEGHINO, FLORENTINO (Fiorino),
paleontology, 1854-1911,
Italy
A 182 (1911) 480
S 34 (1911) 600
AMEND, BERNARD, chemistry,
1821?-1911,
S 33 (1911) 575

AMES, HOWARD E., medicine,
-1918, U.S.A.
S 49 (1919) 167
AMES, JOSEPH SWEETMAN, physics,
1864-1943, U.S.A.
N 66 (1902) 315-316
AMES, MRS. MARY L. PULSIFER,
botany, 1845?-1902, U.S.A.
S 15 (1902) 517
AMON, FRANK, chemistry,
-1918, U.S.A.
S 49 (1919) 42
AMORY, ROBERT, physiology,
1842-1910, U.S.A.
S 32 (1910) 303
AMPÈRE, ANDRÉ MARIE, physics,
1775-1836, France
L 3 (1830-1837) 440
PM III 10 (1837) 152-153
AMSLER (AMSLER-LAFFON), JACOB,
mathematics, 1823-1912,
Switzerland
S 35 (1912) 332
ANAXIMANDER, mathematics,
c.610-c.546 B.C., Greece
P 67 (1905) 701-706
d'ANCHIETÁ, JOSÉ, zoology,
1831?-1897, Portugal?
S 7 (1898) 421
ANDERSON, DAVID (OF MOREDUN),
finance, 1793?-1882,
Scotland
E 12 (1882-1884) 28
ANDERSON, MRS. ELIZABETH
GARRETT, medicine, 1836-
1917, England
N 100 (1917) 309
S 47 (1918) 266
ANDERSON, SIR HUGH KERR,
biology-physiology, 1865-
1928, England
L B104 (1929) xx
ANDERSON, JOHN, zoology, 1833-
1900, Scotland
L 75 (1905) 113-116
N 62 (1900) 529-531
S 12 (1900) 379-380
ANDERSON, JOHN MACVICAR,
architecture, 1834-1915,
Scotland
E 36 (1915-1916) 27-28
ANDERSON, MALCOLM PLAYFAIR,
exploration-zoology, 1879-
1919, U.S.A.
S 49 (1919) 282

ANDERSON, NILS J., botany,
1820?-1880, Sweden
A 123 (1882) 333
A 127 (1884) 243
ANDERSON, RICHARD JOHN,
geology-medicine, 1848-
1914, Ireland
A 188 (1914) 490
S 40 (1914) 236
ANDERSON, TEMPEST, ophthal-
mology, 1846-1913, England
S 38 (1913) 359
ANDERSON, THOMAS, botany,
1832-1870, Scotland
A 103 (1872) 153
ANDERSON, THOMAS, chemistry,
1819-1874, Scotland
A 109 (1875) 76
E 3 (1850-1857) 337-341
ANDERSON, THOMAS DAVID,
astronomy,
E 23 (1899-1901) 449-450
ANDERSON, SIR THOMAS M'CALL,
medicine, 1837?-1908,
Scotland
S 27 (1908) 276
ANDERSON, SIR WILLIAM,
engineering, 1835-1898,
Russia
N 44 (1891) 15
ANDERSON, WILLIAM, anatomy,
1842-1900, England
S 12 (1900) 771
ANDERSON, WILLIAM, geology,
1860-1915, Scotland
E 36 (1915-1916) 28
ANDRAE, CARL JUSTUS, geology-
paleontology, -1885,
Switzerland
Sl 6 (1885) 20
ANDRÉ, CHARLES LOUIS FRANÇOIS,
astronomy, 1842-1912, France
A 184 (1912) 404
S 36 (1912) 14, 48
ANDRÉ, ÉDOUARD FRANÇOIS,
horticulture, 1840-1911,
France
S 34 (1911) 709
ANDRÉ, JOHN, soldier, 1751-
1780, England
A 9 (1825) 395-396
ANDRÉE, RICHARD, ethnography-
geography, 1835-1912,
Germany
P 41 (1892) P 63

ANDRÉE, RICHARD (continued)
S 21 (1905) 557
S 35 (1912) 415, 449
ANDRÉE, SALOMON AUGUST,
ballooning-engineering,
1854-1897, Sweden
S 9 (1899) 268
ANDREWS, CHARLES WILLIAM,
geology, 1866-1924, England
L B100 (1926) P i-iii
ANDREWS, E.B., geology, 1820-
1880, U.S.A.
A 120 (1880) 255
ANDREWS, THOMAS, chemistry-
physics, 1813-1885, Ireland
L 5 (1843-1850) 523
L 41 (1887) xi-xv
N 20 (1879) 507-508
N 33 (1885) 157-159
N 38 (1888) 11
N 39 (1889) 554-556
ANDREWS, THOMAS, metallurgy,
1847-1907, England
L A81 (1908) lxxxii-lxxxiv
ANDREWS, WILLIAM HOLMES,
chemistry,   -1905,
U.S.A.
S 22 (1905) 726
ANGEL, ANDREA, chemistry,
1877-1917?, England
S 45 (1917) 163
ANGELIN, NILS PETER,
paleontology, 1805-1876,
Sweden
A 112 (1876) 80
ANGELL, JOHN, chemistry,
1824-1916, England
N 98 (1916) 56
ANGLIOUS, BARTHOLOMEW, science,
fl. c. 1260, England
N 71 (1905) 559
ÅNGSTRÖM, ANDERS JONAS,
astrophysics, 1814-1874,
Sweden
L 25 (1877) xviii-xxii
N 10 (1874) 376-377
ÅNGSTRÖM, JOHAN, biology,
1814-1880, Sweden
A 119 (1880) 77
ÅNGSTRÖM, KNUT JOHAN, physics,
1857-1910, Sweden
A 179 (1910) 566
N 83 (1910) 134-135
S 31 (1910) 499
ANNADALE, THOMAS NELSON,
zoology, 1876-1924

Scotland?
L B97 (1925) xviii-xxi
ANNINGSON, BUSHELL, law,
1838?-1916, England
S 44 (1916) 236
ANSELL, CHARLES, commerce,
1794-1881, England
L 34 (1883) vii-viii
ANSTED, DAVID THOMAS, geology,
1814-1880, England
L 31 (1881) i-ii
ANSTIE, FRANCIS EDMUND, medi-
cine, 1833-1874, England
N 10 (1874) 398-399
ANTHONY, JOHN GOULD, conchol-
ogy, 1804-1877, U.S.A.
A 114 (1877) 432
ANTHONY, WILLIAM ARNOLD,
physics, 1835-1908, U.S.A.
A 176 (1908) 100
S 27 (1908) 902
ANTON, FERDINAND, astronomy-
meteorology, 1844?-1900,
Italy
S 12 (1900) 693
APGAR, AUSTIN CRAIG, geography,
1838-1908, U.S.A.
S 27 (1908) 518
APGAR, ELLIS A., botany,
-1905, U.S.A.
S 22 (1905) 319
APJOHN, JAMES, chemistry,
1796-1875, Ireland
L 41 (1887) i-iii
APOLANT, HUGO, medicine,
1867?-1915, Germany
S 41 (1915) 606
APPLE, ANDREW THOMAS GEIGER,
astronomy-mathematics,
1858-1918, U.S.A.
S 47 (1918) 236-237
APPLETON, CHARLES EDWARD CUTTS
BIRCH, administration,
1841-1879, England
N 19 (1879) 374, 386-387
APPLETON, WILLIAM HENRY,
publisher, 1814-1899,
U.S.A.
P 56 (1899-1900) 265-267
APPOLD, JOHN GEORGE, engineer-
ing-invention, 1800-1865,
England
L 15 (1867) i-vi
ARAGO, DOMINIQUE FRANÇOIS JEAN,
astronomy-physics, 1786-
1853, France

ARAGO, DOMINIQUE FRANÇOIS JEAN
  (continued)
  A 66 (1853) 447
  A 67 (1854) 113-116
  A 68 (1854) 120
  A 69 (1855) 416
  A 73 (1857) 444-445
  A 79 (1860) 420-421
  A 90 (1865) 395
  L 5 (1843-1850) 1011
  L 6 (1850-1854) 3, 359-
    365
  N 20 (1879) 546-547
  N 21 (1880) P 418-420
  N 33 (1886) 254
  N 48 (1893) P 223-224
  P 16 (1879-1880) 114-115
  P 30 (1886-1887) P fp 145,
    259-266
ARAUJO, PAULO SILVA, micro-
  biology,   -1918, Brazil
  S 49 (1919) 167
ARBER, EDWARD ALEXANDER NEWELL,
  paleobotany, 1871?-1918,
  England
  S 48 (1918) 162
ARCHER, THOMAS CROXEN, curator,
  1817-1885, Scotland
  E 13 (1884-1886) 356
  E 14 (1886-1887) 110-114
  Sl 5 (1885) 264
ARCHER, WALTER E., ichthyology,
  1855-1917, England
  E 38 (1917-1918) 10-11
  S 46 (1917) 310
ARCHER, WILLIAM, biology,
  1827-1897, Ireland
  L 62 (1898) xl-xlii
  S 6 (1897) 519
ARCHIMEDES, science, c.287-
  c.212 B.C., Greece
  N 57 (1898) 409-410
  P 78 (1911) P 327
  S 48 (1918) 430-431
ARCHYTAS, mathematics, c.428
  B.C. - c.347 B.C., Greece
  N 30 (1884) 315-316
ARDERNE (ARDEN), JOHN OF,
  surgery, c.1307-1377? or
  after, England
  S 12 (1900) 258-259
ARGELANDER, FRIEDRICH WILHELM
  AUGUST, astronomy, 1799-
  1875, Germany
  A 109 (1875) 327-328
  A 112 (1876) 113

  P 39 (1891) P fp 433, 549-
    555
ARGENTO, G., surgery, 1847?-
  1917, Italy
  S 45 (1917) 381
ARGYLL, GEORGE JOHN DOUGLAS,
  DUKE OF, aeronautics-geology,
  1823-1900, England
  A 159 (1900) 462
  N 62 (1900) 13-14
ARISTARCHUS OF SAMOS, astron-
  omy, c.320 B.C.-c.250 B.C.
  Greece
  N 91 (1913) 499-500
ARISTOTLE, science, 384-322
  B.C., Greece
  A 118 (1879) 325
  N 25 (1882) 453-456, 505,
    528-529
  N 78 (1908) 106
  N 88 (1911) 1-2
  N 89 (1912) 653
  N 91 (1913) 201-204
  N 92 (1914) 584-585, 606
  N 93 (1914) 428
  N 96 (1916) 699-700
  N 97 (1916) 217
  P 26 (1884-1885) 796-802
  Sl 17 (1891) 128-133
  S 33 (1911) 730-738
  S 48 (1918) 431-432
ARMSTRONG, SIR ALEXANDER,
  medicine, 1818-1899, Ireland
  L 75 (1905) 50-51
  S 10 (1899) 63
ARMSTRONG, GEORGE FREDERICK,
  engineering, 1842-1900,
  Scotland
  S 12 (1900) 893
ARMSTRONG, HENRY EDWARD,
  chemistry, 1848-1937,
  England
  N 88 (1911) 184
ARMSTRONG, JOSEPH R., explora-
  tion,   -1919?, U.S.A.
  S 50 (1919) 565
ARMSTRONG, ROBERT YOUNG, elec-
  tricity, 1839-1894, Ireland
  L 57 (1895) xxii-xxiv
  N 46 (1892) 35
ARMSTRONG, SIR WILLIAM GEORGE,
  engineering-physics, 1810-
  1900, England
  L 75 (1905) 217-227
  N 63 (1901) 235-236
  S 13 (1901) 78

ARMSTRONG, SIR WILLIAM GEORGE
(continued)
S 14 (1901) 1021
ARNAUD, ALBERT, chemistry,
1853-1915, France
S 42 (1915) 242
ARNEGHINO, FLORENTINO,
paleontology, c. 1858-1911,
P 80 (1912) P 303-307
ARNISON, WILLIAM CHRISTOPHER,
surgery, 1837-1899, England
S 10 (1899) 782
ARNOLD, DELOS, geology,
-1909, U.S.A.
S 30 (1909) 437
ARNOLD, FERDINAND, botany,
1828?-1901, Germany
S 14 (1901) 501
ARNOLD, FRIEDRICH, anatomy,
1803- , Germany
S 17 (1903) 438
ARNOLD, JOHN OLIVER, metal-
lurgy, 1858-1930, England
L A130 (1931) P xxiii-
xxxvii
N 74 (1906) P 541-543
ARNOLD, JULIUS, anatomy,
1835?-1915, Germany
S 41 (1915) 422
ARNOLD, THEODOR KARLOVITCH,
forestry, -1903, Russia
S 18 (1903) 158
ARNOTT, NEIL, medicine-physics,
1788-1874, Scotland
A 113 (1877) 244
L 25 (1877) xiv-xviii
N 9 (1874) 364
P 10 (1876-1877) P fr,
100-101
ARON, HERMANN, engineering-
physics, 1845-1913, Germany
S 38 (1913) 662
ARÓSTEGUI, GONZALO, surgery,
1803?-1899, Cuba
S 10 (1899) 782
AROUET -- see Voltaire
d'ARREST, HEINRICH LOUIS,
astronomy, 1922-1875,
Denmark
A 110 (1875) 160
ARRHENIUS, SVANTE AUGUST,
chemistry-physics, 1859-
1927, Sweden
L A119 (1928) P ix-xix
N 64 (1901) P 429

N 67 (1902) 109-110
N 82 (1910) 401-402
P 65 (1904) P 89-91
P 66 (1904-1905) P 14
S 50 (1919) 584
ARROL, SIR WILLIAM, engineer-
ing, 1839-1913, England
N 90 (1913) 705
S 37 (1913) 443
ARTEDI, PETER, ichthyology,
1705-1735, Sweden
S 22 (1905) 378-379
ARTH, GEORGES MARIE FLORENT,
chemistry, 1853-1909,
Alsace-Lorraine
S 30 (1909) 203
ARZRUNI, ANDREAS, mineralogy,
1847-1898, Russia
S 8 (1898) 591
ASCHERSON, PAUL FRIEDRICH
AUGUST, botany, 1834-1913,
Germany
S 30 (1909) 81
ASCHKINASS, EMIL, physics,
1873-1909, Germany
S 29 (1909) 542
ASHBURNER, CHARLES ALBERT,
geology, 1854-1889, U.S.A.
A 139 (1890) 166
S1 9 (1887) 462
ASHHURST, JOHN, JR., surgery,
1839-1900, U.S.A.
S 12 (1900) 117
ASHMEAD, WILLIAM HARRIS,
entomology, 1855-1908,
U.S.A.
P 76 (1910) P 476-477
S 29 (1909) 875-876
ASHMOLE, ELIAS, alchemy-history,
1617-1692, England
N 99 (1917) 234-235
ASKENASY, EUGEN, botany, 1845-
1903, Germany
S 18 (1903) 382
S 19 (1904) 39
ASP, GEORG AUGUST, anatomy,
-1901, Sweden
S 13 (1901) 877
ASSHETON, RICHARD, embryology-
zoology, 1863-1915, England
A 191 (1916) 152
L B97 (1925) P i-vi
N 96 (1915) 266
S 42 (1915) 722

von ASTEN, FRIEDRICH EMIL,
astronomy, 1842-1878,
Germany
A 116 (1878) 410
ASTRUP, ELVIND, exploration,
1871-1895, Norway
S 3 (1896) 165-166
ATHERTON, GEORGE W., education,
1837-1906, U.S.A.
S 24 (1906) 159
ATKINSON, EDMUND, chemistry,
1831-1900, England
S 11 (1900) 877
ATKINSON, EDWARD, economics,
1827-1905, U.S.A.
P 34 (1888-1889) P fr,
113-121
ATKINSON, GEORGE FRANCIS,
botany, 1854-1918, U.S.A.
P 197 (1919) 84
S 48 (1918) 571
S 49 (1919) 230, 371-372
ATKINSON, JOHN, biology,
-1828,
PM II 4 (1828) 395-396
ATKINSON, W.E.G., botany,
-1915, England
S 42 (1915) 373
ATTFIELD, JOHN, pharmacy,
1835-1911, England
L A86 (1911-1912) xliv-
xlvi
N 86 (1911) 117
ATWATER, WILBUR OLIN,
chemistry-physiology,
1844-1907, U.S.A.
A 197 (1919) 84
P 71 (1907) P 568
S 26 (1907) 423, 523-524
ATWOOD, MELVILLE, geology,
1812-1898, England
S 7 (1898) P 635
AUBERT, ALEXANDER, astronomy,
1730-1805, France?
PM 24 (1806) P fr
AUDOUIN, JEAN VICTOR, zoology,
1797-1841, France
A 43 (1842) 215
d'AUBENTON -- see Daubenton
AUDUBON, JOHN JAMES, orni-
thology-zoology, 1785-1851,
Haiti
A 61 (1851) 295
A 141 (1891) 337
N 57 (1898) 386-387
P 31 (1887) P fp 577, 687-
697

P 70 (1907) P 301-303
S1 6 (1885) 140
S1 10 (1887) 68-69, 108
S1 11 (1888) 159
S1 13 (1889) 23
S1 21 (1893) 271
S 4 (1896) 47
S 7 (1898) P fp 289,
289-296
von AUENBRUGGER, JOSEPH
LEOPOLD, medicine, 1722-
1809, Austria
S 28 (1908) 882
AUERBACH, LEOPOLD, anatomy,
1828-1897, Germany
S 6 (1897) 700
AUGHEY, SAMUEL, geology,
1831?-1912, U.S.A.
S 35 (1912) 414
d'AUMALE, HENRI EUGÈNE PHILIPPE
LOUIS d'ORLÉANS, duc, 1822-
1897, government, France
S 5 (1897) 800
AUSTEN, PETER TOWNSEND, chem-
istry, 1852-1907, U.S.A.
A 175 (1908) 168
S 27 (1908) 77
AUSTIN, B.J., physiology,
1829?-1912, England
S 35 (1912) 958
AUSTIN, COE FINCH, bryology-
muscology, 1831-1880,
U.S.A.
A 119 (1880) 423
A 123 (1882) 332
A 127 (1884) 242
AUSTIN, W.H., mathematics,
1857?-1902, England
S 15 (1902) 957
von AUWERS, GEORG FRIEDRICH
JULIUS ARTHUR, astronomy,
1838-1915, Germany
A 189 (1915) 486
E 36 (1915-1916) 26
L A92 (1916) xvi-xx
N 94 (1915) 703-704
S 41 (1915) 355, 495-497
AVEBURY, SIR JOHN LUBBOCK,
geography, 1834-1913,
England
L B87 (1914) i-iii
AVELING, EDWARD BIBBINS,
socialism, 1851-1898,
England
S 8 (1898) 218

AVELOT, RENÉ ANTOINE,
archeology-exploration,
1871-1914, France
S 41 (1915) 859-860
AVENARIUS, RICHARD HEINRICH
LUDWIG, philosophy-
psychology, 1843-1896
France
S 4 (1896) 355
AVERROËS (ABU-AL-WALID
MUHAMMAD IBN-AHMAD IBN-
RUSHD), science, c.1126-
c.1198, Spain
P 25 (1884) P fp 289,
405-409
AVERY, CHARLES ELLERY,
pharmacy, 1848?-1916,
U.S.A.
S 44 (1916) 743
AVILINE, WILLIAM TALBOT,
geology, 1822?-1903,
England
S 17 (1903) 917
AVOGADRO, AMADEO, CONTE DI
QUAREGNA, mathematics-
physics, 1776-1856, Italy
A 178 (1909) P 87
N 78 (1906) 537-538
N 88 (1911) 142-143
AXENFELD, DAVIDE, physiology,
1848?-1912, Italy?
S 36 (1912) 823
AYRES, BROWN, astronomy-
physics, 1856-1919, U.S.A.
S 49 (1919) 146
AYRES, WILLIAM O., ichthyology-
zoology,   -1887?, U.S.A.
Sl 10 (1887) 24
AYRTON, SARAH HERTHA MARKS
(MRS. W.E.), physics, 1854-
1923, England
N 75 (1906) 133-134
N 112 (1923) 800-801
N 113 (1924) 48
AYRTON, WILLIAM EDWARD,
engineering-physics, 1847-
1908, England
A 177 (1909) 100
L A85 (1911) i-viii
N 65 (1901) 108
N 79 (1908) 74-75
S 28 (1908) 722
AYTOUN, WILLIAM EDMONSTOUNE,
literature, 1813-1865,
E 5 (1862-1866) 481-483

BABBAGE, CHARLES, mathematics,
1792-1871, England
A 103 (1872) 74-77
N 5 (1871) 28-29
BABBINGTON, BENJAMIN GUY,
medicine, 1794-1866,
England
L 16 (1868) i-ii
BABCOCK, JAMES FRANCIS,
chemistry, 1844-1897,
U.S.A.
S 6 (1897) 167
BABINGTON, CHARLES CARDALE,
botany, 1808-1895, England
L 59 (1896) viii-x
N 52 (1895) 371-372
N 57 (1898) 314-315
S 2 (1895) 133
BABINGTON, WILLIAM, geology-
medicine,   -1833,
L 3 (1830-1837) 227-228
von BABO, CLEMENS LAMBERT,
chemistry, 1818-1899,
Germany
S 9 (1899) 692
BACCELLI, GUIDO, medicine,
1832-1916, Italy
N 96 (1916) 603-604
S 43 (1916) 167
BACCIALLI, ..., bacteriology,
-1903, Italy
S 18 (1903) 253
BACHE, ALEXANDER DALLAS,
geodesy-physics, 1806-1867,
U.S.A.
A 93 (1867) 282-283
E 6 (1866-1869) 187-188
L 16 (1868) lxiv
P 48 (1895-1896) P fr,
112-120
P 82 (1913) P 612
S 10 (1899) 629-630, 632
S 44 (1916) 46
BACHE, THOMAS H., medicine,
1826?-1912, U.S.A.
S 36 (1912) 79
BACHMANN, ISIDOR, geology,
1837-1884, Switzerland
Sl 4 (1884) 76
BACK, SIR GEORGE, geography,
1796-1878, England
N 18 (1878) 227-228
BACKHOUSE, THOMAS WILLIAM,
astronomy-meteorology,
1842-1920,
A 200 (1920) 82

BACKLUND, JOHANN OSKAR, astron-
omy, 1846-1916, Sweden
L   A94 (1918) xx-xxiv
N   70 (1904) 418
N   98 (1916) 192
S   44 (1916) 782
BACON, CHARLES A., astronomy,
1860?-1901, U.S.A.
S   14 (1901) 780
BACON, SIR FRANCIS, Viscount
St. Albans, Baron Verulam,
philosophy-science, 1561-
1626, England
A   26 (1839) 219-223
N   19 (1879) 262-264
N   39 (1888) 3-4
N   72 (1905) 373-374
N   89 (1912) 454
N   90 (1912) 236
P   76 (1910) 495-499
Sl   7 (1886) 143
Sl 12 (1888) 189
BACON, JOHN MACKENZIE, astron-
omy-meteorology, 1846-
1904, England
S   21 (1905) 237
BACON, ROGER, science, c.1214-
1294, England
A   83 (1862) 110-111
N   77 (1908) 268
N   93 (1914) P 405-406
*   N   94 (1914) 443-445
BAEYER, JOHANN JAKOB, geodesy,
1794-1885, Germany
P   32 (1887-1888) P fp 145,
261-265
Sl   6 (1885) 429
BAGEHOT, WALTER, economics,
1826-1877, England
P   12 (1887-1888) P fp 385,
489-490
BAHNSON, KRISTIAN, ethnology,
-1897, Denmark
S   5 (1897) 270
BAILEY, BERT HEALD, ornithol-
ogy, 1875-1917, U.S.A.
S   46 (1917) 14, 450-451
BAILEY, FRANK KELTON, physics,
-1909, U.S.A.
S   30 (1909) 111
BAILEY, FREDERICK, forestry,
-1912,
E   34 (1913-1914) 5-6
BAILEY, FREDERICK MANSON, botany,
1827-1915, England
N   96 (1915) 10-11
S   42 (1915) 373

BAILEY, JACOB WHITMAN, botany-
geology, 1811-1857, U.S.A.
A   73 (1857) 447-448
A   75 (1858) 153
S   10 (1899) 672-673
BAILEY, JAMES SPENCER, ento-
mology,   -   , U.S.A.
Sl   2 (1883) 148
BAILEY, P.G., genetics,
-1917, England
S   45 (1917) 562
BAILEY, WILLIAM WHITMAN,
botany, 1843-1914, U.S.A.
A 187 (1914) 366
S   39 (1914) 323
BAILLIE, JOHN, oriental lan-
guages,   -1833,
L   3 (1830-1837) 229
BAILLIE, CHARLES WILLIAM,
meteorology, 1844-1899,
England
N   60 (1899) 204
S   10 (1899) 63
BAILLON, HENRI ERNEST, botany,
1827-1895, France
L   59 (1886) lxvii-lxix
N   52 (1895) 371
S   2 (1895) 133
BAILLY, JULES, osteology,
1831-1908, Canada
S   27 (1908) 237
BAILY, FRANCIS, astronomy,
1774-1844, England
L   5 (1843-1850) 524-525
PM III 26 (1845) 38-75
BAIN, ALEXANDER, electricity-
invention, 1810-1877,
Scotland
N   15 (1877) 218
P   9 (1876) P 360-361
BAIN, ALEXANDER, psychology,
1818-1903, Scotland
S   18 (1903) 414
BAIN, SIR JAMES, commerce,
1818-1898, Scotland
E   23 (1899-1901) 6
BAINBRIDGE, FRANCIS ARTHUR,
physiology, 1874-1921,
England
L   B93 (1922) xxiv-xxvi
BAIRD, ANDREW WILSON, mathe-
matics, 1842-1908, England
L   A82 (1909) xvii-xxi
BAIRD, JOHN WALLACE, psychol-
ogy, 1873-1919, Canada
A 197 (1919) 454
S   49 (1919) 213, 393-394

*See page 290 for entries inadvertently omitted.

Sl   3 (1884) 368-369
BALFOUR, THOMAS A.G., medi-
cine, 1825?-1895, Scotland
E   21 (1895-1897) 12
BALL, SIR CHARLES BENT, sur-
gery, 1851-1916, Ireland
S   43 (1916) 530
BALL, JOHN, physics, 1818-
1889, Ireland
L   47 (1890) v-ix
BALL, SIR ROBERT STAWELL,
astronomy-mathematics,
1840-1913, Ireland
A   187 (1914) 208
E   35 (1914-1915) 2
L   A91 (1914-1915) xvii-xxi
N   92 (1913) 403-404
S   38 (1913) 813
BALL, VALENTINE, geology,
1843-1895, Ireland
L   58 (1895) xlvii-xlix
S   1 (1895) 723
BALLARD, ADDISON, philosophy,
1822-1914, U.S.A.
S   40 (1914) 848
BALLARD, EDWARD, hygiene,
1820-1897, England
L   62 (1898) iii-v
N   57 (1897) 106
S   5 (1897) 270
BALLEINE, C.F., archeology,
-1915, England
S   42 (1915) 242
BALLET, CHARLES, horticulture,
-1908, France
S   28 (1908) 921
BALLINGALL, SIR GEORGE,
medicine, 1786?-1856
E   3 (1850-1857) 408
BALTZER, RICHARD ARMIN, geol-
ogy, 1842-1913, Germany
S   38 (1913) 813
BALY, WILLIAM, medicine, 1814-
1861, England
L   12 (1863) i-iii
BANCROFT, HUBERT HOWE, author-
publisher, 1832-1918,
U.S.A.
Sl   1 (1883) 379-380
BANCROFT, WILDER DWIGHT, chem-
istry, 1867-1953, U.S.A.
P   64 (1903-1904) P 377
BANDELIER, ADOLPH FRANCIS
ALPHONSE, archeology, 1840-
1914, Switzerland
P   41 (1892) P 302

S   39 (1914) 461
BANGS, LEMUEL BOLTON, surgery,
1842-1914, U.S.A.
S   40 (1914) 516
BANKS, SIR JOHN, medicine,
1811?-1908, Ireland
S   28 (1908) 207
BANKS, SIR JOSEPH, adminis-
tration-botany, 1743-1820,
England
A   178 (1909) 566
N   55 (1896) 73-74
N   82 (1910) 362
PM   8 (1800) P fr
PM 56 (1820) 40-46, 161-
174, 241-257
S   33 (1911) 368
BANKS, SIR WILLIAM MITCHELL,
surgery, 1842-1904, Scot-
land
S   20 (1904) 255
BANNISTER, RICHARD, chemistry,
1835?-1909, England
S   30 (1909) 594
BARAJAS, CARLOS, medicine,
-1918?, Mexico
S   49 (1919) 89
BARBERA, LUIGI, philosophy,
1829-1904, Italy
N   19 (1904) 358
BARBIER, JOSEPH VICTOR,
geography, 1840-1898,
France
S   8 (1898) 668
BARBOUR, VOLNEY G., engineer-
ing,   -1901, U.S.A.
S   13 (1901) 956
BARBOZA DU BOCAGE, JOSÉ
VICENTE, zoology, 1824?-
1908, Portugal
S   28 (1908) 143, 232
BARCLAY, GEORGE, commerce,
1820-1910, Scotland
E   31 (1910-1911) 684-686
BARCLAY, L.P., optics,
-1908, U.S.A.
S   28 (1908) 370
von BARDELEBEN, HEINRICH ADOLF,
medicine, 1819-1895,
Germany
S   2 (1895) 483
von BARDELEBEN, KARL HEINRICH,
anatomy, 1849-1919, Germany
A   197 (1919) 454
BARDENHEUER, FRANZ BERNHARD
HUBERT, surgery, 1839-1913,

Germany
S 38 (1913) 440
BARDWELL, MISS ELIZABETH M.,
astronomy, 1832?-1899,
U.S.A.
S 9 (1899) 821-822
BARING, EVELYN, Earl of Cromer,
archeology, 1841-1917,
England
N 98 (1917) 433-434
BARKER, GEORGE FREDERIC,
chemistry-physics, 1835-
1910, U.S.A.
A 180 (1910) 96, 225-232
N 83 (1910) 434, 464
P 15 (1879) P fp 577,
693-697
P 77 (1910) P 206-207
S 31 (1910) 853
BARKER, T., electricity, math-
ematics, 1838?-1907,England
S 26 (1907) 886
BARKLA, CHARLES GLOVER,
physics, 1877-1944, England
N 100 (1917) 277
BARKLY, SIR HENRY, administra-
tion, 1815-1898, England
L 75 (1905) 23-25
BARLOW, ALFRED ERNEST, geol-
ogy, 1961-1914, Canada
A 188 (1914) 116
BARLOW, CALEB, biology,
-1908, England
S 27 (1908) 903
BARLOW, PETER, physics, 1776-
1862, England
A 17 (1829-1830) 367-368
L 12 (1863) xxxiii-xxxiv
BARLOW, PETER WILLIAM, en-
gineering,   -1885,
England
L 38 (1885) xxxix-xl
BARLOW, SIR ROBERT, navy,
1758-1843,
L 5 (1843-1850) 527
BARLOW, WILLIAM HENRY, en-
gineering, 1812-1902,
England
S 16 (1902) 877, 974
BARNABY, SIR NATHANIEL, naval
engineering, 1829-1915,
England
S 42 (1915) 88
BARNARD, EDITH ETHEL, chem-
istry, 1880-1914, U.S.A.
S 39 (1914) 421

BARNARD, EDWARD EMERSON,
astronomy, 1857-1923,
U.S.A.
S 36 (1912) 423
BARNARD, FREDERICK AUGUSTUS
PORTER, mathematics-physics,
1809-1889, U.S.A.
A 137 (1889) 504
N 54 (1896) 409-410
P 11 (1877) P fr, 100-103
P 49 (1896) P 505
Sl 13 (1889) 358
S 3 (1896) 608
S 4 (1896) 273-275
S 10 (1899) 676-678
BARNARD, JOHN GROSS, mathe-
matics, 1815-1882, U.S.A.
A 123 (1882) 498
BARNES, CHARLES REID, botany,
1858-1910, U.S.A.
A 179 (1910) 464
P 76 (1910) P 516-517
S 31 (1910) 532-533
BARNES, DANIEL H., conchology,
-1828, U.S.A.
A 15 (1829) 401-402
BARNES, J. H., chemistry
-1917, England
S 46 (1917) 159
BARNES, OLIVER WELDON, en-
gineering, 1823-1908,
U.S.A.
S 28 (1908) 792
BARNES, THOMAS, medicine,
1793-1872, England
E 8 (1872-1875) 3-4
BARR, PETER, horticulture,
1826-1909, Scotland
N 81 (1909) 400
BARRAL, JEAN AUGUSTE, science,
1819-1884, France
N 30 (1884) 517
von BARRANDE, JOACHIM, baron,
geology-paleontology,
1799-1883, France
A 126 (1883) 416
N 28 (1883) 564
Sl 2 (1883) P 699-701,
P 725, 727-729
S 3 (1884) 584
S 4 (1884) 139
BARRAZA, F.C., chemistry,
1862?-1917, Argentina
S 46 (1917) 614
BARRELL, FRANCIS RICHARD,
mathematics-physics,

1860?-1915, England
A 191 (1916) 226
N 96 (1915) 402-403
BARRELL, JOSEPH, geology,
1869-1919, U.S.A.
A 197 (1919) 454
A 198 (1919) P 251-280
S 49 (1919) 467, 605-607
BARRETT, CHARLES GOLDING,
entomology, 1836?-1904,
England
S 21 (1905) 78
BARRETT, SIR WILLIAM FLETCHER,
physics, 1844-1925, Jamaica
N 60 (1899) 31
BARRETT-HAMILTON, GERALD EDWIN
HAMILTON, biology,
-1914, England
S 39 (1914) 355
BARRINGTON, RICHARD MANLIFFE,
biology-ornithology, 1841?-
1915, Ireland
S 42 (1915) 567
BARRIS, WILLIS HERVEY, geology,
1821?-1901, U.S.A.
S 14 (1901) 117
BARROIS, CHARLES EUGÈNE,
geology, 1851-1939, France
N 76 (1907) 605
BARROW, ISAAC, mathematics,
1630-1677, England
A 82 (1861) 299-300
N 100 (1917) 222-223
BARROW, JOHN, physiography,
1808-1898, England
S 9 (1899) 118
BARROWS, CHARLES CLIFFORD,
gynecology, 1857-1916,
U.S.A.
S 43 (1916) 64-65, 528
BARROWS, JOHN HENRY, education,
1847-1902, U.S.A.
S 15 (1902) 957
BARRY, ALEXANDER, chemistry,
-1832,
L 3 (1830-1837) 149
BARRY, SIR CHARLES, architec-
ture, 1795-1860, England
L 11 (1862) i-iii
BARRY, SIR JOHN WOLFE,
engineering, 1836-1918,
England
L A94 (1918) P xxxv-xxxviii
S 47 (1918) 189
BARRY, MARTIN, embryology,
L 4 (1837-1843) 172

BARTEL, . . ., archeology,
-1915, Germany
S 42 (1915) 335
BARTELS, MAX KARL AUGUST,
anthropology, 1843-1904,
Germany
S 20 (1904) 653
BARTH, MAX, agriculture,
1855?-1899,
S 10 (1899) 463
de BARTHÉLMY, ANATOLE,
archeology, 1821?-1904,
France
S 20 (1904) 95
BARTLETT, ABRAHAM DEE,
zoology, 1812-1897, England
N 61 (1900) 267-268
S 5 (1897) 839
BARTLETT, CLARENCE, zoology,
-1903, England
S 17 (1903) 878
BARTLING, FRIEDRICH GOTTLIEB,
botany, 1798?-1875,
Germany
A 111 (1876) 326
BARTON, BENJAMIN SMITH,
biology-physics, 1766-1815,
U.S.A.
A 17 (1829-1830) 367-368
P 48 (1895-1896) P fp 721,
834-840
BARTON, EDWIN HENRY, physics,
1858-1925, England
L A111 (1926) P xl-xliii
BARTON, GEORGE HUNT, geology,
1852-1933, U.S.A.
P 55 (1899) P 644
BARTRAM, JOHN, botany, 1699-
1777, U.S.A.
A 59 (1850) 85-105
P 40 (1891-1892) 827-839
BARTRAM, WILLIAM, biology,
1739-1823, U.S.A.
P 40 (1891-1892) 827-839
P 41 (1892) 561-562,
P fp 577
de BARY, HEINRICH ANTON,
botany, 1831-1888, Germany
N 37 (1888) 297-299
S 11 (1888) 85
BASCH, KARL, physiology,
1859?-1913, Germany
S 38 (1913) 328
BASEVI, GEORGE, architecture,
-1845,
L 5 (1843-1850) 582

BASHFORTH, FRANCIS, mathemat-
ics-physics, 1819-1912,
England
S 35 (1912) 332
BASSANI, FRANCESCO, geology-
paleontology, 1853-1916,
Italy
S 44 (1916) 493
BASSET, ALFRED BARNARD, mathe-
matics, 1854-1930, England
L A131 (1931) i-ii
BASSOT, JEAN ANTONIN LÉON
PIERRE, geodesy, 1841-1917,
France
S 45 (1917) 334
BASTIAN, ADOLF, ethnology,
1826-1905, Germany
P 41 (1892) P 60
S 4 (1896) 223
BASTIAN, HENRY CHARLTON,
neurology, 1837-1915,
England
A 191 (1916) 152
L B89 (1917) xxi-xxiv
N 96 (1915) 347-348
P 8 (1875-1876) P 108-110
S 42 (1915) 762
BASTIAN, EDSON SEWELL, botany,
1843?-1897, U.S.A.
S 5 (1897) 617
BATE, CHARLES SPENCE, zoology,
1818-1889, England
L 46 (1890) xli-xlii
BATEMAN, SIR FREDERIC, medicine,
1824-1904, England
S 20 (1904) 255
BATEMAN, JAMES, botany, 1811-
1897, England
S 6 (1897) 955
BATEMAN, JOHN FREDERIC LA
TROBE, engineering, 1810-
1889, Scotland
L 46 (1890) xlii-xlviii
S1 13 (1889) 501
BATES, EDWARD PAYSON, engineer-
ing, 1844?-1919, U.S.A.
S 50 (1919) 302
BATES, HENRY WALTER, entomol-
ogy, 1825-1892, England
N 45 (1892) 398-399
P 42 (1892-1893) P fr,
118-122
BATESON, WILLIAM, morphology,
1861-1926, England
L B101 (1927) P i-v
N 50 (1894) 55

N 71 (1904) 110
BATTELLI, ANGELO, physics,
1862-1916, Italy
S 45 (1917) 257, 381
BATTEN, EDMOND CHISHOLM, law,
1817-1897, Scotland
E 22 (1897-1899) 4, iii-iv
BATTEN, JOSEPH HALLETT,
classics, -1837,
L 4 (1837-1843) 15
BATTY, JOSEPH H., taxidermy,
-1906, U.S.A.
S 24 (1906) 190
BAUER, ALEXANDER ANTON EMIL,
chemistry, 1836-1921,
Hungary
S 43 (1916) 459
BAUER, CONRAD GUSTAV, mathe-
matics, 1820-1906, Germany
S 23 (1906) 798
BAUER, FRANCIS, botany, 1758-
1841, Austria
L 4 (1837-1843) 342-344
BAUER, FRANZ, geology-tech-
nology, 1870?-1903,
Germany
S 18 (1903) 125, 221
BAUER, GEORG -- see Agricola,
Georgius
BAUER, LOUIS AGRICOLA, ter-
restrial magnetism, 1865-
1932, U.S.A.
P 66 (1904-1905) P 14
P 76 (1910) P 203
BAUER, MAX HERMANN, mineralogy,
1844-1917, Germany
S 41 (1915) 392-395
BAUERMAN, HILARY, geology-
metallurgy, 1833-1909,
England
N 82 (1909) 195-196
S 30 (1909) 914
BAUMANN, ERNEST, exploration,
1871?-1895,
S 2 (1895) 483
BAUMANN, EUGEN, chemistry-
physiology, 1846-1896,
Germany
S 4 (1896) 793
S 5 (1897) 51-53
BAUMANN, OSKAR, geography,
1864-1899, Austria
S 10 (1899) 702
von BAUMHAUER, ÉDOUARD HENRI,
chemistry, 1820-1885, Belgium
A 130 (1885) 408

BAUR, GEORG HERMANN CARL LUDWIG,
paleontology, 1859?-1898,
Germany
N 58 (1898) 350
S 8 (1898) 20, 68-71
BAUSCH, HENRY, optics, 1859?-
1909, U.S.A.
S 29 (1909) 451
BAXENDELL, JOSEPH, astronomy-
meteorology, 1815-1887,
England
L 43 (1888) iv-vi
N 36 (1887) 585
BAYEN, PIERRE, chemistry,
1725-1798,
PM 1 (1798) 212-218
von BAYER, K. ERNST, embryol-
ogy, 1792-1876.
P 67 (1905) P 111-117
BAYLISS, SIR WILLIAM MADDOCK,
physiology, 1860-1924,
England
L B99 (1926) P xxvii-xxxii
N 88 (1911) 183-184
BAYMA, T., bacteriology, 1863?-
1918?, Brazil
S 49 (1919) 167
BAYNE, HERBERT A., chemistry,
-1886, Canada
N 34 (1886) 553
Sl 8 (1886) 270, 432
BAZIN, ERNEST, invention,
1826-1898, Algiers
S 7 (1897) 129
BAZIN, HENRI ÉMILE, hydraulics,
1829-1917, France
S 45 (1917) 499
BEACH, ALFORD ELY, invention,
1826-1896, U.S.A.
S 3 (1896) 66
BEACH, HENRY HARRIS AUBREY,
anatomy, 1843-1910, U.S.A.
S 32 (1910) 54
BEACON, G.F., engineering,
-1909, England
S 30 (1909) 82
BEAL, FOSTER ELLENBOROUGH
LASCELLES, ornithology,
1840-1916, U.S.A.
S 44 (1916) 528
BEAL, SAMUEL EDWARD, astron-
omy-geography, 1836?-1897.
S 6 (1897) 364
BEALE, LIONEL SMITH, medi-
cine-physiology, 1828-1906,
England

A 171 (1906) 408
L B79 (1907) lvii-lxiii
N 73 (1906) 540
S 23 (1906) 599
BEALS, A.H.B., philosophy,
-1898, U.S.A.
S 8 (1898) 129
BEAN, TARLETON HOFFMAN,
ichthyology-zoology,
1846-1916, U.S.A.
S 41 (1915) 749
S 45 (1917) 14
de BEAUCHAMP, PIERRE JOSEPH,
astronomy, 1752-1801,
France
PM 7 (1800) P fr
PM 12 (1802) P 353-356
BEAUTEMPS-BEAUPRÉ, CHARLES
FRANÇOIS, hydrography,
1766-1854, France
A 68 (1854) 115-116
BEBB, MICHAEL SCHUCK, botany,
1833?-1895, U.S.A.
A 151 (1896) 78
S 2 (1895) 890
BÉCHAMP, PIERRE JACQUES
ANTOINE, chemistry, 1816-
1908, France
A 176 (1908) 100
N 78 (1908) 13-14
S 27 (1908) 837
BECK, CARL, surgery, 1856-
1911, Germany
S 33 (1911) 959
BECK, LEWIS CALEB, biology-
mineralogy, 1798-1853,
U.S.A.
A 66 (1853) 149-150
P 73 (1908) 488-499
BECK, PHILLIP, medicine,
-1915, Germany
S 41 (1915) 460
BECK, T.S., physiology,
L 5 (1843-1850) 575-576
BECK, THEODRIC ROMEYN, medi-
cine, 1791-1855, U.S.A.
A 71 (1856) 152
BECKER, ERNST EMIL HUGO,
astronomy, 1843-1912,
Germany
S 36 (1912) 431
BECKER, GEORGE FERDINAND,
geology, 1847-1919, U.S.A.
A 197 (1919) 390
A 198 (1919) 242-245
S 49 (1919) 396

BECKER, LUDWIG, astronomy-
physics, 1860-1947,
E 19 (1891-1892) 272-273
BECQUEREL, ALEXANDRE EDMOND,
physics, 1820-1891, France
L 51 (1892) xxi-xxiv
BECQUEREL, ANTOINE CÉSAR,
chemistry-physics, 1788-
1878, France
A 115 (1878) 239-240
L 4 (1837-1843) 22-23
N 17 (1878) 244-245
BECQUEREL, ANTOINE HENRI,
chemistry-physics, 1852-
1908, France
A 176 (1908) 404
L A83 (1909-1910) xx-xxiii
N 70 (1904) 418
N 71 (1904) P 177-179
N 74 (1906) 322-323
N 78 (1908) 414-416
P 13 (1878) 20-25
S 28 (1908) 301
S 36 (1912) 79
BECQUEREL, DUMERIL,
-1871, France
A 101 (1871) 392, 479
BEDDARD, FRANK EVERS, zoology,
1858-1925, England
L B99 (1926) xxxvi-xxxvii
N 46 (1892) 35
BEDDOE, JOHN, anthropology,
1826-1911, England
L B84 (1912) xxv-xxvii
N 87 (1911) 116-117
S 34 (1911) 147
BEDDOME, R.M., botany, 1828?-
1911, England
S 33 (1911) 421
BEDFORD, F.R., zoology,
-1900?, England
S 13 (1901) 118
BEDFORD, JOHN RUSSELL, Duke of,
botany, 1766-1839, England
A 40 (1840-1841) 219
BEEBE, WILLIAM, astronomy-
mathematics, 1851-1917,
U.S.A.
A 193 (1917) 342
S 45 (1917) 289
BEECHER, CHARLES EMERSON,
paleontology, 1856-1904,
U.S.A.
A 167 (1904) 252, P 411-
422
A 193 (1917) 196

P 64 (1903-1904) P 567-
568
S 19 (1904) 318, 453-455
BEETHAM, ALBERT WILLIAM, law,
1802-1895, England
L 57 (1885) xxv
van BEETHOVEN, LUDWIG, music,
1770-1827, Germany
P 84 (1914) 265-270
BEEVOR, CHARLES EDWARD,
neurology, 1854-1908,
England
S 29 (1909) 73
BEG, ULUGH, astronomy, 1394-
1467, Persia
S 46 (1917) 365-366
BEGAN, P. VAUGHAN, physics,
1875-1913, England
N 92 (1913) 481
BEGBIE, JAMES, medicine,
1789-1869, Scotland
E 7 (1869-1872) 2-6
BEGBIE, JAMES WARBURTON,
medicine, 1826-1876,
Scotland
E 9 (1875-1878) 209-212
BEHM, ERNST, geography, 1830-
1884, Germany
Sl 3 (1884) 468
BEHN, ULRICH ANDREAS RICHARD,
physics, 1868-1908, Germany
S 27 (1908) 966
BEHR, HANS HERMANN, entomology,
1818-1904, Germany
S 19 (1904) 636
BEHRENS, PAUL, chemistry,
-1905, Germany
S 21 (1905) 758
BEHRENS, WILHELM JULIUS,
botany,   -1904, Germany
S 19 (1904) 199
von BEHRING, EMIL ADOLPH,
bacteriology-medicine,
1854-1917, Germany
N 99 (1917) 169, 228-229
S 45 (1917) 407
BEILBY, SIR GEORGE T., chem-
istry-engineering, 1850-
1924,
L A109 (1925) P i-xvii
BEILSTEIN, FRIEDRICH KONRAD
(Fedor Fedorovich), chem-
istry, 1838-1906, Russia
S 24 (1906) 605
BEIT, ALFRED, philanthropy,
1853-1906, Germany

S 24 (1906) 125
BEITH, DONALD, law, 1815-1894,
    Scotland
    E 20 (1892-1895) xxvi-
       xxxviii
BEKETOV, A.N., botany, 1825?-
    1902, Russia
    S 16 (1902) 399
BELFIELD, HENRY HOLMES,
    technology,   -1912,
    U.S.A.
    S 35 (1912) 982
BELKNAP, GEORGE EUGENE, hydro-
    graphy, 1832-1903, U.S.A.
    A 165 (1903) 418
    S 17 (1903) 636
BELL, A. BEATSON, law, 1832?-
    1913, Scotland
    E 34 (1913-1914) 6
BELL, AGRIPPA NELSON, medicine,
    1820-1911, U.S.A.
    P 65 (1904) P 282-283
BELL, ALEXANDER GRAHAM,
    physics-telephony, 1847-
    1922, Scotland
    N 92 (1913) 406
    S 22 (1905) 221
    S 23 (1906) 278, 797
BELL, ALEXANDER MELVILLE,
    phonetics, 1819-1905,
    England
    S 22 (1905) 221
BELL, ANDREW, education,
    1753-1832, England
    A 23 (1832-1833) 370
BELL, SIR CHARLES, anatomy-
    neurology, 1778-1842,
    Scotland
    E 1 (1832-1844) 427
    L 3 (1830-1837) 221
    L 4 (1837-1843) 402-406
BELL, CHARLES DAVIDSON, artist,
    1813-1882, Scotland
    E 12 (1882-1884) 14-22
BELL, CHARLES J. (or C.?),
    chemistry, 1854-1903, U.S.A.
    A 165 (1903) 242
    S 17 (1903) 79, 119
BELL, CLARK, law, 1832-1918,
    U.S.A.
    S 47 (1918) 217
BELL, SIR ISAAC LOWTHIAN,
    metallurgy, 1816-1904,
    Scotland
    L A78 (1907) xiv-xviii
    N 71 (1905) 230

S 21 (1905) 78
BELL, JAMES, chemistry,
    1825-1908, England
    L A82 (1909) v
    N 77 (1908) 539
BELL, JOHN, law,   -1836,
    L 3 (1830-1837) 437-438
BELL, JOSEPH, surgery, 1837-
    1911, Scotland
    S 34 (1911) 600
BELL, ROBERT, surgery, 1782-
    1860, Scotland
    E 4 (1857-1862) 483-484
BELL, SIR ROBERT, geography-
    geology, 1841-1917,
    Canada
    A 194 (1917) 338
    L B90 (1919) xxvi-xxvii
    N 56 (1897) 54-55
    N 99 (1917) 370
    S 46 (1917) 135
BELL, THOMAS, zoology, 1792-
    1880, England
    N 21 (1880) 499-500
BELLEVILLE, JULIUS, invention,
            -1896, France
    S 3 (1896) 592
BĚLCHOUBEK, AUGUST J., chem-
    istry, 1847-1908
    Czechoslovakia
    S 27 (1908) 966
    S 28 (1908) 46
BELON, PIERRE, anatomy-biology,
    1517-1564, France
    P 34 (1888-1889) P fp 577,
       692-697
BELT, THOMAS, geology, 1832-
    1878, England
    A 116 (1878) 410
    N 18 (1878) 570
BELTRAMI, EUGENIO, mathematics-
    physics, 1835-1900, Italy
    N 61 (1900) 568-569
    N 67 (1903) 79
    S 11 (1900) 437
BENDIRE, CHARLES EMIL, oology-
    ornithology, 1836-1897?,
    Germany
    S 5 (1897) 261-262, 304
    S 7 (1898) 241
BENECKE, ERICH, medicine,
            -1904, Germany
    S 20 (1904) 351
BENNDORF, FRIEDRICH AUGUST
    OTTO, archeology, 1838-1907,
    Austria

S   25 (1907) 198
BENNER, HENRY, mathematics,
    -1901, U.S.A.
S   14 (1901) 339
BENNET, EDWARD TURNER, zoology,
    -1837, England
A   32 (1837) 215-216
BENNETT, ALFRED WILLIAM, botany,
    1833-1902, England
N   65 (1902) 321
S   14 (1901) 821
S   15 (1902) 318
BENNETT, SIR JAMES, medicine,
    . . . ,
L   51 (1892) xli-xliii
BENNETT, JOHN HUGHES, medicine,
    1812-1875, England
E   9 (1875-1878) 15-17
BENNETT, JOHN JOSEPH, botany,
    1801-1876, England
A 113 (1877) 237-238
BENT, CLINTON THOMAS, explora-
    tion, 1851?-1912, England
S   36 (1912) 370
BENT, JAMES THEODORE, archeology,
    1852-1897, England
N   56 (1897) 35
S   5 (1897) 839
BENTE, F., agriculture,
    -1911, Germany
S   34 (1911) 838
BENTHAM, GEORGE, botany, 1800-
    1884, England
A 128 (1884) 319
A 129 (1885) 103-113, 172
L   38 (1885) i-v
N   30 (1884) 539-543, 591
Sl   4 (1884) P 352-353
Sl   5 (1885) 122
BENTHAM, JEREMY, philanthropy,
    1748-1832, England
A   23 (1832-1833) 370
BENZENBERG, JOHANN FRIEDRICH,
    astronomy-physics, 1777-
    1846, Germany
A   52 (1846) 297
BERCKMANS, PROSPER J.A.,
    horticulture, 1829?-1910,
    U.S.A.
S   32 (1910) 711
BEREND, NICOLAUS, medicine,
    -1919, Hungary
S   50 (1919) 109
BERG, CARLOS, biology?, 1843?-
    1902, Argentina
S   15 (1902) 318

BERG, OTTO, botany, 1815?-
    1866, Germany
A   95 (1868) 124
BERGÉ, HENRI, chemistry,
    -1911, Belgium?
S   33 (1911) 723
BERGEN, JOSEPH YOUNG, botany-
    physics, 1851-1917, U.S.A.
S   46 (1917) 379-380
S   47 (1918) 14-15
BERGER, ALEXANDER FREDERIK,
    mathematics, 1844-1901,
    Sweden
S   14 (1901) 660
BERGER, PAUL, surgery, 1845-
    1908, France
S   28 (1908) 642
BERGH, LUDWIG RUDOLPH SOPHUS,
    medicine, 1824-1909,
    Denmark
S   30 (1909) 55, 304
BERGHAUS, HEINRICH KARL WILHELM,
    mathematics, 1797-1884,
    Germany
Sl   3 (1884) 468
BERGMAN, TOBERN OLOF, chemistry-
    physics, 1735-1784, Sweden
PM   3 (1799) P fr
PM   9 (1801) P 193-200
von BERGMANN, ERNST, medicine,
    1836-1907, Germany
S   24 (1906) 381
S   25 (1907) 559
BERGSTRÖM, JOHN ANDREW,
    pedagogy, 1867-1910, Sweden
S   31 (1910) 410
BERINGER, JOHANN BARTHOLOMAEUS
    ADAM, paleontology, c.1667-
    1738, Germany
A 118 (1879) 332
BERKELEY, MYLES JOSEPH,
    mycology, 1803-1889,
    England
A   87 (1864) 111-112
L   47 (1890) ix-xii
N   40 (1889) 371-372
Sl 14 (1889) 112
BERNADOU, JOHN BAPTISTE,
    chemistry, 1858-1908, U.S.A.
S   21 (1905) 879
BERNARD, CLAUDE, physiology,
    1813-1878, France
A   69 (1855) 105
E   10 (1878-1880) 6-10
N   17 (1878) 304-305
N   27 (1883) 317-319

P 13 (1878) 20-25, P fp
641, 742-744
P 84 (1914) P 567-578
Sl 5 (1885) 20
Sl 6 (1885) 117
S 39 (1914) 206
BERNARD, FÉLIX, malacology,
1863?-1898,
S 8 (1898) 613
BERNARD, JOHN MACKAY, meteor-
ology, 1857-1919, Scotland
E 40 (1919-1920) 2-3
BERNHARDI, JOHANN JACOB,
botany, 1774-1850,
A 63 (1852) 45
BERNHARDT, MARTIN, neurol-
ogy, 1845?-1915, Germany
S 41 (1915) 722
BERNIER, PIERRE FRANÇOIS
astronomy, 1779-1803,
PM 20 (1804) 103-106
BERNOULLI, JACQUES (II),
mathematics, 1759-1789,
Switzerland
PM 3 (1799) 92-99
BERNSTEIN, JULIUS, physiol-
ogy, 1839-1917, Germany
S 41 (1915) 203
BERRY, GEORGE, commerce,
1795-1874, Scotland
E 8 (1872-1875) 476-477
BERT, PAUL, physiology-zool-
ogy, 1833-1886, France
N 35 (1886) 54
P 33 (1888) P fp 289,
401-407
Sl 8 (1886) 445, 584
BERTELLI, TIMOTEO, physics-
seismology, 1826-1905, Italy
S 21 (1905) 399, 557
BERTHEIM, B. ALFRED, chemis-
try, 1879?-1914, Germany
S 40 (1914) 479
BERTHELOT, PIERRE EUGÈNE MARCE-
LIN, chemistry, 1827-1907,
France
A 173 (1907) 324
L A80 (1908) iii-x
N 65 (1901) 80-83
N 75 (1907) 493, 512-514
P 27 (1885) P fr, 113-116
P 70 (1907) 475-477
Sl 2 (1883) 839
S 25 (1907) 516, 557,
592-595

BERTHIER, PIERRE, mineralogy,
1782-1861, France
A 83 (1862) 108, 150-151
BERTILLON, ALPHONSE, anthro-
pometry, 1853-1914, France
S 39 (1914) 355
BERTKAU, PHILIPP, zoology,
-1895, Germany
S 2 (1895) 691
BERTOLONI, ANTONIO, botany,
1775-1869, Italy
A 99 (1870) 129
BERTRAND, CHARLES EUGÈNE, bot-
any, 1851-1917, France
S 46 (1917) 538
BERTRAND, JOSEPH LOUIS FRANÇOIS
mathematics, 1822-1900,
France
A 159 (1900) 462
N 61 (1900) P 614-616
S 11 (1900) 596
S 26 (1907) 629-630
BERTRAND, MARCEL ALEXANDRE,
geology-mathematics, 1847-
1907, France
A 173 (1907) 324
N 75 (1907) 441-442
S 25 (1907) 517
von BERZELIUS, JÖNS JAKOB,
baron, chemistry, 1779-
1848, Sweden
A 47 (1844) 218-220
A 56 (1848) 448-451
A 66 (1853) 1-15, 173-186,
305-313
A 67 (1854) 103-113
N 31 (1885) 196-197
L 3 (1830-1837) 442
L 5 (1843-1850) 872-876
N 48 (1893) 561-562
N 63 (1901) 77-78
N 67 (1902) 49-50
S 15 (1902) 422, 740-742
BESANT, WILLIAM HENRY, mathe-
matics, 1828-1917, England
N 99 (1917) 310-311
S 46 (1917) 14
BESSEL, FRIEDRICH WILHELM, as-
tronomy-mathematics, 1784-
1846, Germany
A 52 (1846) 145
A 54 (1847) 305-320
L 5 (1843-1850) 644-649
P 27 (1885) 340-344
PM III 30 (1847) 201-206

S 10 (1899) 962-963
BESSELS, EMIL, exploration,
1857-1888, Germany
Sl 11 (1888) 169, 219-220
BESSEMER, SIR HENRY, metal-
lurgy, 1813-1898, England
N 57 (1898) 487-488
S 7 (1898) 458
BESSEY, CHARLES EDWIN, bot-
any, 1845-1915, U.S.A.
A 189 (1915) 486
P 72 (1908) P 191
P 78 (1911) P 200-201
S 41 (1915) 355, 420-421,
599
BESSEY, EDWARD A., engineer-
ing,   -1910, U.S.A.
S 32 (1910) 151
BETTONI, EUGENIO, ichthyology,
1845?-1898, Italy
S 8 (1898) 476
BEUSHAUSEN, HERMANN ERNST LOUIS,
geology-paleontology, 1863-
1904, Germany
S 19 (1904) 478, 559
BEVAN, PENRY VAUGHAN, physics,
1875-1913, England
A 187 (1914) 208
S 39 (1914) 20
BEVERIDGE, ERSKINE, commerce,
-1920, Scotland
E 40 (1919-1920) 191
BEVERLY, CHARLES JAMES, sur-
gery, 1788-1868, England
L 17 (1869) lxxxvii-
lxxxviii
BEVIS (BEVANS), JOHN, astron-
omy-medicine, 1693-1771,
PM 23 (1806) 247-252
BEWICK, THOMAS, biology,
1753-1823, England
A 37 (1839) 158-161
BEYER, HENRY GUSTAV, surgery,
1850-1918, Germany
S 48 (1918) 616
BEYRICH, HEINRICH ERNST, geol-
ogy, 1815-1896, Germany
S 4 (1896) 310
BEZJIAN, H. ALEXAN, science,
1837?-1913, Turkey
S 37 (1913) 626
von BEZOLD, JOHANN FRIEDRICH
WILHELM, meteorology-physics,
1837-1907, Germany
A 170 (1905) 470

A 173 (1907) 324
N 75 (1907) 397
N 76 (1907) 28-29
S 22 (1905) 510
S 25 (1907) 398, 674
BIART, LUCIEN, ethnology, 1829-
1897, France
S 5 (1897) 692
BIASOLETTO, B., botany, 1793?-
1858, Italy
A 77 (1895) 442
von BIBRA, ERNST, Baron, biol-
ogy, 1806-1878, Germany
A 116 (1878) 164
BICHAT, ERNEST ADOLPHE, physics,
1845-1905, France
S 22 (1905) 254
BICHAT, MARIE FRANÇOIS XAVIER,
physiology, 1771-1802, France
S 16 (1902) 239
BICKERTON, SIR RICHARD HUSSEY,
navigation,   -1832,
L 3 (1830-1837) 149
BICKMORE, ALBERT SMITH, geogra-
phy-geology, 1839-1914, U.S.A.
A 188 (1914) 370
S 40 (1914) 267
BIDWELL, SHELFORD, physics,
1848-1909, England
A 179 (1910) 276
N 82 (1909) 252-253
S 31 (1910) 105
BIERI, ROBERT, biology, 1878?-
1904, Switzerland
S 20 (1904) 287
BIERMANN, AUGUST LEO OTTO, mathe-
matics, 1858-1909, Austria
S 29 (1909) 893-894
BIGELOW, FRANK HAGAR, meteorol-
ogy, 1851-   , U.S.A.
S 5 (1897) 692
BIGELOW, JACOB, botany, 1787?-
1879, U.S.A.
A 117 (1879) 180, 263-266
A 119 (1880) 77
BIGSBY, JOHN JEREMIAH, geology,
1792-1881, England
A 121 (1881) 338
L 33 (1882) xvi-xvii
N 23 (1881) 389
BILGUER, JEAN ULRIC, surgery,
1720-1796, Switzerland
S 12 (1900) 258
BILLINGS, ELKANAH, paleontology,
1820-1876, Canada

A 112 (1876) 80
A 114 (1877) 78-80
BILLINGS, FRANK SEAVER, medi-
cine, 1845-1912, U.S.A.
S 36 (1912) 552
BILLINGS, JOHN SHAW, medicine,
1838-1913, U.S.A.
A 185 (1913) 468
N 91 (1913) 62
S 37 (1913) 408, 512
S 38 (1913) 827-833
S 39 (1914) 210
S 43 (1916) 536
BILLWILLER, ROBERT AUGUST,
meteorology, 1849-1905,
Switzerland
S 22 (1905) 319
BINET, ALFRED, psychology,
1857-1911, France
S 34 (1911) 558
BINET, JACQUES PHILIPPE MARIE,
mathematics, 1786-1856, France
A 72 (1856) 264
BINNEY, AMOS, conchology-
geology, 1803-1847, U.S.A.
A 53 (1847) 451-452
BINNEY, EDWARD WILLIAM, geol-
ogy, 1812-1881, England
N 25 (1882) 293
N 90 (1913) 539
BINNIE, SIR ALEXANDER RICH-
ARDSON, engineering, 1839?-
1917, England
N 99 (1917) 267
S 45 (1917) 634
BINOT, JEAN, anatomy,
-1909, France
S 30 (1909) 874
BINZ, CARL, pharmacology,
1832-1913, Germany
S 36 (1912) 168
S 37 (1913) 251
BION, H.S., geology,
-1915
S 42 (1915) 242
BIOT, JEAN BAPTISTE, mathe-
matics-physics, 1774-1862,
France
A 83 (1862) 441
A 84 (1862) 120-122
E 5 (1862-1866) 25-27
L 12 (1863) xxxv-xlii
BIRD, C., geography, 1843?-
1910, U.S.A.
S 31 (1910) 663

BIRKELAND, KRISTIAN R., chem-
istry-physics, 1867-1917,
Norway
N 99 (1917) 349
S 46 (1917) 135
BIRMINGHAM, JOHN, astronomy,
c. 1816-1884, Ireland
Sl 5 (1885) 122
BIRNBACHER, ALOIS, ophthalmology,
1849?-1915, Germany
S 41 (1915) 608
BIRSCH-HIRSCHFELD, ..., pathol-
ogy, 1842?-1899, Germany
S 10 (1899) 979
BIRTWELL, FRANCIS J., ornithol-
ogy,   -1901, U.S.A.
S 14 (1901) 77
BISCHOF, CARL GUSTAV CHRISTOPH,
chemistry-geology, 1792-
1870, Germany
A 101 (1871) 151
N 3 (1871) 212
BISCHOFF, GOTTLIEB WILHELM,
botany, 1797-1854, Germany
A 69 (1855) 129
BISCHOFFSHEIM, ...,astronomy,
-1906,
S 23 (1906) 990
BISHOP, GEORGE, astronomy,
1785-1861, England
L 12 (1863) iii-iv
BISHOP, HEBER R., anthropol-
ogy-philanthropy, 1840-
1902, U.S.A.
S 17 (1903) 35-36
S 24 (1906) 23-25
BISHOP, JOHN, medicine, 1797-
1873, England
L 21 (1873) v-vi
BISHOP,SERENO EDWARDS, geology,
1827-1909, U.S.A.
S 29 (1909) 654
BISSELL, WILLIAM GROSVENOR,
bacteriology, 1870-1919, U.S.A
S 50 (1919) 480
BISSETT, JOHN J., engineering,
1836?-1915, U.S.A.
S 42 (1915) 157
BITTNER, ALEXANDER, geology-
paleontology, 1850-1902,
Austria
A 163 (1902) 480
S 15 (1902) 758
BIZZOZERO, GIULIO, pathology,
1846?-1901, Italy
S 13 (1901) 717

BJERKNES, CARL ANTON, mathe-
matics-physics, 1825-1903,
Norway
N 62 (1900) 3, 200
N 68 (1903) 133, 172-173
S 17 (1903) 799
BJERKNES, VICTOR, meteorology,
A 185 (1913) 202-203
BLACK, ADAM, publisher, 1784-
1874, Scotland
E 8 (1872-1875) 467-468
BLACK, CAMPBELL, medicine,
1843?-1898, Scotland
E 23 (1899-1901) 6-7
BLACK, CHARLES W. M., mathe-
matics,   -1902, U.S.A.
S 16 (1902) 318
BLACK, GREENE VARDIMAN, den-
tistry, 1836-1915, U.S.A.
S 42 (1915) 496-497
BLACK, JAMES, medicine, 1787-
1867, Scotland
E 6 (1866-1869) 188-189
BLACK, JOSEPH, chemistry-
physics, 1728-1799, France
E 2 (1844-1850) 238
E 12 (1882-1884) 462-463
N 18 (1878) 346-347
N 64 (1901) 420
N 69 (1904) 612-613
PM 5 (1799) 312
PM 5 (1800) P fr
PM 10 (1801) P 157-158
S 19 (1904) 678
BLACKBURN, HUGH, mathematics,
1823?-1909, Scotland
N 81 (1909) 522-523
S 30 (1909) 594
BLACKBURN, ISAAC W., pathology,
1851?-1911, U.S.A.
S 33 (1911) 991
BLACKFORD, EUGENE GILBERT,
ichthyology, 1839-1904,
U.S.A.
S 21 (1905) 38, 232-233
BLACKIE, JOHN STUART, litera-
ture, 1809-1895, Scotland
E 21 (1895-1897) vi-ix
BLACKWOOD, JOHN, publisher,
1818-1878, Scotland
E 10 (1878-1880) 329-331
BLACKWOOD, FREDERIC TEMPLE
HAMILTON-TEMPLE, marquis of
Dufforin and Ava, diplomacy,
1826-1902, England
S 16 (1902) 974

BLAGDEN, SIR CHARLES, science,
1748-1820, England
A 2 (1820) 344
BLAIKIE, W. GARDEN, theology,
1820-1862, Scotland
E 23 (1899-1901) 7
de BLAINVILLE, HENRI MARIE
DUCROTAY, anatomy, 1777-
1850, France
A 60 (1850) 138
L 5 (1843-1850) 1011-1013
S 26 (1907) 496-497
BLAIR, . . .,   ,   ,
A 17 (1829-1830) 367-368
BLAIR, H. W., geography,
-1884, U.S.A.
Sl 5 (1885) 264
BLAIR, R. A., geology,
-1902, U.S.A.
S 17 (1903) 37
BLAKE, CLARENCE JOHN, otology,
1843-1919, U.S.A.
S 49 (1919) 167
BLAKE, ELI WHITNEY, JR.,
physics, 1836-1895?, U.S.A.
A 150 (1895) 434
S 2 (1895) 483
BLAKE, FRANCIS, invention-
physics, 1850-1913, U.S.A.
S 37 (1913) 172
BLAKE, HENRY WOLLASTON,   ,
1815-1899, England
S 10 (1899) 63
BLAKE, JOHN FREDERICK, geology,
1839-1906, England
S 24 (1906) 126
BLAKE, JOHN MARCUS, crystal-
lography, 1831?-1920, U.S.A
A 200 (1920) 316
BLAKE, LUCIAN IRA, physics,
1854-1916, U.S.A.
S 43 (1916) 684
BLAKE, WILLIAM PHIPPS, geol-
ogy-mining, 1826-1910,
U.S.A.
A 180 (1910) 95-96
S 31 (1910) 853
BLAKISTON, PEYTON, medicine,
1801-1878, England
L 29 (1879) i-ii
BLANCHARD, CHARLES ÉMILE,
entomology, 1819-1900,
France
A 159 (1900) 395
N 61 (1900) 473
S 11 (1900) 399

BLANCHARD, RAPHAEL ANATOLE
ÉMILE, medicine, 1857-1919,
France
A 197 (1919) 454
P 87 (1915) P 74
S 49 (1919) 234, 391-392
BLANCHET, PAUL, archeology-
exploration, 1870-1900,
France
S 12 (1900) 652
BLAND, THOMAS, biology-conchol-
ogy, 1809-1885, England
A 130 (1885) 407-408
Sl 6 (1885) 440
BLANDFORD, G. F., psychology,
1829?-1911, England
S 34 (1911) 376
BLANE, WILLIAM, chemistry,
-1836,
L 3 (1830-1837) 437
BLANFORD, HENRY FRANCIS, geol-
ogy-meteorology, 1834-
1893, England
L 54 (1894) xii-xix
N 47 (1893) 522-523
BLANFORD, WILLIAM THOMAS,
geology-zoology, 1832-1905,
England
L B79 (1907) xxvii-xxxi
N 65 (1901) 108
N 72 (1905) 202-203
S 22 (1905) 63-64
BLASCHKA, . . ., glassblowing,
A 149 (1895) 242-245
BLASERNA, PIETRO, physics,
1836-1918, Italy
S 47 (1918) 415
BLATIN, JEAN BAPTISTE ANTOINE,
physiology, 1841-1911,
France
S 34 (1911) 680
BLEEKER, PIETER, ichthyology,
1819-1878, Netherlands
N 17 (1878) 286
BLEICHER, MARIE GUSTAVE,
geology-pharmacy, 1838-1901,
France
S 13 (1901) 1038
BLIX, MAGNUS, physiology, 1849?-
1904, Sweden
S 19 (1904) 478
BLOXAM, ANDREW, botany, 1802?-
1878, England
A 117 (1879) 178
BLOXAM, WILLIAM POPPLEWELL,
chemistry, 1860?-1913,

A 187 (1914) 208
S 39 (1914) 136
BLUE, RUPERT, sanitation,
1867- , U.S.A.
P 82 (1913) P 373-375
BLUM, JOHANN REINHARD,
mineralogy, 1802-1883,
Germany
A 126 (1883) 332
BLUME, CARL LUDWIG, botany,
1796-1862, Germany
A 83 (1862) 428
BLUMENBACH, JOHANN FRIEDRICH,
medicine, 1752-1840,
Germany
A 40 (1840-1841) 219
L 4 (1837-1843) 265-267
BLUMENTRITT, FERDINAND, eth-
nology, -1913,
Czechoslovakia
S 38 (1913) 738
BLUMSTRAND, WILHELM, chemistry,
-1897, Sweden
S 6 (1897) 876
BLUNT, EDMUND, geodesy, 1799-
1866, U.S.A.
A 92 (1866) 433-434
BLYTH, BENJAMIN HALL, engi-
neering, 1849-1917, Scotland
E 37 (1916-1917) 387-390
E 38 (1917-1918) 11
BLYTH, JAMES, mathematics-
physics, -1906, Scot-
land
S 23 (1906) 959
BLYTT, AXEL GUDBRAND, botany,
1844-1898, Norway
S 8 (1898) 263
BLYTT, M. N., botany, 1792?-
1862, Norway
A 85 (1863) 449
BOARDMAN, T. H., physics,
-1917, England
S 46 (1917) 337
BOAS, FRANZ, anthropology,
1858-1942, Germany
A 72 (1908) P 288
BÔCHER, MAXIME, mathematics,
1867-1918, U.S.A.
S 48 (1918) 291, 534-535
BOCOURT, MARIE FIRMIN, bio-
logy, 1819-1904, France
S 19 (1904) 358
BODE, JOHANN ELERLT, astron-
omy, 1747-1826, Germany
A 15 (1829) 177

BODINE, DONALDSON, geology-
zoology, 1866-1916, U.S.A.
S 43 (1916) 131
BODINUS, KARL AUGUST HEINRICH,
zoology, 1813?-1884, Ger-
many
Sl 5 (1885) 62
BÖCK, RUPERT, mechanics,
-1899, Austria
S 9 (1899) 301
BOECKH, . . ., statistics,
1825?-1908?, Hungary?
S 27 (1908) 118
BÖCKING, ADOLF, zoology,
-1898, Germany
S 8 (1898) 76
BOEDEKER, CARL HEINRICH DETLEV,
chemistry, 1815-1895, Ger-
many
S 1 (1895) 364
BOEHM, GEORG, geology, 1854-
1913, Germany
S 37 (1913) 626
BÖHM, RICHARD JOHANN CONSTAN-
TIN, zoology, 1854-1884,
Germany
Sl 6 (1885) 20
BÖLCKERS, KARL, ophthalmology,
1836?-1914, Germany
S 39 (1914) 355
BOER, OSCAR, medicine,
-1897, Germany
S 6 (1897) 211
BÖRGEN, CARL NICOLAI JENSEN,
astronomy, 1843-1909,
Germany
S 30 (1909) 411
BOERHAAVE, HERMANN, medicine,
1668-1738, Netherlands
P 47 (1895) P fr, 110-120
BOETHOR, ELLIOUS, philology,
1782?-1822, Egypt
A 5 (1822) 180
BÖTTCHER, ALBR., physics,
-1900, Germany
S 12 (1900) 1014
BOGDANOF, ANATOLY PETROVICH,
zoology, 1834-1896, Russia
N 53 (1896) 584
S 3 (1896) 702
BOGDANOF, ALEXANDER, pathology,
1854?-1906, Russia
S 24 (1906) 318
BOGDANOF, MODEST NIKOLAEVICH,
zoology, 1841-1888, Russia
N 37 (1888) 567

Sl 11 (1888) 209
BOGDANOFSKY, VERA EVSTAFJEVNA
(MRS. POPOF), chemistry,
-1897
N 56 (1897) 132
S 6 (1897) 96
BOGGIANI, GUIDO, exploration,
-1903, Italy
S 18 (1903) 317
BOGGS, GILBERT HILLHOUSE,
chemistry, 1875-1941, U.S.A.
S 14 (1901) 334
BOGOMOLOF, T., chemistry
-1897, Russia
S 6 (1897) 519
BOGUE, ERNEST EVERETT, forest-
ry, 1864-1907, U.S.A.
S 26 (1907) 295
BOGUE, VIRGIL GAY, engineering,
1846-1916, U.S.A.
S 44 (1916) 604
von BOGUSLAFSKI, GEORG HEIN-
RICH, hydrography, 1827-
1884, Germany
Sl 4 (1884) 76
BOHM VON BAWERK, EUGEN, eco-
nomics, 1851-1914, Austria
S 40 (1914) 516
BOHN, JOHANN CONRAD, mathe-
matics-physics, 1831-1897,
Germany
S 6 (1897) 591
BOILEAU, JOHN THEOPHILUS, en-
gineering, 1805-1886, India
L 42 (1887) i-vii
BOISSIER, PIERRE EDMOND,
botany, 1810-1885, Switzer-
land
A 131 (1886) 20-21
BOISTEL, ALPHONSE, botany-
geology, 1836-1908, France
S 28 (1908) 556
BOJER, . . ., botany, 1800?-
1856, Mauritius?
A 73 (1857) 148, 279
BOLDONI, SIGISMONDO, medicine,
1597- , Italy
S 8 (1898) 591
BOLTER, ANDREW, entomology,
1820?-1900, U.S.A.
S 11 (1900) 518-519
BOLLES, WILLIAM PALMER, botany,
-1916, U.S.A.
S 43 (1916) 566
von BOLLINGER, OTTO, pathology,
1843-1909, Germany

S 30 (1909) 335
BOLTON, HENRY CARRINGTON,
  chemistry, 1843-1903, U.S.A.
  A 166 (1903) 475
  P 43 (1893) P fp 577,
     688-695
  S 18 (1903) 278, 703, 798
  S 21 (1905) 884
  S 22 (1905) 304-305
BOLTZMANN, LUDWIG EDUARD,
  physics, 1844-1906, Austria
  A 172 (1906) 476
  L A80 (1908) xi-xiii
  N 48 (1893) 435
  N 49 (1894) 381-382
  N 74 (1906) 569-570
  S 24 (1906) 415
  S 25 (1907) 2
BOLUS, HARRY, botany,
     -1911, South Africa
  N 86 (1911) 490
BOLYAI DE BOLYA, FARKAS (WOLF-
  GANG), mathematics, 1775-
  1856, Hungary
  S 13 (1901) 463
BOLYAI, JÁNOS (JOHANN), mathe-
  matics, 1802-1860, Hungary
  S 2 (1895) 843
  S 12 (1900) 842-846
  S 13 (1901) 462-465
BONAPARTE, CHARLES LUCIEN
  JULES LAURENT, Prince,
  ornithology, 1803-1857,
  France
  A 74 (1857) 299
BONAPARTE, LOUIS CHARLES
  NAPOLEON, administration,
  1769-1821, Corsica
  A 12 (1827) 390-391
BONAPARTE, PRINCE ROLAND,
  biology-geography, 1858-
  1924, France
  N 81 (1909) 12
BONAR, WILLIAM, patron, 1798-
  1866, Scotland
  E 6 (1866-1869) 33-34
BONAVIA-HUNT, HENRY GEORGE,
  theology,   -1917, Malta
  E 39 (1918-1919) 10-13
BOND, GEORGE PHILLIPS, astron-
  omy, 1825-1865, U.S.A.
  A 89 (1865) 235-236
  N 57 (1897) 171-172
  S 6 (1897) 997-999
BOND, WILLIAM CRANCH, astron-
  omy, 1789-1859, U.S.A.

A 77 (1859) 303
N 57 (1897) 171-172
P 47 (1895) P fp 289,
   400-408
S 5 (1897) 934
S 6 (1897) 997-999
BONDY, O., gynecology,
     -1915, Germany
  S 42 (1915) 335-336
BONNEY, THOMAS GEORGE, geology,
  1833-1923, England
  L B99 (1926) P xvii-xxvii
  P 75 (1909) P 412-414
  S 3 (1890) 65
BONPLAND, GOUJAUD AIMÉ JACQUES
  ALEXANDRE, biology, 1773-
  1858, France
  A 4 (1822) 197
  A 52 (1846) 297
  A 76 (1858) 301-304
  A 77 (1859) 442
BONSDORF, EVERT JULIUS, anatomy,
  1810?-1898, Sweden
  S 8 (1898) 367
de BONSTETTEN, CHARLES VICTOR,
  sociology, 1745-1832,
  Switzerland
  A 23 (1832-1833) 370,
     374-376
BONTAIN, ..., physics,
     -1900, France
  S 12 (1900) 39
BOOLE, GEORGE, mathematics,
  1815-1864, England
  E 4 (1857-1862) 85-87
  L 5 (1843-1850) 522
  L 15 (1867) vi-xi
  N 99 (1917) 221
  P 17 (1880) P fp 721,
     840-842
  S 13 (1901) 517
BOONE, C. J., geometry, 1866?-
  1896, U.S.A.
  S 4 (1896) 616
BOOTH, CHARLES, sociology,
  1840-1916, England
  N 60 (1899) 31
BOOTH, EDWARD, chemistry,
     -1917, U.S.A.
  S 46 (1917) 337
BOOTH, JAMES CURTIS, chemistry,
  1810-1888, U.S.A.
  A 135 (1888) 346
  P 40 (1891-1892) P fr,
     116-122
  S 15 (1902) 741-742

S   21 (1905) 876-877
BOOTH, SAMUEL C., mineralogy,
        -1895, U.S.A.
S   2 (1895) 452
BOOTT, FRANCIS, botany, 1792-
1863, U.S.A.
A   87 (1864) 288-292
BOOTT, WILLIAM, botany, 1805-
1887, U.S.A.
A   134 (1887) 160
A   135 (1888) 262
de BOOY, THEODORE, archeology,
1883?-1919, Netherlands
S   49 (1919) 213
BOPP, KARL, mathematics-physics,
1877-1904, Germany
S   19 (1904) 967
BORCHERT, OSCAR, exploration,
        -1895,
S   2 (1895) 770
BORDA, JEAN CHARLES, physics,
1733-1799, France
PM   3 (1799) 332
PM   4 (1799) 222-224
BORDIER, ARTHUR, anthropology,
1841-1910, France
S   31 (1910) 411
BOREAU, ALEXANDRE, botany,
1803-1875, France
A   111 (1876) 326
BORELLI, GIOVANNI ALFONSO,
physics, 1608-1679, Italy
N   64 (1901) 418
BORGER, W.A., bacteriology,
1875?-1915?, France
S   43 (1916) 65
BORGHÈSE, CAMILLE, . . . ,
        -1832, Italy
A   23 (1832-1833) 370
BORGMANN, IVAN IVANOVICH,
physics, 1849-1914, Russia
A   189 (1915) 230
S   40 (1914) 812
BORICKÝ, EMANUEL, mineralogy,
1840-1881, Czechoslovakia
A   121 (1881) 338
BORN, GUSTAV JACOB, anatomy,
1851?-1900, Germany
S   12 (1900) 237
BORNET, JEAN BAPTISTE EDOUARD,
botany, 1828-1911, France
A   183 (1912) 296
N   88 (1912) 321
S   35 (1912) 143
BORNTRAGER, ARTHUR, chemistry,
1820?-1905, Germany

S   21 (1905) 439
BORRER, WILLIAM, botany, 1781-
1862, England
A   85 (1863) 449
L   12 (1863) xlii
BORSHCHOV, ILYA GRIGOREVICH,
botany,   -1878, Russia
A   117 (1879) 179
BORUP, GEORGE, exploration,
        -1912,
A   183 (1912) 598
BORY DE SAINT-VINCENT,
GENEVIÈVE JEAN BAPTISTE
MARCELLIN, baron, geography,
1778-1846, France
A   53 (1847) 452
BOSANQUET, ROBERT HOLFORD
MACDOWALL, physics, 1841-
1912, England
N   42 (1890) 14
S   36 (1912) 273
BOSCOVICH, RUGGIERO GIUSEPPE,
astronomy-mathematics,
1711-1787, Italy
PM   4 (1799) P fr
PM   10 (1801) P 74-76
BOSS, LEWIS, astronomy, 1846-
1912, U.S.A.
A   184 (1912) 495
N   90 (1912) 226-227
P   81 (1912) P 618-619
S   36 (1912) 472
BOSSCHA, JOHANNES, physics,
1831-1911, Netherlands
A   181 (1911) 582
N   86 (1911) 419-420
S   33 (1911) 767
BOSSERT, JOSEPH FRANÇOIS,
astronomy, 1851-1906,
France
S   24 (1906) 382
BOSSO, GIUSEPPE, bacteriology,
        -1899, Italy
S   9 (1899) 158
BOSTOCK, JOHN, medicine,
1774-1846, England
L   5 (1843-1850) 636-638
PM   III 30 (1847) 196-198
BOTFIELD, BERIAH, literature,
1807-1863, England
E   5 (1862-1866) 131-133
BOTTINI, E., medicine,
        , Italy
S   24 (1906) 382
BOTTOMLEY, JAMES THOMSON,
physics, 1845-1926, Ireland

L   A113 (1927) P xii-xiii
N   38 (1888) 11
N   117 (1926) 830
BOTTOMLEY, WILLIAM, physics,
  1849?-1912, Scotland
N   90 (1912) 226
S   36 (1912) 669
BOUCHARD, CHARLES JACQUES,
  biology-pathology, 1837-
  1915, France
A   191 (1916) 152
S   42 (1915) 827
BOUCHARDAT, GUSTAVE, chemistry-
  pharmacy, 1842-1918, France
S   49 (1919) 42
BOUCHER DE CRÈVECOEUR DE
  PERTHES, JACQUES, archeol-
  ogy, 1788-1868, France
S   28 (1908) 83-84
BOUÉ, AMÉDÉE AMI, geology,
  1794-1881, Germany
N   25 (1881) 109-111
de BOUGAINVILLE, LOUIS ANTOINE,
  comte, geography, 1729-1811,
  France
N   80 (1909) P 430
PM   43 (1814) 371-378
BOULENGER, GEORGE ALBERT,
  zoology, 1858-1937, Belgium
N   50 (1894) 55
BOULTON, MATTHEW, engineering-
  invention, 1728-1809,
  England
P   12 (1877-1878) P 139-140
PM   15 (1803) P fr, 59-63
BOUQUET, JEAN CLAUDE, mathe-
  matics, 1819-1885, France
Sl   6 (1885) 429
BOUQUET DE LA GRYE, JEAN
  JACQUES ANATOLE, astronomy-
  engineering, 1827-1909,
  France
N   82 (1910) 286-287
S   31 (1910) 105
BOURGEAU, EUGÈNE, botany,
  1813-1877, France
A   115 (1878) 225
BOURKE, JOHN GREGORY, anthro-
  pology, 1846-1896, U.S.A.
S   3 (1896) 899
S   4 (1896) 820-822
BOURLET, CARLO ÉMILE ERNEST,
  mechanics, 1866-1913,
  France
S   38 (1913) 359
BOURLON, . . ., archeology,

-1915, France
S   41 (1915) 819-820
BOURNE, SIR ALFRED GIBBS,
  zoology, 1859-1940,
  England
N   52 (1895) 31
BOUSFIELD, SIR WILLIAM,
  education, 1842-1910,
  England
N   83 (1910) 195-196
BOUSSINGAULT, JEAN BAPTISTE
  JOSEPH DIEUDONNÉ, agricul-
  ture-chemistry, 1802-1887,
  France
N   36 (1887) 134-135
P   33 (1888) P fp 721,
  836-841
S   2 (1895) 186
BOUTIGNY, PIERRE HIPPOLYTE,
  chemistry-physics, 1798-
  1884, France
Sl   4 (1884) 76
BOUVARD, ALEXIS, astronomy,
  1767-1843, France
L   5 (1843-1850) 478
BOUVEAULT, LOUIS, chemistry,
  1864-1909, France
S   30 (1909) 403
BOVERI, THEODOR HEINRICH,
  cytology-zoology, 1862-
  1915, Germany
A   190 (1915) 524
N   96 (1915) 372-373
S   43 (1916) 263-270
BOVEY, HENRY TAYLOR, educa-
  tor-engineering, 1852?-
  1912, England
L   A88 (1913) x-xi
N   88 (1912) 520-521
S   35 (1912) 299
BOWDITCH, HENRY PICKERING,
  physiology-zoology, 1840-
  1911, U.S.A.
A   181 (1911) 340
N   58 (1898) 428
P   66 (1904-1905) P 381
P   78 (1911) P 618-620
P   85 (1914) P 416
S   23 (1906) 758, 988
S   33 (1911) 451, 598-601,
  651-652
BOWDITCH, NATHANIEL, mathe-
  matics-physics, 1773-1838,
  U.S.A.
A   19 (1830-1831) 202
A   34 (1838) 220-224

A 35 (1838) 1-47
A 36 (1839) 214-216
A 38 (1839-1840) 155
L 4 (1837-1843) 95-97
PM III 14 (1839) 63-65
Sl 10 (1887) 32
S 5 (1897) 932
BOWEN, GEORGE T., chemistry-
mineralogy, 1803-1828,
U.S.A.
A 15 (1829) 403-404
BOWER, FREDERICK ORPEN, botany,
1855-1948, Scotland
N 44 (1891) 15
N 85 (1910) 144
BOWMAN, SIR WILLIAM, anatomy,
1816-1892, England
L 4 (1837-1843) 422
L 52 (1893) i-vii
N 45 (1892) 517-518,
564-566
N 48 (1893) 26
BOWNE, BORDEN PARKER, philos-
ophy, 1847-1910, U.S.A.
S 31 (1910) 576
BOWSER, EDWARD ALBERT, en-
gineering, 1845-1910,
U.S.A.
S 31 (1910) 454
BOYCE, SIR RUBERT WILLIAM,
pathology, 1863-1911,
England
L B84 (1912) iii-ix
N 86 (1911) 589
S 34 (1911) 12
BOYÉ, MARTIN HANS, chemistry-
medicine, 1812-1909,
Denmark
P 49 (1896) P 503
S 29 (1909) 448-449
BOYESON, HJALMAR HJORTH,
linguistics, 1848?-1895,
S 2 (1895) 483
BOYLE, SIR COURTENAY EDMUND,
administration, 1845-1901,
England
N 64 (1901) 82-83
S 13 (1901) 918
BOYLE, ROBERT, chemistry-
physics, 1627-1691,
Ireland
A 114 (1877) 268
E 2 (1844-1850) 208-214
N 29 (1884) 333-334, 356-
357
N 38 (1888) 11

N 50 (1894) 349-352
N 55 (1896) P 116-117
N 79 (1906) 152-154
N 100 (1918) 477-478
P 42 (1892-1893) P fp 433,
548-553
S 17 (1903) 548
S 18 (1903) 278-280
BOYS, SIR CHARLES VERNON,
physics, 1855-1944, England
N 29 (1884) 333-334, 356-
357
N 38 (1888) 11
N 55 (1896) P 116-117
N 79 (1906) 152-154
N 100 (1918) 477-478
BOZAREINGUES, CHARLES GIROU,
biology, -1857, France
A 75 (1858) 293
BRABOURNE, WYNDHAM WENTWORTH
KNATCHBULL-HEGESSEN, Baron,
ornithology, 1885-1915
England
S 42 (1915) 373
BRACE, DE WITT BRISTOL, physics,
1859-1905, U.S.A.
A 170 (1905) 470
A 22 (1905) 476, 510,
513-514
S 23 (1906) 161-163
BRACKEBUSCH, LUIS, geology,
1849?-1906, Germany
A 172 (1906) 194
BRACKETT, CYRUS FOGG, physics,
1833-1915, U.S.A.
A 189 (1915) 326
S 41 (1915) 204, 523-525
BRACONNOT, HENRI, chemistry-
geology, 1781-1855, France
A 69 (1855) 415
A 71 (1856) 117-119
BRADBURY, JOHN, botany,
P 73 (1908) 488-499
BRADFORD, SIR JOHN ROSE,
Baron of Mawddwy, medicine,
1863-1935, England
N 50 (1894) 55
BRADFORD, THOMAS,
1745-1838,
A 38 (1839-1840) 156
BRADLEY, FRANK HOWE, geology,
1838-1879, U.S.A.
A 117 (1879) 415-416
BRADLEY, GUY M., ornithology,
-1905, U.S.A.
S 22 (1905) 190

BRADSHAW, HENRY, bibliography,
    -1886, England
    N 33 (1886) 366
BRADSHEAR, WILLIAM S., edu-
    cation, 1850?-1902, U.S.A.
    S 16 (1902) 276
BRADY, SIR ANTONIO, geology,
    1811-1881, England
    N 25 (1881) 174-175
BRADY, GEORGE STEWARDSON,
    zoology, 1832-1921, England
    L B93 (1922) P xx-xxiii
BRADY, HENRY BOWMAN, pharmacy-
    physiology, 1835-1891,
    England
    A 141 (1891) 338
    L 50 (1892) x-xiii
    N 43 (1891) 278, 299
BRADY, SAMUEL, exploration,
    1758-1796,
    A 31 (1837) 19-21
BRÄNDZA, DIMITRI, botany,
    -1895, Romania
    S 2 (1895) 586
BRAGG, SIR WILLIAM HENRY,
    physics, 1862-1942, England
    N 98 (1916) 278
    S 44 (1916) 137-138
BRAGG, WILLIAM LAWRENCE, phys-
    ics, 1890-   , Australia
    S 44 (1916) 138
BRAHE, TYCHO (TYGE), astron-
    omy, 1546-1601, Denmark
    N 15 (1877) P 405-410
    N 16 (1877) 501-502
    N 18 (1878) 306
    N 43 (1890) 98-100
    N 63 (1900) P 206-207
    N 65 (1901) 5-9, 104-106,
        181
    N 78 (1907) 81-82
    N 95 (1915) 141-142
    N 96 (1915) 252-253
    P 78 (1911) P 323
    Sl 17 (1891) 40-41
    S 13 (1901) 399
BRAID, ANDREW, hydrography,
    1846?-1919, U.S.A.
    S 49 (1919) 167
BRAIDWOOD, THOMAS, education,
        , Scotland
    Sl 11 (1888) 12
BRAKEBUSCH, LUDWIG, geology,
    1849?-1906, Germany
    S 24 (1906) 61

BRAMWELL, SIR FREDERICK JOSEPH,
    engineering, 1818-1903,
    England
    N 69 (1903) 110
    S 18 (1903) 799
BRANCHAT, R., hygiene,
    -1897,
    S 6 (1897) 700
BRAND, WILLIAM, botany, 1807-
    1869, Scotland
    E 7 (1869-1872) 6-7
BRANDE, WILLIAM THOMAS, chem-
    istry, 1786-1866, England
    A 91 (1866) 428-429
    E 6 (1866-1869) 34-36
    L 16 (1868) i-vi
BRANDIS, SIR DIETRICH, botany-
    forestry, 1824-1907,
    Germany
    L B80 (1908) iii-vi
    N 76 (1907) 131-132
    S 25 (1907) 950
BRANDT, MAX, botany,   -1915,
    Germany
    S 41 (1915) 204
BRANICKI, CONSTANTINE, count,
    biology,   -1884,
    Sl 4 (1884) 409
BRASHEAR, JOHN ALFRED, astron-
    omy-optics, 1840-1920
    U.S.A.
    A 199 (1920) 390
    P 72 (1908) P 438, 447-450
    S 42 (1915) 761
    S 45 (1917) 287
BRASSAI, SAMUEL, mathematics,
    1797?-1897, Hungary
    S 6 (1897) 127
BRAUN, ALEXANDER CARL HEINRICH,
    botany, 1805-1877, Germany
    A 113 (1877) 471-472
    N 15 (1877) 490
BRAUN, FREDERICK, mineralogy,
    1841-1919, Germany
    A 198 (1919) 402
BRAUN, KARL FERDINAND, physics,
    1850-1918, Germany
    S 47 (1918) 438
BRAUNDET, LOUIS, anatomy,
    -1911, France
    S 34 (1911) 436
BRAUNGART, RICHARD, agricul-
    ture, 1839?-1916, Germany
    S 43 (1916) 710
von BRAUNMÜHL, ANTON EDLER,

mathematics, 1853-1908,
Russia
S   27 (1908) 597
de BRAZZA, PIERRE PAUL
FRANÇOIS CAMILLE SAVORGNAN,
comte, exploration,
-1905, France
S   22 (1905) 381
BRAUNS, DAVID AUGUST, geology-
travel, 1827-1893, Germany
A   147 (1894) 160
BRAVAIS, AUGUSTE, physics,
1811-1863, France
A   86 (1863) 401-402
BREADALBANE, . . . , Marquis
of, geology,   -1863,
A   86 (1863) 278
de BRÉBISSON, LOUIS ALPHONSE,
biology, 1798-1872, France
A   105 (1873) 395
BREDICHIN, FEDOR ALEKSANDRO-
VICH, astronomy, 1831-1904,
Russia
N   70 (1904) 252
S   19 (1904) 967
BREGUET, ABRAHAM LOUIS, in-
strumentation, 1747-1823,
France
PM   62 (1823) 239
PM   63 (1824) 252-259
BREHM, ALFRED EDMUND, biology,
1829-1884, Germany
P   27 (1885) P fp 145,
263-267
Sl   5 (1885) 62
BREISLAK, SCIPIONE, geology,
1748-1826, Italy
A   12 (1827) 192-193
BREITENLOHNER, JAKOB, meteorol-
ogy,   -1897, Austria
S   5 (1897) 653, 728
BREITHAUPT, JOHANN FRIEDRICH
AUGUSTE, mineralogy, 1791-
1873, Germany
A   106 (1873) 474
BRÉLAZ, GEORGES, chemistry,
1831?-1906, France
S   23 (1906) 798
BRERETON, C.A., engineering,
1851?-1910, England
S   32 (1910) 426
BRETENSCHNEIDER, E., medicine,
-1901,
S   13 (1901) 877
BRETONNEAU, PIERRE FIDÈLE,

medicine, 1778-1862, France
S   39 (1914) 684
BRETT, JACOB, telegraphy,
A   71 (1856) 257-258
BREWER, WILLIAM HENRY, agri-
culture-biology, 1828-1910,
U.S.A.
A   180 (1910) 431
A   181 (1911) 71-74
S   32 (1910) 662
BREWSTER, SIR DAVID, physics,
1781-1868, Scotland
A   95 (1868) 284
E   6 (1866-1869) 282-284
E   12 (1882-1884) 468
L   3 (1830-1837) 11, 221
L   17 (1869) lxix-lxxiv
N   1 (1870) 650
N   25 (1881) 157-159
P   26 (1884-1885) P fp 433,
546-552
BREZINA, MARIA ARISTIDES
SEVERIN FERDINAND, mineral-
ogy, 1848-1909, Austria
S   30 (1909) 15
BRICKNER, SAMUEL MAX, gynecol-
ogy, 1867-1916, U.S.A.
S   43 (1916) 710
BRIDGE, BEWICK, mathematics,
-1833,
L   3 (1830-1837) 228
BRIDGE, THOMAS WILLIAM, zoology,
1848-1909, England
L   B82 (1910) vii-x
N   81 (1909) 42-43
S   30 (1909) 111
BRIDGES, JOHN HENRY, philos-
ophy, 1832-1906
N   80 (1909) 217
BRIDGES, THOMAS, botany,
-1865,
A   91 (1866) 265
BRIDGMAN, LAURA, deaf-mute,
1829-1889, U.S.A.
S   10 (1887) 319
S   11 (1888) 89-91, 160-161
S   13 (1889) 421
BRIGGS, THOMAS, mathematics,
, England
N   33 (1886) 223
BRIGHT, SIR CHARLES TILSTON,
telegraphy, 1832-1888,
England
N   60 (1899) 613-615
BRIGHT, RICHARD, medicine,

1789-1858, England
L 10 (1860) i-iv
BRIGHTWEN, MRS. ELIZA ELDER,
biology, 1830-1906,
Scotland
N 80 (1909) 426
S 23 (1906) 827-828
BRINCKERHOFF, WALTER REMSEN,
pathology, 1874-1911,
U.S.A.
S 33 (1911) 368
BRINTON, DANIEL GARRISON,
anthropology-archeology,
1837-1899, U.S.A.
A 158 (1899) 318
N 60 (1899) 374
P 38 (1890-1891) P fp 721,
836-840
P 41 (1892) P 293
S 10 (1899) P fp 193,
193-196
S 11 (1900) 401-402,
594-595
BRINTON, J. BERNARD, botany,
-1895?,
S 1 (1895) 448
BRINTON, WILLIAM, physiology,
1823-1867, England
L 16 (1868) vi-viii
BRIOSCHI, FRANCESCO, mathe-
matics, 1824-1897, Italy
N 57 (1898) 279
N 66 (1902) 221-222
N 67 (1903) 79
S 7 (1898) 60
BRISBANE, SIR THOMAS MACDOUGALL,
astronomy, 1773-1860,
Scotland
E 4 (1857-1862) 350-355
L 11 (1862) iii-vii
BRISSAUD, ÉDOUARD, neurology,
1852-1909, France
S 31 (1910) 65
BRISTOW, HENRY WILLIAM,
geology, 1817-1889, England
N 40 (1889) 178, 206-207
Sl 14 (1889) 9
BIRSTOWE, JOHN SYER, medicine,
1827-1895, England
L 59 (1896) x-xii
S 2 (1895) 341
BROADBENT, RALPH L., geology,
1859?-1911, Canada
S 34 (1911) 110
BROADBENT, SIR WILLIAM HENRY,

physiology, 1835-1907,
England
L B82 (1910) vii-x
N 56 (1897) 55
S 26 (1907) 126
BROCA, PIERRE PAUL, anthro-
pology-medicine, 1824-1880,
France
N 22 (1880) 249, 292-293
P 20 (1881-1882) P fp 145,
261-266
BROCH, OLE JACOB, mathematics,
1819-1889, Norway
N 39 (1889) 375
Sl 13 (1889) 180
BROCK, EDWARD PHILIP LOFTUS,
archeology,   -1895,
England
S 2 (1895) 732
BROCK, REGINALD WALTER, geology,
1874-1935, Canada
P 76 (1910) P 204
BROCKWAY, FRED JOHN, anatomy,
1860-1901, U.S.A.
S 13 (1901) 676
BRODERIP, WILLIAM JOHN, zoology,
1789-1859, England
L 10 (1860) iv-vii
BRODIE, SIR BENJAMIN COLLINS,
chemistry, 1817-1880,
England
A 121 (1881) 86
L 5 (1843-1850) 1011
L 12 (1863) xlii-lvi
N 23 (1880) 126-127
BRODIE, PETER BELLINGER,
geology, 1815-1897, England
N 57 (1897) 31-32
S 6 (1897) 805
BRODIE, THOMAS GREGOR, physiol-
ogy, 1866-1916, England
L B91 (1920) xxviii-xxx
N 98 (1916) 3-10
S 44 (1916) 349
BRODIE, WILLIAM, biology,
1831-1909, Canada
S 30 (1909) 305
BRÖGGER, WALDEMAR CHRISTOFER,
geology, 1851-1940, Norway
N 76 (1907) 604
BROME, FRED, archeology,
-1870, England
N 1 (1870) 509
N 2 (1870) 24
BROMWELL, CHARLES SUMMERS,

engineering, 1869-1915,
U.S.A.
S 42 (1915) 898
BROMWICH, THOMAS JOHN L'ANSON,
mathematics, 1875-1929,
England
L A129 (1930) P i-x
BRONGNIART, ADOLPHE THÉODORE,
biology, 1801-1876, France
A 111 (1876) 326
A 113 (1877) 237
E 9 (1875-1878) 229-230
L 28 (1879) iv-vii
BRONGNIART, ALEXANDRE, geology-
mineralogy, 1770-1847,
France
A 55 (1848) 141-144,
155-159
L 5 (1843-1850) 718-719
PM III 32 (1848) 228
BRONGNIART, CHARLES JULES
EDME, entomology, 1859-
1899, France
S 9 (1899) 726
BRONN, HEINRICH GEORG, biology,
1800-1862, Germany
A 84 (1862) 304
A 86 (1863) 278
BROOK, GEORGE, zoology, 1857-
1893, England
N 48 (1893) 420-421
BROOKE, CHARLES, surgery,
1804-1879, England
L 30 (1880) i-ii
BROOKE, JOHN MERCER, physics,
1826-1906, U.S.A.
S 25 (1907) 115-116
BROOKE, SIR WILLIAM
O'SHAUGNESSY, surgery,
1809-1889, Ireland
L 46 (1890) xviii-xix
BROOKES, JOSHUE, anatomy,
-1833,
L 3 (1830-1837) 229
BROOKS, THOMAS BENTON, geology,
1836-1900, U.S.A.
S 13 (1901) 460-462
BROOKS, WILLIAM EDWIN, orni-
thology, 1830?-1900,
Canada
S 11 (1900) 635
BROOKS, WILLIAM KEITH, zoology,
1848-1908, U.S.A.
A 176 (1908) 591
P 55 (1899) P fp 289,
400-409

S 9 (1899) 529-532
S 28 (1908) 722, 777-786
S 29 (1909) 614-616
BRORSEN, THEODOR JOHANN
CHRISTIAN AMBDERS, astron-
omy, 1819-1895, Germany
S 1 (1895) 585, 667
BROTHERHOOD, PETER, engineer-
ing, 1837?-1902, England
S 16 (1902) 755
BROTHERS, ALFRED, optics-
photography, 1826?-1912,
England
S 36 (1912) 343
BROTHWICK, JOHN LIVINGSTON
DINWIDDIE, engineering,
1840?-1904, U.S.A.
S 20 (1904) 573
BROUARDEL, PAUL CAMILLE
HIPPOLYTE, pathology, 1837-
1906, France
N 74 (1906) 412-413
BROUGH, BENNETT HOOPER, metal-
lurgy-mining, 1860-1908,
England
N 78 (1908) 575
S 28 (1908) 556
BROUGHTON, J.D., surgery,
-1837,
L 4 (1837-1843) 17
BROUN, JOHN ALLAN, magnetism-
meteorology, 1817-1879,
England
L 30 (1880) iii-iv
N 21 (1879) 112-114
BROUN, WILLIAM LE ROY, educa-
tion, 1827-1902, U.S.A.
S 15 (1902) 198, 316-317
BROUSSINGAULT, JEAN BAPTISTE,
chemistry, 1802-   ,
France
N 19 (1878) 39-40
BROWN, ALEXANDER RUSSELL,
chemistry-physics, 1889-
1916, Scotland
E 37 (1916-1917) 11-12
S 44 (1916) 421
BROWN, ADDISON, botany, 1830-
1913, U.S.A.
S 37 (1913) 830
BROWN, ADRIAN JOHN, biochem-
istry, 1852-1919, England
L B93 (1922) iii-ix
S 50 (1919) 109
BROWN, ALEXANDER CRUM, chem-
istry, 1838-1922, Scotland

S 11 (1900) 476
BRUCE, SIR DAVID, microbiology,
1855-1931, Austria
N 60 (1899) 31
N 71 (1904) 109-110
BRUCE, WILLIAM SPEIRS, explora-
tion-geography,   ,
E 34 (1913-1914) 310
BRÜHL, JULIUS, WILHELM, chem-
istry, 1850-1911, Germany
A 181 (1911) 340
N 70 (1904) 418
N 85 (1911) 517-518
BRÜHL, KARL BERNHARD, zoology,
1819?-1899, Austria
S 10 (1899) 382
BRÜNNOW, FRANZ FRIEDRICH ERNST,
astronomy, 1821-1891,
Germany
N 44 (1891) 449-450
BRUGNATELLI, LODOVIGO (LUIGI),
chemistry, 1761-1818, Italy
PM 53 (1819) 321-326
BRUGNATELLI, TULLIO, chemistry,
-1906, Italy
S 23 (1906) 677
BRUMBACK, ARTHUR MARION, chem-
istry, 1869-1916, U.S.A.
S 44 (1916) 306
BRUMMER, JOHANNES, agriculture,
1852?-1895, Germany
S 1 (1895) 473
BRUNCHORST, JØRGEN, botany,
1862?-1917, Norway
S 45 (1917) 657-658
BRUNEL, ISAMBARD KINGDOM,
engineering, 1806-1859?,
England
L 10 (1860) vii-xi
BRUNER, HENRY LANE, biology,
1861-1945, U.S.A.
S 41 (1915) 751
BRUNHES, ANTOINE JOSEPH BERNARD,
meteorology, 1867-1910, France
S 31 (1910) 901
BRUNHUBER, . . . , explora-
tion,   -1909, Germany
S 30 (1909) 404
BRUNLEES, SIR JAMES, engineer-
ing, 1816-1892, Scotland
E 20 (1892-1895) 7-8
von BRUNN, FERDINAND ALBERT
WILHELM, anatomy,   -1895?,
Germany
N 3 (1890) 66
BRUNO, GIORDANO, cosmology-

philosophy, c.1545-1600,
Italy
N 62 (1900) 77
N 69 (1904) 505-507
Sl 15 (1890) 236
BRUNTON, SIR THOMAS LAUDER,
medicine-pharmacology,
1844-1916, Scotland
L B89 (1917) P xliv-xlviii
N 98 (1916) 72-73
S 44 (1916) 461
BRUSH, CHARLES BENJAMIN, en-
gineering, 1848?-1897,
U.S.A.
S 5 (1897) 916
BRUSH, GEORGE JARVIS, mineral-
ogy, 1831-1912, U.S.A.
A 108 (1874) 144, 240
A 183 (1912) 296, P 389-
396
P 20 (1881-1882) P fr,
117-121
P 80 (1912) P 519
S 35 (1912) 213, 509-411
BRYAN, E.E., law, 1835?-1903,
U.S.A.
S 18 (1903) 253
BRYAN, ELIZABETH LETSON (MRS.
WILLIAM ALANSON), conchol-
ogy, 1875?-1919, U.S.A.
S 49 (1919) 305
BRYAN, GEORGE HARTLEY, thermo-
dynamics, 1864-1928,
England
N 52 (1895) 31
N 122 (1928) 657, 849-850
BRYANT, JOSEPH DECATUR,
surgery, 1845-1914, U.S.A.
S 39 (1914) 573
BRYANT, THOMAS, surgery,
1829?-1915, England
S 41 (1915) 163
BRYCE, DAVID, architecture,
1803-1876, Scotland
E 9 (1875-1878) 216-218
BRYCE, JAMES, geology-physics,
1806-1877, Ireland
E 9 (1875-1878) 514-518
BRYCE, THOMAS H., zoology,   ,
E 27 (1906-1907) 382-383
BRYSON, ALEXANDER, biology
geology, 1816-1866,
Scotland
E 6 (1866-1869) 189
BUCCLEUCH, . . . , DUKE OF
-1884, Scotland

E 12 (1882-1884) 938
von BUCH, CHRISTIAN LEOPOLD,
baron, geology, 1774-1853,
Germany
A 65 (1853) 464-465
A 67 (1854) 1-11
S 6 (1897) 928
BUCHAN, ALEXANDER, meteorology,
1829-1907, Scotland
E 20 (1892-1895) 510-511
L A90 (1914) i-iii
N 58 (1898) 32
N 76 (1907) 83-84
S 25 (1907) 879
S 26 (1907) 26-27
BUCHANAN, GEORGE, engineering,
-1852,
PM 36 (1810) P at end
BUCHANAN, SIR GEORGE, medi-
cine, 1831-1895, England
L 59 (1896) xli
N 52 (1895) 58
S 1 (1895) 640
BUCHANAN, JOHN YOUNG, physics,
1844-1925, Scotland
E 16 (1888-1889) 813-815
L 110 (1926) P xii-xiii
N 36 (1887) 5
BUCHANAN, ROBERDEAU, astronomy-
mathematics, 1839-1916,
U.S.A.
S 45 (1917) 112
BUCHHEIM, ARTHUR, mathematics,
1859-1888, England
N 38 (1888) 515-516
BUCHNER, EDUARD, chemistry,
1860-1917, Germany
A 194 (1917) 338
S 46 (1917) 208
BUCHNER, HANS ERNST ANGASS,
bacteriology, 1850-1902,
Germany
S 15 (1902) 676
BUCK, LEFFERT LEFFERTS, en-
gineering, 1837-1909,
U.S.A.
S 30 (1909) 111
BUCKHOUT, WILLIAM A., botany,
1846-1912, U.S.A.
A 185 (1913) 120
S 36 (1912) 822
BUCKINGHAM, CHARLES LUMAN, law,
1852-1909, U.S.A.
S 29 (1909) 966
BUCKLAND, FRANCIS TREVELYAN,
biology, 1826-1880, England

N 23 (1880) 175
N 32 (1885) 385-386
P 18 (1880-1881) 812-820
P 28 (1885-1886) P fp 289,
401-406
BUCKLAND, WILLIAM, geology,
1784-1856, England
A 72 (1856) 449-452
N 51 (1895) 457-458
S 1 (1895) 329-330
BUCKLEY, SAMUEL BOTSFORD,
botany, 1809-1883, U.S.A.
A 129 (1885) 171-172
BUCKNILL, SIR JOHN, neurology,
1817-1897, England
L 75 (1905) 130-131
S 6 (1897) 211
BUCKTON, GEORGE BOWDLER, en-
tomology, 1818-1905,
England
A 170 (1905) 412
L B79 (1907) xlv-xlviii
N 72 (1905) 587-588
S 22 (1905) 476
BUDD, GEORGE, medicine, 1808-
1882, England
L 34 (1883) i-iii
BUDD, J.L., horticulture,
-1904, U.S.A.
S 20 (1904) 933
BUDGETT, JOHN SAMUEL, biology,
1873-1904, England
N 69 (1904) 300-301
N 78 (1908) 313-315
P 72 (1908) P 478-479
S 28 (1908) 452-454
BUDIN, PIERRE CONSTANT,
gynecology, 1846-1907,
France
S 25 (1907) 318
BUCHNER, FRIEDRICH KARL
CHRISTIAN LUDWIG, medicine,
1824-1899, Germany
S 9 (1899) 692
BUEK, H.W., botany, 1796?-
1879, Germany
A 119 (1880) 77
von BÜLOW, FRIEDRICH GUSTAV,
Baron, astrophysics, 1817-
1893, Germany
Sl 22 (1893) 334
BÜRGI, JOOST, mathematics,
1552-1632, Switzerland
S 44 (1916) 429
deBUFFON, GEORGES LOUIS
LECLERC, comte, science,

1707-1788, France
N 90 (1912) 1-2
BUGAEFF, NIKOLAI VASILIEVICH,
mathematics, 1837-1903,
Russia
S 16 (1902) 755
S 18 (1903) 286
BUIST, GEORGE, geology, 1805-
1860, Scotland
E 4 (1857-1862) 356-357
BUIST, J.B., medicine,   -1915,
Scotland
E 36 (1915-1916) 28
BUKA, FELIX, geometry, 1851?-
1896, Germany
S 5 (1897) 56
BULL, CHARLES STEDMAN, ophthal-
mology, 1845-1911, U.S.A.
S 33 (1911) 686
BULL, EPHRAIM WALES, horti-
culture-legislation, 1806-
1895, U.S.A.
S 2 (1895) 484
BULL, STORM, engineering,
1856-1907, Norway
S 26 (1907) 767
BULL, WILLIAM TILLINGHAST,
surgery, 1850-1909, U.S.A.
S 29 (1909) 381, 498
BULLEN, ROBERT ASHINGTON,
biology, 1850?-1912, England
S 36 (1912) 370
BULLER, SIR WALTER LAWRY,
ornithology, 1838-1906,
New Zealand
A 172 (1906) 352
N 74 (1906) 354-355
S 24 (1906) 190
BULLOCK, OTIS E., biology,
-1897,
S 5 (1897) 692
BULMER, THOMAS SANDERSON,
archeology,   -1898,
U.S.A.
S 8 (1898) 866
BULSTRODE, HERBERT TIMBRELL,
medicine, 1858?-1911, Isle
of Wight
N 87 (1911) 117-118
BUMPUS, HERMON CAREY, biology,
S 12 (1900) 869
BUNBURY, SIR CHARLES JONES FOX,
paleobotany, 1809-1886,
Sicily
L 46 (1890) xiii-xiv
N 75 (1907) 433-434

BUNIAKOVSKI, VIKTOR JAKOVLEVICH,
mathematics, 1804-1889,
Russia
S 21 (1905) 518
BUNSEN, ROBERT WILHELM EBERHARD,
chemistry-physics, 1811-1899,
Germany
A 116 (1878) 392-393
A 158 (1899) 318
L 75 (1905) 46-49
N 23 (1881) P 597-600
N 24 (1881) 53, 339
N 45 (1892) 469-470
N 60 (1899) 424-425
N 73 (1905) 147-148
N 86 (1911) 79
P 19 (1881) P fp 433,
550-553
S 10 (1899) 259, 447-451,
865-870
S 15 (1902) 423
BURBANK, LUTHER, botany, 1849-
1926, U.S.A.
N 80 (1909) 337
P 67 (1905) P 329-347,
363-374
BURBIDGE, FREDERICK WILLIAM
THOMAS, botany, 1847-1906,
England
S 23 (1906) 78-79
BURBURY, SAMUEL HAWKESLEY,
mathematics-physics, 1831-
1911, England
L A88 (1913) i-iv
N 42 (1890) 14-15
N 87 (1911) 281-282
S 34 (1911) 309
BURCH, GEORGE JAMES, physics-
physiology, 1852-1914,
England
N 62 (1900) 56-57
N 93 (1914) 114-115
S 39 (1914) 530
BURCHAM, J.S., ichthyology,
-1905,
S 22 (1905) 807
BURCKHARDT, KARL RUDOLF,
zoology, 1866?-1908,
S 27 (1908) 358
BURDON SANDERSON, SIR JOHN
SCOTT -- see Sanderson,
Sir J.S.B.
BUREAU, LOUIS ÉDOUARD, botany,
1831?-1919, France
S 49 (1919) 191
BURGESS, EDWARD S., entomology,

anatomy, 1813-1889, U.S.A.
P 52 (1897-1898) P 224-
228
CABOT, SAMUEL, ornithology,
-1885, U.S.A.
Sl 6 (1885) 20
CACCIATORE, GAETANO, astron-
omy, 1814-1889, Italy
N 40 (1889) 255
Sl 14 (1889) 27
CAESARO, ERNST, mathematics,
-1906, Italy
S 24 (1906) 638
CAGNIARD DE LATOUR, CHARLES,
Baron, physics, 1777-1859,
France
A 76 (1858) 97
A 78 (1859) 424-425
A 79 (1860) 266-268
CAILLETET, LOUIS PAUL, chem-
istry-physics, 1832-1913,
France
A 185 (1913) 336
S 37 (1913) 145
CAIRD, SIR JAMES, agriculture,
1816-1892, Scotland
L 50 (1892) xiii-xiv
CAIRD, JOHN, philosophy-
theology, 1820-1898,
Scotland
E 22 (1897-1899) 718
S 8 (1898) 158
CAIRD, ROBERT, engineering,
-1915, Scotland
E 37 (1916-1917) 12
CAIRNES, DELORME DONALDSON,
geology, 1879-1917, Canada
A 194 (1917) 338
CAIUS (KAYE, KEY), JOHN,
medicine, 1510-1573,
England
N 92 (Feb. 5, 1914 Sup-
plement) vi
CALDERWOOD, HENRY, philosophy,
1830-1898?, Scotland
E 22 (1897-1899) 718-719
S 6 (1897) 805
CALDESI, LUDOVICO, botany,
-1884, Italy
Sl 4 (1884) 409
CALDWELL, EUGENE WILSON,
radiology, 1870-1918,
U.S.A.
S 47 (1918) 635
CALLANDREAU, PIERRE JEAN
OCTAVE, astronomy, 1852-

1904, France
N 69 (1904) 441
S 19 (1904) 439
CALLAWAY, CHARLES, geology,
1838?-1915, England
S 42 (1915) 826
CALLENDAR, HUGH LONGBOURNE,
physics, 1863-1930, England
L A134 (1932) P xviii-
xxvi
N 50 (1894) 55
N 75 (1906) 132-135
CALORI, LUIGI, anatomy,
1808?-1897, Italy
S 5 (1897) 143
S 6 (1897) 876
CALVER, EDWARD KILLWICK,
physics, 1813-1892, England
L 52 (1893) xviii-xix
CALVIN, SAMUEL, geology,
1840-1911, Scotland
A 181 (1911) 468
S 34 (1911) 106-107
S 35 (1911) 767
CAMEIL, LOUIS FLORENTINE,
neurology-psychiatry,
1798?-1895, France
S 1 (1895) 499
CAMERON, AUGUSTUS JOHN DARLING,
engineering, 1841-1884,
Scotland
E 14 (1886-1887) 137-138
CAMERON, JOHN, medicine,
1818?-1906, England
S 24 (1906) 382
CAMERON, PETER, biology,
-1912, England
S 36 (1912) 901
CAMERON, VERNEY LOVETT, ex-
ploration-geography, 1844-
1894, England
A 147 (1894) 484
N 49 (1894) 537
CAMICIA, L.S., geophysics,
-1912, Switzerland
S 36 (1912) 862
CAMISSO, ..., botany,
, Germany
S 12 (1900) 934
CAMPBELL, GEORGE DOUGLAS,
Duke of Argyll, geology,
1823-1900, Scotland
A 159 (1900) 462
N 62 (1900) 13-14
CAMPBELL, SIR JOHN, law,
1781-1860, Scotland

E   4 (1857-1862) 484-491
CAMPBELL, JOHN ARCHIBALD,
  writer, 1788-1866, Scotland
  E   6 (1866-1869) 20
CAMPBELL, JOHN EDWARD, mathe-
  matics, 1862-1924, Ireland
  L   A107 (1925) P ix-xii
CAMPBELL, JOHN FRANCIS,
  geology, 1821-1885, Scotland
  Sl   5 (1885) 264
CAMPBELL, JOHN L., chemistry-
  geology, 1820-1886, U.S.A.
  A   131 (1866) 240
CAMPBELL, JOHN PENDLETON, biol-
  ogy-physiology, 1863-1918,
  U.S.A.
  S   49 (1919) 21
CAMPBELL, WILLIAM WALLACE,
  astronomy, 1862-1938,
  U.S.A.
  P   86 (1915) P 306
CANCANI, ADOLFO, physics-
  seismology,   -1904,
  Italy
  N   70 (1904) 128-129
  S   19 (1904) 967
CANDÈZE, ERNEST CHARLES
  AUGUSTE, entomology, 1827-
  1898, Belgium
  S   8 (1898) 263
CANDOLLE -- see DECANDOLLE
CANET, GUSTAVE, engineering,
  1848-1908, France
  S   28 (1908) 679
CANNIZZARO, STANISLAO, chem-
  istry, 1826-1910,   Italy
  N   45 (1891) 111
  N   55 (1896) 203-204
  N   56 (1897) P 1-4
  N   83 (1910) 343-344
  N   85 (1910) 2
  S   4 (1896) 753
  S   24 (1906) 253
  S   31 (1910) 813
CANTOR, GEORG FERDINAND LUDWIG
  PHILIPP, mathematics, 1845-
  1918, Russia
  N   71 (1904) 110-111
CANTOR, MORITZ BENEDIKT,
  mathematics, 1829-1920,
  Germany
  S   20 (1904) 381
  S   30 (1909) 363
CAPOCCI DE BELMONTE, ERNESTO,
  astronomy, 1798-1864, Italy
  A   87 (1864) 304

CAPSHAW, WALTER L., anatomy,
  -1915, U.S.A.
  S   43 (1916) 64
CARBUTT, SIR EDWARD H.,
  engineering,   -1905,
  England
  S   22 (1905) 542
CARDANO, GIROLAMO (GERONIMO),
  mathematics, 1501-1576,
  Italy
  P   44 (1893-1894) 106-110
CARDEW, PHILIP, engineering,
  1851-1910, England
  N   83 (1910) 404
CAREY, JOHN, botany, 1797?-
  1880, England
  A   119 (1880) 421-423
  A   127 (1884) 242
CAREY-FOSTER -- see FOSTER
CARLINI, FRANCESCO, astronomy,
  1783-1862, Italy
  L   12 (1863) lvi-lix
CARLISLE, SIR ANTHONY, anatomy,
  1768-1840,
  L   4 (1837-1843) 260-261
CARLISLE, NICHOLAS, archeology,
  1771-1847,
  L   5 (1843-1850) 706-707
CARNEGIE, ANDREW, invention-
  philanthropy, 1835-1919,
  Scotland
  P   59 (1901) P 3-20
CARNEGIE, DAVID WYNFORD, ex-
  ploration, 1871-1900,
  Scotland
  S   13 (1901) 79
CARNEL, T., botany,   -1899,
  Italy
  S   9 (1899) 188
CARNELL, FREDERICK JAMES,
  physics,   -1902, U.S.A.
  S   16 (1902) 877
CARNELLEY, THOMAS, chemistry,
  1852-1890, England
  N   42 (1890) 522-523
  Sl   16 (1890) 202
CARNOT, LAZARE NICOLAS
  MARGUERITE, mathematics,
  1753-1823, France
  P   62 (1902-1903) P 119-
  120
  PM   30 (1808) P fr
CARNOT, NICOLAS LÉONARD SADI,
  physics, 1796-1832, France
  A   118 (1879) 405
  N   42 (1890) 365-366

P 62 (1902-1903) P 118
S 36 (1912) 322-329
CARNOY (LE CHANOINE), JEAN
BAPTISTE, biology, 1836-
1899, Belgium
S 10 (1899) 622
CARO, HEINRICH, chemistry,
1834-1910, Germany
S 19 (1904) 558
CARPENTER, GEORGE, medicine,
1859-1910, England
S 31 (1910) 697-698
CARPENTER, PHILIP HERBERT,
biology, 1853?-1891,
England
A 143 (1892) 80
L 51 (1892) xxxvi-xxxviii
N 44 (1891) 628-629
CARPENTER, PHILIP PEARSALL,
conchology, 1819-1877,
England
A 114 (1877) 80
N 16 (1877) 84
CARPENTER, ROLLA CLINTON, engi-
neering, 1852-1919, U.S.A.
S 49 (1919) 118
CARPENTER, WILLIAM BENJAMIN,
physiology, 1813-1885,
England
A 130 (1885) 490
L 41 (1887) ii-ix
N 33 (1885) 83-85, 112
P 1 (1872) P 745-750
P 28 (1885-1886) P 538-544
Sl 6 (1885) 429, 493-494
CARPUE, JOHN CONSTANTINE, anat-
omy, 1764?-1846
L 5 (1843-1850) 638-639
CARR, WILLIAM HOLWELL, patron,
-1831,
L 3 (1830-1837) 84
CARRÉ, GUILLAUME LOUIS JULIEN,
law, 1777-1832, France
A 23 (1832-1833) 371
CARREL, ALEXIS, physiology-
surgery, 1873-1944, France
P 81 (1912) P 614-617
CARRENO,..., botany, 1818?-1841,
A 43 (1842) 215
CARRIÈRE,..., botany, 1817?-
1896, France
S 4 (1896) 404
CARRINGTON, BENJAMIN, botany,
1827-1895, England
E 21 (1895-1897) i-v, 12
CARRION, DANIEL A., medicine,
-1885, Peru?
S 40 (1914) 163

CARROLL, CHARLES GEIGER, chem-
istry, 1875-1916, U.S.A.
S 43 (1916) 346
CARROLL, JAMES, pathology,
1854-1907, England
P 87 (1915) P 177
S 26 (1907) 390, 453
S 28 (1908) 752
CARROLL, LEWIS (pseud.)--
see DODGSON
CARRUTHERS, JOHN BENNETT,
botany-mycology, 1869-
1910, England
N 84 (1910) 114-115
S 32 (1910) 173
CARRUTHERS, WILLIAM, botany,
1830-1922, Scotland?
L B97 (1925) vi-viii
CARSON, JOSEPH, botany, 1808-
1876, U.S.A.
A 113 (1877) 238
CARSTANJEN, ERNST, chemistry,
1836-1884, Germany
Sl 4 (1884) 409
CART, J. T., chemistry,
-1908, England
S 28 (1908) 556
CARTEIGHE, MICHAEL, pharmacy,
1842?-1910, England
S 31 (1910) 947
CARTER, HENRY JOHN, surgery,
1813-1895, England
L 58 (1895) liv-lvii
S 1 (1895) 615
CARTER, JAMES, paleontology,
1814-1895, England
S 2 (1895) 483
CARTER, ROBERT BRUDENELL,
ophthalmology, 1828?-1918,
England
S 48 (1918) 617
CARTON, G., archeology,
-1896, Belgium
S 4 (1896) 874
CARUS, JULIUS VICTOR, zoology,
1823-1903, Germany
N 67 (1903) 613-614
S 17 (1903) 598
CARUS, PAUL, philosophy,
1852-1919, Germany
S 49 (1915) 233-234
CARY, PHILLIP H., geology,
-1916, U.S.A.
S 44 (1916) 672
CASATI, GAETANO, exploration,
1839?-1902, Italy
S 15 (1902) 438

CASATI, LUIGI, medicine, 1830?-
1906, Italy
S 24 (1906) 789
CASE, EDWARD, engineering-
meteorology, -1899,
England
S 10 (1899) 582
CASE, WILLARD ERASTUS, electric-
ity, 1857-1918, U.S.A.
S 48 (1918) 467
CASEY, JOHN, mathematics,
1820-1891, Ireland
L 49 (1891) xxiv-xxv
CASEY, THOMAS LINCOLN, engi-
neering, 1831-1896, U.S.A.
S 3 (1896) 510
CASH, JOHN THEODORE, pharmacol-
ogy, 1854-1936, England
N 36 (1887) 5
CASSEDAY, S. A., paleontology,
-1860, U.S.A.
A 81 (1861) 155
CASSIE, WILLIAM RIACH, physics,
1861-1908, England
N 78 (1908) 179
S 28 (1908) 84
CASSIN, JOHN, ornithology,
1813-1869, U.S.A.
A 97 (1869) 291-293, 435
CASSINI, GIOVANNI DOMENICO
(JEAN DOMINIQUE), astron-
omy, 1625-1712, Italy
L 5 (1843-1850) 582-583
N 19 (1878) 122-123
PM III 28 (1846) 412-413
S 16 (1902) 61
CASSINI, JEAN JACQUES, astron-
omy, 1677-1756, France
L 5 (1843-1850) 582-583
PM III 28 (1846) 412-413
de CASSINI, A HENRI G., vicomte,
botany-law, 1784-1832, France
L 5 (1843-1850) 582-583
PM III 28 (1846) 412-413
CASSINI, JACQUES (or JEAN)
DOMINIQUE, Comte de Thury,
astronomy, 1748-1845, France
A 52 (1864) 145
L 5 (1843-1850) 582-583
PM III 28 (1846) 412-413
CASSINI DE THURY, CÉSAR FRAN-
ÇOIS, astronomy, 1714-1884,
France
L 5 (1843-1850) 582-583
PM III 28 (1846) 412-413
S 16 (1902) 60-61, 399

del CASTILLO, ANTONIO, geology,
-1895, Mexico
A 157 (1896) 78
CASTNER, HAMILTON YOUNG, chem-
istry, 1859-1899, U.S.A.
S 10 (1899) 620
S 21 (1905) 881
CASTRACANE DEGLI ANTELMINELLI,
FRANCESCO, conte, microscopy,
1817-1899, Italy
S 9 (1899) 692
CASWELL, ALEXIS, astronomy-
meteorology, 1799-1877,
U.S.A.
S 10 (1899) 673-674
CATANOSO OF MESSINI, ... sur-
gery, , Italy
A 5 (1822) 179
CATHCART (LORD GREENOCK), ...,
geology, 1785-1859, Scotland
E 4 (1857-1862) 222-224
CATLIN, CHARLES ALBERT, chem-
istry, 1849-1916, U.S.A.
S 43 (1916) 639
CATLIN, GEORGE, anthropology-
ethnology, 1796-1871, U.S.A.
S 35 (1912) 263-264
N 7 (1873) 222-223
P 39 (1891) P fp 289, 402-
409
CATON, F. W., chemistry,
-1916, England
S 44 (1916) 270
CATTANEO, GIACOMO, surgery,
1832?-1915, Italy
S 42 (1915) 416
CATTON, THOMAS, astronomy,
1758?-1838,
L 4 (1837-1843) 94-95
CAUCHOIX, ROBERT AGLAÉ, instru-
mentation, 1776-1845, France
A 19 (1830-1831) 390
PM 63 (1824) 252-259
CAUCHY, AUGUSTIN LOUIS, baron,
mathematics, 1789-1857, France
A 74 (1857) 299, 408-409
E 4 (1857-1862) 33-40
CAURO, J., physics, -1900,
France
S 11 (1900) 198
CAVAFY, JOHN, physiology,
1841?-1901, England
S 9 (1899) 59-63
S 13 (1901) 796-797
CAVALLO, TIBERIO, physics,
1749-1809, Italy

S   22 (1905) 286
CAVENDISH, HENRY, chemistry-
  physics, 1731-1810, France
  N   43 (1890) 1-3
  P   59 (1901) P 431-440
CAVENDISH, SPENCER COMPTON,
  Duke of Devonshire, govern-
  ment, 1833-1908, England
  L   82 (1909) xi-xvii
CAVENTOU, EUGÈNE, chemistry,
  1824-1912, France
  S   35 (1912) 369, 814
CAVERLY, CHARLES S., hygiene,
  -1918, U.S.A.
  S   48 (1918) 467
CAVOLINI, FILIPPO, biology,
  1756-1810, Italy
  S   32 (1910) 405
CAY, JOHN, law, 1790-1865,
  Scotland
  E   6 (1866-1869) 19-20
CAYLEY, ARTHUR, mathematics,
  1821-1895, England
  A   149 (1895) 248
  E   21 (1895-1897) 15
  L   58 (1895) i-xliii
  N   28 (1883) P 481-485
  N   49 (1894 supplement, Jan.
   18) iv-vi
  N   51 (1894-1895) 323
  N   53 (1895) 110
  N   57 (1898) 217-218
  N   58 (1898) 50
  N   99 (1917) 221-222
  S   1 (1895) 166, 450-451
   615
  S   9 (1899) 59-63
  S   13 (1901) 516-517
  S   43 (1916) 781
  S   44 (1916) 173, 465
CECCARINI,..., sculpture,
  , Italy
  A   4 (1822) 197
CECIL, ROBERT ARTHUR TALBOT
  GASCOIGNE, Marquis of
  Salisbury, administration,
  1838-1903, England
  N   68 (1903) 392-393
CELAKOVSKY, LADISLAV, botany,
  1835-1902, Czechoslovakia
  N   67 (1903) 302
  S   16 (1902) 1040
  S   17 (1903) 37
CELLI, ANGELO, medicine, 1857-
  1914, Italy

P   87 (1915) P 72
S   40 (1914) 888
S   43 (1916) 235
CENTER, WILLIAM, medicine,
  -1900, England
  S   11 (1900) 877
CERRUTI, VALENTINO, mathematics,
  1850-1909, Italy
  S   30 (1909) 363
CERTES, LOUIS ADOLPHE ADRIEN,
  bacteriology, 1835-1903,
  France
  S   18 (1903) 509
CESARIS, GIOVANNI ANGELO,
  astronomy, 1749-1832, Italy
  A   23 (1832-1833) 370
CESATI, VINCENZO, barone, bot-
  any, 1806?-1883, Italy
  A   127 (1884) 243
CHABANEAU, FRANÇOIS, chemistry,
  1754-1842, France
  P   84 (1914) 64-70
CHACORNAC, JEAN, astronomy,
  1823-1873, France
  N   8 (1873) 512
CHAGAS, MANUEL PINHEIRO, biol-
  ogy, 1842-1895, Portugal
  S   1 (1895) 615
CHAILLÉ, STANFORD EMERSON, phys-
  iology, 1830-1911, U.S.A.
  S   27 (1908) 517
  S   33 (1911) 339
CHAILLON,..., bacteriology,
  -1915, France
  S   42 (1915) 119
CHAIX, PAUL GEORGES GABRIEL,
  geography, 1808-1901
  Switzerland?
  S   13 (1901) 717
CHALMERS,..., philanthropy,
  -1849?, Scotland
  E   2 (1844-1850) 226-227
CHALMERS, DAVID, printing,
  1820-1899, Scotland
  E   23 (1899-1901) 7-8
CHALMERS, JAMES, anthropology,
  1841-1901, Scotland
  N   64 (1901) 38
  S   13 (1901) 796
CHALMERS, MEUNIER, geology,
  1903, France
  S   18 (1903) 317
CHALMERS, ROBERT, geology,
  1834-1908, Canada
  A   176 (1908) 100

S   21 (1905) 879
CHESELDEN, WILLIAM, anatomy-
    surgery, 1688-1752, England
    S   12 (1900) 259
CHESNEVIEUX, VINCENT LECHE,
    geology, 1816?-1902, France
    S   16 (1902) 638
CHESTER, ALBERT HUNTINGTON,
    chemistry, 1843-1903, U.S.A.
    A 165 (1903) 418
    S   17 (1903) 677
CHESTER, H. C., navigation,
    U.S.A.
    S   41 (1915) 750
CHEVALLIER, JEAN BAPTISTE AL-
    PHONSE, dentistry-pharmacy,
    1793-1879, France
    N   21 (1879) 132-133
CHEVREUL, MICHEL EUGÈNE, chem-
    istry-gerontology, 1786-
    1889, France
    N   6 (1872) 420
    N   39 (1889) 565
    N   64 (1901) P 332
    P   27 (1885) P fp 433, 548-
    552
    P   30 (1886-1887) P 33-40
    P   70 (1907) P 482
    Sl   6 (1885) 140, 258-259
    Sl   7 (1886) 213
    Sl   8 (1886) 29, P 248-251
    Sl 13 (1889) P 271, 341
    S   14 (1901) 339
    S   45 (1917) 293
CHEVREUX, MAURICE, naval archi-
    tecture,   -1918, France
    S   48 (1918) 244
CHEVROLAT, LOUIS ALEXANDRE
    AUGUSTE, entomology, 1799?-
    1884, France
    Sl   5 (1885) 122
CHEYNE, ..., exploration, 1827?-
    1902,
    S   15 (1902) 318
CHEYNE, WILLIAM WATSON, surgery,
    1852-1932, at sea, off Tas-
    mania
    N   50 (1894) 55
    N   79 (1907) 235
CHIERICI, GAETANO, anthropol-
    ogy,   -1885, Italy
    Sl   7 (1886) 123-124
CHIEVITZ, J. H., anatomy,
    -1901?, Denmark
    S   15 (1902) 79
CHILD, CHARLES T., engineering,

1867?-1902, U.S.A.
    S   16 (1902) 38
CHILDREN, JOHN GEORGE, science,
    1777-1852,
    L   6 (1850-1854) 245-247
CHILTON, GEORGE, invention,
    1767-1836, England
    A   31 (1837) 421-424
CHILTON, JAMES RENWICK, chem-
    istry, 1809?-1863, U.S.A.
    A   86 (1836) 314
CHISHOLM, HENRY WILLIAMS,
    standardization, 1809-1901,
    England
    N   63 (1901) 304
CHITTENDEN, RUSSEL HENRY, chem-
    istry-physiology, 1856-1943,
    U.S.A.
    P   53 (1898) P fr, 115-121
CHIZZONI, FRANCESCO, mathemat-
    ics,   -1904, Italy
    S   20 (1904) 774
CHLADNI, ERNST FLORENS FRIED-
    RICH, physics, 1756-1827,
    Germany
    A   15 (1829) 177
    S   14 (1901) 988
CHODAT, ROBERT HIPPOLYTE,
    botany, 1865-1934, Switzer-
    land
    N   81 (1909) 12
CHOFFAT, PAUL, geology,
    -1919, Portugal
    A 198 (1919) 250
CHOLMELEY, WILLIAM, medicine,
    1823?-1896, England
    S   4 (1896) 75
CHOUTEAU, CHARLES P.,   ,
    ,
    P   52 (1897-1898) P 630
CHREE, CHARLES, physics, 1860-
    1928, Scotland
    L A122 (1929) P vii-xiv
    N   56 (1897) 55
    N 122 (1928) 248, 321-322
CHRISTIAN FRIEDRICH VIII, King
    of Denmark, geology, 1786-
    1848, Denmark
    A   23 (1832-1833) 371
    A   60 (1850) 297
CHRISTIANSEN, CHRISTIAN, physics,
    1843-1917, Denmark
    S   47 (1918) 92
CHRISTIE, SAMUEL HUNTER, mathe-
    matics, 1784-1865, England
    L   15 (1867) xi-xiv

CLARK, JOHN WILLIS, anatomy-
biology, 1833-1910, England
N 84 (1910) 501
N 91 (1913) 525-528
CLARK, JONAS GILMAN, educa-
tion, 1815-1900, U.S.A.
S 8 (1898) 704-705
CLARK, JOSIAH LATIMER, elec-
tricity, 1822-1898, England
N 59 (1898) 38
N 81 (1909) 512-513
S 8 (1898) 704-705
CLARK, SHELDON, education,
1785-1840, U.S.A.
A 29 (1835-1836) 155
A 41 (1841) P fp 217,
217-231
CLARK, SIR THOMAS, publisher,
-1901?, Scotland
E 24 (1901-1903) 4
CLARK, WILLIAM BULLOCK, geol-
ogy, 1860-1917, U.S.A.
A 194 (1917) 247-248
N 99 (1917) 527-528
CLARK, WILLIAM SMITH, chemis-
try-education, 1826-1886,
U.S.A.
S 27 (1908) 172-180
CLARK, WILLIAM TIERNEY, engi-
neering, -1852,
L 6 (1850-1854) 244-245
CLARKE, ALEXANDER ROSS, geodesy,
1828-1914, England
A 187 (1914) 366
E 35 (1919-1915) 3
L A90 (1914) xvi-xviii
N 37 (1887) 118
N 92 (1914) 692-693
S 39 (1914) 390
CLARKE, CHARLES BARON, botany,
1832-1906, England
L B79 (1907) xlix-lvi
N 74 (1906) 495
S 24 (1906) 350
CLARKE, MISS CORA HUIDEKOPER,
botany, 1851-1916, U.S.A.
S 43 (1916) 815
CLARKE, EDWARD DANIEL, miner-
alogy, 1769-1822, England
PM 59 (1822) 316-319
CLARKE, FRANK WIGGLESWORTH,
chemistry-geology, 1847-
1931, U.S.A.
N 128 (1932) 59, 214-215
P 54 (1898-1899) P fr,
110-117

CLARKE, FREDERICK C.,
sociology, -1903, U.S.A.
S 18 (1903) 414
CLARKE, SIR GEORGE SYDENHAM,
Baron of Combe, engineering,
1848-1933,
N 54 (1896) 1-10
CLARKE, SIR JAMES, medicine,
1788-1870, Scotland
L 19 (1871) xiii-xix
CLARKE, HENRY JAMES -- see JAMES
CLARKE
CLARKE, JOHN MASON, paleontolo-
gy, 1857-1925, U.S.A.
P 66 (1904-1905) P 10
CLARKE, T.C., engineering,
1827-1901, U.S.A.
S 13 (1901) 1038-1039
CLARKE, WILLIAM BRANWHITE,
geology, 1798-1878, England
A 116 (1878) 334
L 28 (1879) i-iv
CLARKE, WILLIAM BULLOCK, geology,
1860-1917, U.S.A.
S 46 (1917) 104-106, 159
CLAUDET, ANTOINE FRANÇOIS JEAN,
photography, 1797-1867, France
L 17 (1869) lxxxv-lxxxvii
CLAUS, ADOLF CARL LUDWIG, chem-
istry, 1838-1900, Germany
S 11 (1900) 877
CLAUS, R.F., zoology, 1836?-
1899, Austria
S 9 (1899) 268
CLAUSEN, THOMAS, astronomy
1801-1885, Estonia
Sl 6 (1885) 260
CLAUSIUS, RODOLF JULIUS EMANUEL,
mathematics-physics, 1822-
1888, Germany
A 136 (1888) 304
L 48 (1891) i-viii
N 38 (1888) 438-439
P 35 (1889) P fr, 117-121
CLAXTON, PHILANDER PRIESTLY,
education, 1862-   , U.S.A.
P 84 (1914) P 207
CLAY, JOSEPH A., mineralogy,
1806?-1881, U.S.A.
A 121 (1881) 338
CLAYPOLE, MISS EDITH JANE,
pathology, -1915, U.S.A.
S 41 (1915) 527, 754
CLAYPOLE, EDWARD WALLER, geology,
1835?-1901, England?
S 14 (1901) 542

S 16 (1902) 276
CLEGHORN, ALLAN MACKENZIE,
   medicine-physiology, 1872-
   1916, Canada
   S 43 (1916) 492
CLEGHORN, HUGH FRANCIS CLARKE,
   botany, 1820-1895, India
   E 20 (1892-1895) li-lx
   E 21 (1895-1897) 13
   S 1 (1895) 667
CLEGHORN, THOMAS, education-law,
   1818-1874, Scotland
   E 8 (1872-1875) 468-469
CLEMENS, BRACKENRIDGE, entomolo-
   gy, 1826-1867, England?
   P 76 (1910) P 470-472
CLERK, HENRY, physics, 1822?-
   1913, England
   S 37 (1913) 479
CLERK MAXWELL, JAMES, physics,
   1831-1879, Scotland
   A 118 (1879) 499-500
   A 123 (1887) 149-150
   A 129 (1885) 347
 . E 10 (1878-1880) 331-339
   L 33 (1882) i-xvi
   N 10 (1874) 480
   N 11 (1875) 359, 377
   N 15 (1877) 391
   N 21 (1879) 43-46
   N 21 (1880) 317-321
   N 24 (1881) P 601-602
   N 25 (1887) 237-240
   N 27 (1882) 26-28
   N 43 (1890) 26-27
   N 44 (1891) 355-358
   N 49 (1894) 357-359, 366
   381-382
   N 50 (1894) 8-11
   N 58 (1898) 219-221
   N 65 (1902) 555-556
   N 99 (1917) 221-222
   N 118 (December 18, 1926
   Supplement) 44
   N 127 (1931) 902-903
   P 17 (1880) P fr, 116-119
   P 78 (1911) P 517-519
   Sl 1 (1883) 360-365
   Sl 5 (1883) 317-318
   S 1 (1895) 141-157
   S 2 (1895) 809-811, 861-
   880
   S 8 (1898) 591
   S 39 (1914) 555
   S 43 (1916) 569-571, 585-
   586

CLERKE, MISS AGNES MARY, as-
   tronomy, 1842-1907,
   England
   S 25 (1907) 238
CLERKE, THOMAS HENRY SHADWELL,
   -1849,
   L 5 (1843-1850) 888-889
CLEVE, PER THEODOR, chemistry-
   oceanography, 1840-1905,
   Sweden
   S 22 (1905) 126
CLEVELAND, PARKER, mineralogy,
   1780-1858, U.S.A.
   A 76 (1858) 448
CLIFFORD, WILLIAM KINGDON,
   mathematics, 1845-1879,
   England
   A 117 (1879) 416
   A 118 (1879) 497
   N 19 (1879) 443-444
   N 26 (1882) 217-219
   N 32 (1885) 4
   N 65 (1902) 584
   N 99 (1917) 221-222
   P 15 (1879) P fp 145, 258-
   264
   S 13 (1901) 516-517
CLIFT, WILLIAM, anatomy,
   1775-1849, England
   L 5 (1843-1850) 876-880
CLIFTON, ROBERT BELLAMY,
   physics, 1836-1921, England
   L A99 (1921) vi-ix
CLINTON, GEORGE W., botany,
   1807-1885, U.S.A.
   A 131 (1886) 17-20
CLISSOLD, HARRY, science,
          -1917?, England
   S 47 (1918) 118
des CLOIZEAUX (DESCLOIZEAUX),
   ALFRED LOUIS OLIVER LEGRAND,
   mineralogy, 1817-1897,
   France
   A 154 (1897) 164
   N 57 (1897) 107
CLOS, DOMINIQUE, botany, 1821-
   1908, France
   S 28 (1908) 511
   S 29 (1909) 225
CLOSE, MAXWELL HENRY, astron-
   omy-geology, 1822-1903
   Ireland
   S 18 (1903) 446
CLOUGH, CHARLES HOMAS, geology,
   1853-1916, Scotland
   E 37 (1916-1917) 12-13

S   44 (1916) 421
CLOUSTON, CHARLES, meteorol-
   ogy, 1800?-1884, England
   N   31 (1884) 104-105
CLOUSTON, SIR THOMAS SMITH,
   psychiatry, 1840-1915,
   Scotland
   E   36 (1915-1916) 28-29
   S   41 (1915) 722
CLOWES, WILLIAM, surgery, 1540-
   1604, England
   S   12 (1900) 259
COAKLEY, GEORGE W., astronomy-
   mathematics, 1814?-1893, West
   Indies
   A   146 (1893) 484
   N   48 (1893) 398
COAN, TITUS MUNSON, geology,
   1801-1882, U.S.A.
   A   124 (1882) 77
   A   125 (1883) 168
   S1   1 (1883) 27
COATS, JOSEPH, pathology, 1846?-
   1899, Scotland
   S   9 (1899) 229
COATS, SIR PETER, commerce-
   philanthropy, 1808?-1890,
   Scotland
   E   17 (1889-1890) 409
COBBOLD, THOMAS SPENCER, helmin-
   thology, 1828-1886, England
   L   47 (1890) iv-v
   N   33 (1886) 534
COCCHI, GAETANO, medicine,
       -1904, Italy
   S   20 (1904) 933
COCCHI, IGINO, geology, 1828-1913,
   Italy
   S   38 (1913) 879
COCK, JULIA, surgery, 1860?-1914,
   U.S.A.
   S   39 (1914) 390
COCKERELL, THEODORE DRU ALISON,
   entomology, 1821?-1901, U.S.A.
   S   14 (1901) 1941
COCKIN, REGINALD PERCY, helmin-
   thology, 1878?-1918, England
   S   49 (1919) 42
COCKLE, SIR JAMES, mathematics,
   1819-1895, England
   L   59 (1896) xxx-xxxix
COCKLE, JOHN, medicine,   -1900,
   England
   S   12 (1900) 893
CODRINGTON, THOMAS, geology,

1829?-1918, England
   S   48 (1918) 617
COE, HOWARD SHELDON, agri-
   culture, 1888-1918, U.S.A.
   S   48 (1918) 467
COFFIN, JAMES HENRY, astron-
   omy-meteorology, 1806-
   1873, U.S.A.
   A   105 (1873) 242
   P   3 (1873) P fp 503-508
   S   15 (1902) 797, 917
COFFIN, JOHN HUNTINGTON CRANE
   astronomy-mathematics,
   1815-1890, U.S.A.
   A   139 (1890) 246
COGGIA, GERONIMO EUGENIO,
   astronomy, 1849-1919,
   France?
   S   49 (1919) 263
COHEN, EMIL WILHELM, astron-
   omy, 1842-1905, Germany
   S   24 (1906) 153
COHN, FERDINAND   JULIUS,
   botany, 1828-1898, Poland
   N   58 (1898) 275
   S   8 (1898) 76
COHN, HERMANN LUDWIG, ophtha
   mology, 1838-1906, German
   S   24 (1906) 447
COINDET, JEAN FRANÇOIS, medi-
   cine, 1774-1834, Switzer-
   land
   A   27 (1834-1835) 404-405
COLBURN, W.W., ornithology,
       -1899, U.S.A.
   S   11 (1900) 159
COLBY, CHARLES EDWARDS, chem
   istry, 1855-1897, U.S.A.
   S   6 (1897) 628
COLBY, THOMAS F., geodesy,
   1784-1852,
   L   6 (1850-1854) 247-250
COLDEN, CADWALLADER, medicin
   physics, 1688-1776, Irela
   A   44 (1842-1843) 85
   S   27 (1908) 59
COLE, AARON HODGMAN, biology
   1856-1913, U.S.A.
   S   39 (1914) 206
COLE, ALFRED DODGE, physics
   1861-1928, U.S.A.
   P   84 (1914) P 200
COLE, FRANK J., anatomy,
   E   28 (1907-1908) 722
COLE, GRENVILLE ARTHUR JAME

geology, 1859-1924, England
L B100 (1926) iv-vii
COLE, SIR HENRY, administra-
tion, 1808-1882, England
N 25 (1882) 611-612
N 31 (1885) 309
COLE, WILLIAM WILLOUGHBY (Earl
of Enniskillen), geology,
1807-1886, England
L 41 (1887) ix-xi
COLEBROOKE, HENRY THOMAS,
mathematics-Sanscrit,
-1837,
L 4 (1837-1843) 10-12
COLEMAN, JOSEPH J., chemistry,
1839?-1888, Scotland
E 17 (1889-1890) xxix-xxx
COLEMAN, W.L., medicine,
-1904, U.S.A.
S 20 (1904) 814
COLENSO, WILLIAM, botany-
ethnology, 1811-1899,
England
L 75 (1905) 57-60
N 59 (1899) 420
S 9 (1899) 339
von COLER, ALWIN, surgery,
1831?-1901, Germany
S 14 (1901) 463
COLES, JOHN, geography, 1833?-
1910, Scotland
S 32 (1910) 272
COLIN, CONSTANT GABRIEL,
physiology, 1825-1896,
France
S 4 (1896) 113
COLLADON, JEAN DANIEL, physics,
1802-1893, Switzerland
N 48 (1893) 396-397
COLLEDGE, THOMAS RICHARDSON,
medicine, 1796?-1879?,
E 10 (1878-1880) 339
COLLETT, JOHN, geology, 1828-
1899, U.S.A.
S 9 (1899) 461
COLLETT, ROBERT, zoology,
1843?-1913, Norway
A 185 (1913) 336
S 37 (1913) 251
COLLIE, JOHN NORMAN, chemistry,
1859-1942, England
E 33 (1912-1913) 354-355
N 54 (1898) 10
COLLIER, PETER, chemistry,
1835-1896, U.S.A.
A 152 (1896) 246

COLLIN, HENRY ALONZO, chem-
istry-physics, 1837-1918,
U.S.A.
S 47 (1918) 533
COLLINGWOOD, CUTHBERT, biology,
1826-1908, England
S 28 (1908) 679
COLLINS, JOSEPH HENRY, geol-
ogy, 1841?-1916, England
S 43 (1916) 684
COLLINS, JOSEPH WILLIAM,
ichthyology, 1839-1904,
U.S.A.
S 41 (1915) 749-750
COLLINS, ZACCHEUS, botany,
-1832?, U.S.A.
A 23 (1832-1833) 398-399
COLMEIRO, MIGUEL, botany,
1815?-1901, Spain
S 14 (1901) 821
COLQUHOUN, ARCHIBALD ROSS,
exploration, 1848?-1914,
England
S 40 (1914) 930
COLUMBUS (COLOMBO), CHRIS-
TOPHER (CRISTOFERO), ex-
ploration, c.1451?-1506,
Italy
N 46 (1892) 185-186
Sl 18 (1891) 163
COLVILE, SIR JAMES, law, 1810-
1883?, England
L 34 (1883) x-xi
COMBE, GEORGE, psychology,
1788-1858, Scotland
P 15 (1879) 109-121
COMBES, EDWARD, engineering,
-1895, Australia
S 2 (1895) 770
COMMERSON, PHILIBERT, botany,
1727-1773, France
N 80 (1909) 430-431
P 46 (1894-1895) 112-115
COMMON, ANDREW AINSLIE, astron-
omy, 1841-1903, England
L 75 (1905) 313-318
N 68 (1903) 132-133
S 17 (1903) 988
COMPTON, ALFRED GEORGE, astron-
omy-physics, 1835-1913,
U.S.A.
S 38 (1913) 879
COMPTON, SPENCER JOSHUA ALWYNE,
Marquis and Earl of North-
ampton, science, 1790-1851,
L 6 (1850-1854) 117-120

COMSTOCK, CYRUS BALLOU, en-
gineering, 1831-1910,
U.S.A.
S 31 (1910) 901
COMSTOCK, JOHN HENRY, ento-
mology, 1849-1931, U.S.A.
S 39 (1914) 718
COMTE, ISIDORE AUGUSTE MARIE
FRANÇOIS XAVIER, philoso-
phy-sociology, 1798-1857,
France
S 19 (1904) 376-380
CONANT, FRANKLIN STORY, biol-
ogy, 1870?-1897, U.S.A.
S 7 (1898) 277
CONANT, LEVI LEONARD, mathe-
matics, 1857-1916, U.S.A.
S 44 (1916) 564
CONARD, HENRY SHOEMAKER,
botany, 1874-   , U.S.A.
S 14 (1901) 334-335
CONDER, CLAUDE REIGNIER, ex-
ploration,   -1910,
England
S 31 (1910) 381
CONDON, THOMAS, geology,
1832-1907, U.S.A.
S 15 (1902) 517
S 25 (1907) 318
de CONDORCET, JEAN ANTOINE
NICOLAS DE CARITAT, marquis,
mathematics-philosophy,
1743-1794, France
A 7 (1824) 200
P 64 (1903-1904) P 528
PM 44 (1814) 81-91
CONGREVE, RICHARD, sociology,
-1899, England
S 10 (1899) 92
CONKLIN, EDWIN GRANT, zoology,
1863-1952, U.S.A.
P 70 (1907) P 185
CONLAN, JOSEPH J.--see
CHRYSOSTOM
CONN, HERBERT WILLIAM, biology,
1859-1917, U.S.A.
S 45 (1917) 407, 451-452,
429
CONNEFFE, JAMES F., bacteriol-
ogy,   -1910, U.S.A.
S 31 (1910) 187
CONNELL, ARTHUR, mineralogy,
1794-1863, Scotland
E 5 (1862-1866) 136-137
L 13 (1864) i
CONOR, ALFRED, bacteriology,

-1914,
S 39 (1914) 573
CONRAD, TIMOTHY ABBOTT,
biology-geology, 1803-1877,
U.S.A.
A 114 (1877) 247-248
P 47 (1895) P fp 145, 257-
263
CONRAD, WALDEMAR, philosophy,
-1915, Germany
S 42 (1915) 335
CONROY, SIR JOHN, chemistry-
physics, 1845-1900, England
L 75 (1905) 246-252
N 44 (1891) 15
N 63 (1900-1901) 186
S 13 (1901) 79
S 14 (1901) 1021
CONSTABLE, ARCHIBALD DAVID,
editor, 1843-1915, Scotland
E 36 (1915-1916) 29
CONSTABLE, JAMES M., biology,
1812?-1900, England
S 11 (1900) 836
CONSTANTINOVICH, CONSTANTINE,
Grand Duke, geology, 1858?-
1915, Russia
P 51 (1897) P 212-222
S 41 (1915) 938
CONTEJEAN, C., bacteriology,
-1897, France
S 5 (1897) 580
CONYBEARE, WILLIAM DANIEL,
geology, 1787-1857, England
A 77 (1859) 63-71
COOK, ALBERT JOHN, entomology,
1842-1916, U.S.A.
S 44 (1916) 528
COOK, GEORGE HAMMELL, geology,
1818-1889, U.S.A.
A 138 (1889) 336, 498-499
Sl 14 (1889) 217
Sl 16 (1890) 8-9
COOK, JAMES, geography, 1728-
1779, England
N 19 (1879) 334-335, 408-
409
N 20 (1879) 6, 7-8
COOK, JOHN, education-physics,
-1915, Scotland
E 37 (1916-1917) 13
COOK, JOSEPH, biology,
-1901, U.S.A.
S 14 (1901) 38
COOK, THOMAS, anatomy,
-1899, England

S 45 (1917) 184
CRYMBLE, C.R., chemistry,
-1914, England
S 41 (1915) 61
CUBITT, SIR WILLIAM, engineer-
ing, 1785-1861, England
L 12 (1863) iv
CULLINGWORTH, CHARLES JAMES,
gynecology, 1841-1908,
England
S 27 (1908) 903
CUMINGS, HUGH, biology, 1791-
1865, England
A 90 (1865) 395
A 91 (1866) 265
CUMMING, JAMES, geology-
physics, 1777-1861,
England
A 86 (1863) 278
CUMMING, JOHN, writer-theology,
1810-1881, Scotland
E 11 (1880-1882) 328-329
CUMMINGS, MISS CLARA EATON
botany, 1855-1906, U.S.A.
S 25 (1907) 77-78
CUMMINGS, J.B., science,
-1896, U.S.A.
S 3 (1896) 555
CUMMINGS, JOHN, tanning, 1785-
1867, U.S.A.
P 55 (1899) P 451-454
CUMMINGS, JOHN, education,
-1898, U.S.A.
S 9 (1899) 24
CUNNINGHAM, ALLAN, botany,
1791-1839, England
A 40 (1840-1841) 219
CUNNINGHAM, DANIEL JOHN,
anatomy, 1850-1909, Ireland
E 30 (1909-1910) 569-579
N 44 (1891) 15
N 81 (1909) 15-16
S 30 (1909) 32
CUNNINGHAM, DAVID DOUGLAS,
pathology, 1843-1914,
England
L B89 (1917) xv-xx
N 94 (1915) 536-537
S 41 (1915) 163-164
CUNNINGHAM, J. M. (T.?), medi-
cine, 1834?-1905,
S 22 (1905) 95
CUNNINGHAM, JAMES, science,
1800-1878, Scotland
E 10 (1878-1880) 13-14
CUNNINGHAM, R. O., geology,

1842?-1918, Ireland
S 48 (1918) 188
CUNNINGHAM, RICHARD, botany,
1793-1835,
A 32 (1837) 215
CURETON, WILLIAM, language-
literature, 1808-1864,
England
L 14 (1865) i
CURIE, MARIE (MARYA) SKLODOWSKA,
chemistry-physics, 1867-
1934, Poland
N 69 (1903) 109
N 86 (1911) 1-3
P 64 (1903-1904) P 477
CURIE, PIERRE, chemistry-
physics, 1859-1906, France
A 171 (1906) 408
N 69 (1906) 109
N 73 (1906) 612-613
N 74 (1906) 357
P 64 (1903-1904) P 477
S 23 (1906) 677
S 24 (1906) 354-355
S 25 (1907) 1-2
CURLING, THOMAS BLIZARD,
surgery, 1811-1888, England
L 44 (1888) xxv-xxvi
CURREY, FREDERICK, mycology,
1819-1881, England
N 24 (1881) 485-486
CURTIN, JEREMIAH, anthropology,
1840-1906, U.S.A.
S 25 (1907) 78
CURTIS, EDWARD, medicine,
1838-1912, U.S.A.
S 36 (1912) 822
CURTIS, JOHN GREEN, physiol-
ogy, 1844-1913, U.S.A.
S 38 (1913) 476
CURTIS, MOSES ASHLEY, botany-
mycology, 1808-1872, U.S.A.
A 103 (1872) 474
A 105 (1873) 391-393
P 34 (1888-1889) P fp 289,
405-410
CURTISS, ALLEN HIRAM, biology,
1845-1907, U.S.A.
S 26 (1907) 606
CURWEN, JOHN, medicine, 1821-
1901, U.S.A.
S 14 (1901) 77
CUSHING, EDWARD FITCH, medi-
cine, 1862?-1911, U.S.A.
S 33 (1911) 523
CUSHING, FRANK HAMILTON,

anthropology-ethnology,
1857-1900, U.S.A.
N 62 (1900) 16
P 41 (1892) P 298
S 11 (1900) 596
CUSHMAN, HOLBROOK, physics,
1857?-1895, U.S.A.
S 2 (1895) 585, 757-761
CUSHNY, ARTHUR ROBERTSON,
pharmacology, 1866-1926,
Scotland
L B100 (1926) P xix-xxvii
CUTBUSH, JAMES, chemistry,
1788-1823, U.S.A.
A 199 (1920) 79
CUTTER, EPHRAIM, microscopy,
1832-1917, U.S.A.
S 45 (1917) 429
CUTTS, RICHARD D., geodesy,
1817?-1883, U.S.A.
Sl 2 (1883) 810
CUVIER, JEAN LÉOPOLD NICOLAS
FRÉDÉRIC (GEORGES), baron,
paleontology-zoology, 1769-
1832, France
A 23 (1832-1833) 303-311,
371
A 30 (1836) 184
A 118 (1879) 338-340
L 3 (1830-1837) 149-152
L 4 (1837-1843) 98-99
PM III 2 (1833) 141-143
S 26 (1907) 495-500
S 49 (1919) 300-301
CZAPSKI, SIEGFRIED, optics,
1861-1907, Germany
S 26 (1907) 126
CZERKAWSKI, E., philosophy,
1822?-1896, Poland
S 4 (1896) 721
CZERMAK (ČERMAK), JOHANN
NEPOMUK, laryngology-
phonetics, 1828-1873,
Czechoslovakia
A 106 (1876) 398
N 9 (1873) 63-64
P 4 (1873-1874) 115-116
von CZERNY, VINCENT JOSEPH,
surgery, 1842-1916,
Czechoslovakia
S 44 (1916) 564
da COSTA, EMMANUEL MENDEZ,
conchology,
A 37 (1839) 155
da COSTA, JACOB MENDEZ, medi-
cine, 1833-1900, U.S.A.

S 12 (1900) 453
von DAECKE, ADOLF ERICH, en-
tomology,   -1918,
Germany
S 48 (1918) 487
da GAMA, VASCO, exploration,
1469?-1524, Portugal
N 58 (1898) 67-69
DAGUERRE, LOUIS JACQUES MANDÉ,
photography, 1787-1851,
France
S 6 (1897) 126
DAGUILLON, AUGUSTE, botany,
-1908, France
S 28 (1908) 232, 404
DAHL, OLAUS, linguistics,
-1897,
S 5 (1897) 473
DAHLANDER, GUSTAV ROBERT,
technology, 1834-1903,
Sweden
S 18 (1903) 573, 703
DAIMLER, GOTTLIEB WILHELM,
invention, 1834-1900,
Germany
S 11 (1900) 437
DAJEE, BHAU, medicine, 1823-
1874, India
N 10 (1874) 270-271
DAKIN, JOHN A., ornithology,
1852?-1900, U.S.A.
S 11 (1900) 635
DAKYNS, JOHN ROCHE, geodesy,
-1910,England
S 32 (1910) 626
DALE, SIR DAVID, engineering,
-1906, England
S 23 (1906) 827
DALEMBERT, J. L.--see
d'ALEMBERT
DALL, CHARLES HENRY APPLETON,
missionary,   -1886,
Sl 8 (1886) 123
DALL, WILLIAM HEALEY, mala-
cology-paleontology, 1845-
1927, U.S.A.
P 86 (1915) P 619
DALLAS, ELMSLIE WILLIAM,
mathematics-physics, 1809-
1879, England
E 10 (1878-1888) 340-346
DALLAS, W. D. (L?), meteorol-
ogy,   -1919, England
S 50 (1919) 326
DALLAS, WILLIAM SWEETLAND,
geology, 1824?-1890, England

N 42 (1890) 132-133
DALLINGER, WILLIAM HENRY,
protozoology, 1842-1909,
England
L B82 (1910) iv-vi
N 82 (1909) 71-72
S 30 (1909) 751
DALRYMPLE, JOHN, pathology,
1804-1852, England
L 6 (1850-1854) 250-251
DALRYMPLE-HAY, SIR JOHN
CHARLES, administration,
1821-1912, Scotland
L A88 (1913) xii-xiv
N 88 (1912) 487-488
DALTON, CHARLES X., instru-
mentation, 1840-1912,
U.S.A.
S 35 (1912) 444-446
DALTON, JOHN, chemistry-
physics, 1766-1844, England
A 73 (1857) 449-450
L 3 (1830-1837) 219-220
L 5 (1843-1850) 528-530
N 52 (1895) 169-170
N 68 (1903) 81-84
N 74 (1906) 537-538
N 75 (1907) 246
N 96 (1915) 344-345
P 63 (1903) P 280-281
P 76 (1910) 500-512
PM III 27 (1845) 139-141
DALTON, JOHN CALL, physiology,
1825-1889, U.S.A.
Sl 8 (1886) 123
DALY, CHARLES PATRICK, geog-
raphy, 1816-1899, U.S.A.
S 10 (1899) 462
DALY, CLARENCE M., technology,
-1904, U.S.A.
S 20 (1904) 509
DALYELL, SIR JOHN GRAHAM,
literature, 1775-1851,
Scotland
A 62 (1851) 302
DALZEL, ANDREW, Greek, 1742-
1806, Scotland
E 4 (1857-1862) 512-514
DALZELL, ALLEN, chemistry-
medicine, 1821-1869, India
E 7 (1869-1872) 7-9
DAMES, WILHELM BARNIM, geol-
ogy-paleontology, 1843-
1898, Germany
N 59 (1898-1899) 276
S 9 (1899) 462

DAMMANN, KARL, medicine,
-1914, Germany
S 40 (1914) 95
de DAMOISEAU, . . ., baron,
astronomy, -1846,
L 5 (1843-1850) 649
DAMON, ROBERT, biology-geology,
-1889, England
N 40 (1889) 44
Sl 13 (1889) 401
DAMON, WILLIAM EMERSON,
ichthyology, 1838-1911,
U.S.A.
S 35 (1912) 175-176
DAMOUR, AUGUSTIN ALEXIS,
chemistry-mineralogy,
1808-1902, France
S 16 (1902) 597
DAMPIER-WHETHAM, W.C.--see
WHETHAM, W.C.D.
DANA, JAMES DWIGHT, education-
geology, 1813-1895, U.S.A.
A 149 (1895) P 329-356
A 159 (1900) 80
E 21 (1897) x-xvi, 15-16
L 58 (1895) lvii-lx
N 51 (1895) 611-612
N 61 (1900) 409-410
P 1 (1872) P 362-365
P 70 (1907) P 306-308
S 1 (1895) 472, 489-490,
545-546
S 2 (1895) 491
S 3 (1896) 106-107, 181-
185
S 10 (1899) 634-635
S 37 (1913) 95-96
DANA, SAMUEL LUTHER, agricul-
ture-chemistry, 1795-1868,
U.S.A.
A 95 (1868) 424-425
P 49 (1896) P fp 577, 692-
697
D'ANCHIETÁ, JOSÉ ALBERTO,
zoology, 1831?-1897,
Portugal
S 7 (1898) 421
DANCKELMANN, BERNHARDT,
forestry, 1831?-1901,
U.S.A.
S 13 (1901) 279
DANIELL, JOHN FREDERIC, chem-
istry, 1790-1845, England
A 52 (1846) 145
L 4 (1837-1843) 23-24,
255-256, 422

62

L   5 (1843-1850) 577-580
PM III   28 (1846) 409-412
DANIELLS, WILLIAM WILLARD,
chemistry, 1840-1912,
U.S.A.
S   36 (1912) 552
DANIELS, ARCHIBALD LAMONT,
mathematics, 1849-1918,
U.S.A.
S   48 (1918) 137
DANNE, JACQUES, physics,
1882-1919, France
A   197 (1919) 454
S   50 (1919) 340-341
DANTE, ALIGHIERI, poetry-
science, 1265-1321, Italy
N   58 (1898) 362-364
N   59 (1899) 417-420
N   94 (1914) 359-360
DARBISHIRE, ARTHUR DUKINFIELD,
genetics, 1879-1915,
Scotland
E   37 (1916-1917) 13-14
S   43 (1916) 131
DARBOUX, JEAN GASTON, mathe-
matics, 1842-1917, France
A   193 (1917) 497
E   38 (1917-1918) 10
L   A94 (1918) xxxi-xxxiv
N   98 (1916) 279
N   99 (1917) 28
S   45 (1917) 306
DARBY, JOHN, education-botany,
1804-1877, U.S.A.
A   114 (1877) 499-500
A   115 (1878) 225
"DARBY, JOHN," pseud.--
see GARRETSON, J.E.
DARLINGTON, WILLIAM, botany,
1782-1863, U.S.A.
A   86 (1863) 132-138
A   87 (1864) 288
DARNLEY, . . ., Earl of,
patron,   -1831,
L   3 (1830-1837) 84
D'ARREST, HEINRICH LOUIS,
astronomy, 1822-1875,
Germany
A   110 (1875) 160
DARWIN, CHARLES ROBERT,
biology-evolution, 1809-
1882, England
A   123 (1882) 422
A   124 (1882) 239, 453-463
A   127 (1884) 243
A   175 (1908) 460

A   178 (1909) 505-506
E   12 (1882-1884) 1-6
L   6 (1850-1854) 355-356
L   44 (1888) i-xxv
N   10 (1874) P 79-81
N   25 (1882) 597
N   26 (1882) 49-51, 73-75,
97-100, 104, 145-147,
169-171, 533-541
N   27 (1883) 557-558
N   32 (1885) 121-122
N   33 (1885) 147-149
N   37 (1887) 73-75, 342-
343, 363-364
N   44 (1891) 337-339
N   55 (1897) 289-290
N   56 (1897) 609-611
N   60 (1899) 187-188
N   67 (1903) 529-530
N   78 (1908) P 221-223
N   80 (1909) P 72-73, 433-
434, 496-498
N   81 (1909) 7-11
N   82 (1909) 91-93
N   85 (1911) 354-359
N   88 (1911) 8-12, 547-548
N   92 (1913) 320, 372, 588-
589
N   95 (1915) 503-504
P   2 (1872-1873) P fp 385,
497-498
P   5 (1874) 475-480
P   6 (1874-1875) 592-598
P   17 (1880) 337-344
P   21 (1882) P fr, 260-265
P   27 (1885) 532-536
P   32 (1887-1888) 208-213,
619-628
P   60 (1901-1902) P fp 5-13,
177-184
P   62 (1901-1902) P 387-414
P   74 (1909) P 416
P   75 (1909) 90-98, 206-207,
499-514, 537-549
P   76 (1910) 23-31, 32-48
Sl   1 (1883) 531
Sl   5 (1885) 471
Sl   6 (1885) P 10-12, 18,
276-277
S   4 (1896) 568
S   10 (1899) 156
S   23 (1906) 986-987
S   27 (1908) 799
S   30 (1909) 199-200
S   31 (1910) 424-425, 903-
904

S   3 (1896) 21
S 13 (1901) 438, P fp 561-
   563
S 14 (1901) 1022
DAWSON, SIR JOHN WILLIAM,
   geology, 1820-1899, Canada
A 158 (1899) 475-476
A 159 (1900) 82-84
N   61 (1899) 80-81
N   65 (1902) 339-341
P   8 (1875-1876) P fp 231-
    234
S 10 (1899) 781, P fp
    905-910
S 12 (1900) 357
DAY, AUSTIN GOODYEAR, chem-
   istry, 1824-1889, U.S.A.
S 21 (1905) 876
DAY, DAVID TALBOT, chemistry-
   geology, 1859-1925, U.S.A.
S 21 (1905) 883
DAY, GEORGE EDWARD, medicine,
   1815-1872, Scotland
N   5 (1872) 383-384
DAY, JEREMIAH, education,
   1773-1867, U.S.A.
A 94 (1867) 291-292
DAY, WILLIAM CATHCART, chem-
   istry, 1857-1905, U.S.A.
S 21 (1905) 880
DEACHAES, WILHELM, geology,
   -1916, Germany
S 43 (1916) 423
DEACON, GEORGE FREDERICK,
   engineering, 1843-1909,
   Scotland
N 81 (1909) 16
DEALTRY, WILLIAM, mathematics-
   theology, 1775-1847,
   England
L   5 (1843-1850) 707-708
DEAN, ALEXANDER, horticulture,
   1832?-1912, England
S 36 (1912) 343
DEAN, GEORGE, pathology,
   1863-1914, Canada
S 39 (1914) 900
S 40 (1914) 22
DEANE, JAMES, geology, 1802?-
   1858, U.S.A.
A 76 (1858) 155
DEARBORN, BENJAMIN, music,
   1755?-1838, U.S.A.
A 38 (1839-1840) 154
DEAS, FRANCIS, law, 1839-1874?,
   Scotland

E   8 (1872-1875) 461-466
DEBAINS, ALFRED, agriculture,
   -1896, France?
S   3 (1896) 737
DE BARY--see BARY . . . de
DEBRAY, HENRI JULES, chemis-
   try, 1827-1888, France
A 136 (1888) 304
N   38 (1888) 396
DE BRUYN, CORNELIUS ADRIAAN,
   biology-chemistry, 1857?-
   1904, Netherlands
S 20 (1904) 287
DEBURAUX, . . ., aeronautics,
   1864?-1904,
S 19 (1904) 598
DEBUS, HEINRICH, chemistry,
   1824-1916, Germany
A 191 (1916) 306
N   96 (1916) 515-516
S 43 (1916) 95
DE BUSH (DEBUS, H.?), Baron,
   chemistry, 1860-1903,
   England?
S 18 (1903) 158
DEBY, JULIEN MARC, biology,
   -1895, Belgium
S   2 (1895) 104
DECAISNE, JOSEPH, botany,
   1807-1882, Belgium
A 123 (1882) 331-332
A 127 (1884) 243
L   34 (1883) iii-vi
N   25 (1882) 390-391
DECANDOLLE (DE CANDOLLE),
   ALPHONSE LOUIS PIERRE
   PYRAMUS, botany, 1806-1893,
   France
A   63 (1852) 150
A 146 (1893) 236-239
E   20 (1895) xxi-xxvi
L   57 (1895) xiv-xx
N   27 (1883) 429-431
N   48 (1893) 269-271
DECANDOLLE (DE CANDOLLE), ANNE
   CASIMIR, botany, 1836-1918,
   Switzerland
S 49 (1919) 167
DECANDOLLE (DE CANDOLLE),
   AUGUSTIN PYRAMUS, botany,
   1778-1841, Switzerland
A   42 (1841-1842) 217-227
A   44 (1842-1843) 217-239
A   85 (1836) 1-16
A   86 (1863) 434
E   20 (1895) xxi-xxvi

A   97 (1869) 142
DELGADO, JOAQUIM FILIPPE NERY,
   geology, 1834?-1908,
   Portugal
   A 176 (1908) 404
DELGADO, R. CLAUDIO,
      -1916, Cuba
   S   44 (1916) 236
DELMAR, F.O.T., philanthropy,
      -1895,
   S   2 (1895) 770
DE LONG, GEORGE WASHINGTON,
   exploration, 1844-1881,
   U.S.A.
   Sl 2 (1883) 540-544
DELPINO, FEDERICO, botany,
   1833?-1905, Italy
   S   21 (1905) 996
DELPONTE, G.B., botany,
      -1884, Italy
   Sl 4 (1884) 409
DELUC (deLUC), JEAN ANDRÉ,
   geology-physics, 1727-
   1817, Switzerland
   S   20 (1904) 729
   S   21 (1905) 111, 274-275
DEMARÇAY, EUGÈNE ANATOLE,
   chemistry, 1852-1903, France
   S   17 (1904) 1020
von DEMBOWSKI, ERCOLE, baron,
   astronomy, 1812-1881, Italy
   N   23 (1881) 322
DEMONTZEY, G.L. PROSPER,
   agriculture,   -1898?,
   France
   S   7 (1898) 710
DE MORGAN, AUGUSTUS, mathe-
   matics, 1806-1871, India
   Sl 1 (1883) 422-425
   S   13 (1901) 516-517
   S   42 (1915) 729-731
DENDY, ARTHUR, zoology, 1865-
   1925, England
   L   B99 (1926) P xxxiii-
      xxxxv
DENHAM, SIR HENRY MANGLES,
   naval science, 1800-1887,
   England
   L   43 (1888) i-ii
DENIKER, JOSEPH, anthropology,
   1852-1918, Russia
   S   47 (1918) 587
DENISON, CHARLES, medicine,
   1845-1909, U.S.A.
   S   29 (1909) 179
DENISON, CHARLES SIMEON,

engineering-stereotomy,
   1849-1913, U.S.A.
   S   38 (1913) 189
   S   43 (1916) 740
DENNY, PETER, engineering,
   1820-1895?, Scotland
   E   21 (1895-1897) 13
DENNY, WILLIAM, naval archi-
   tecture, 1847-1887,
   Scotland
   E   14 (1886-1887) 162-163
   N   39 (1889) 241-244
DENZA, FRANCESCO, astronomy,
   1834-1894, Italy
   A   149 (1895) 80
   N   51 (1894) 179
DEPPE, FERDINAND, botany,
      -1861,
   A   83 (1862) 427
DEPREZ, MARCEL, physics, 1843-
   1918, France
   A   197 (1919) 240
   Sl 8 (1886) 297
DERBY, ORVILLE ADELBERT,
   geology, 1851-1915, U.S.A.
   A   191 (1916) 152
   S   42 (1915) 826
   S   43 (1916) 596
DERENBOURG, JOSEPH, philology,
   1811?-1895, France
   S   2 (1895) 188
DESAINS, QUENTIN PAUL, physics,
   1817-1885, France
   Sl 6 (1885) 20
DESAULLE, GASTON DUBOIS, ex-
   ploration,   -1903,
   S   17 (1903) 956
DESCARTES, RENÉ, mathematics-
   philosophy, 1596-1650,
   France
   A   4 (1822) 390
   N   41 (1889) 171-172
   N   72 (1905) 292-293
   P   37 (1890) P fp 721,
      833-840
   S   39 (1914) 461-462
DES CLOIZEAU, ALFRED LOUIS
   OLIVER LEGRAND, mineralogy,
   1817-1897, France
   L   63 (1898) xxv-xxviii
   S   5 (1897) 839, 916
DES FONTAINES, RENÉ LOUICHE,
   botany, 1750-1833, France
   A   27 (1834-1835) 201-215
   L   3 (1830-1837) 233-234
DESHAYES, GERARD PAUL, geology,

DIEULAFOY, GEORGES, medicine,
1839-1911, France
S 34 (1911) 376
DIGGES (DIGGS), LEONARD,
mathematics,   -1571,
England
N 81 (1909) 517-518
DILLENIUS, JOHN JAMES, botany,
1687-1747, England
N 76 (1907) 289
DILLER, JOSEPH SILAS, geology,
1850-1928, U.S.A.
P 84 (1914) P 203
DILLWYN, LEWIS WESTON, biol-
ogy, 1778-1855, England
A 75 (1858) 293
DILTHEY, WILHELM, philosophy,
1833-1911, Germany
S 34 (1911) 508
DINES, WILLIAM HENRY, meteorol-
ogy, 1855-1927, England
L A119 (1928) P xxiii-
xxxii
DIONNE, NARCISSE E., archeol-
ogy,   -1917, Canada
S 45 (1917) 407
DIRICHLET, PETER GUSTAV
LEJEUNE, mathematics, 1805-
1859, Germany
L 10 (1860) xxxviii-xxxix
DITTE, ALFRED, chemistry, 1843-
1908, France
S 28 (1908) 752
von DITTEL, LEOPOLD, surgery,
1815-1898, Austria
S 8 (1898) 367
DITTMAR, WILLIAM, chemistry,
1833-1892, Germany
E 20 (1892-1895) 8, vi-vii
N 45 (1892) 493-494
DITTRICH, GEORG PAUL MAX, chem-
istry, 1864-1913, Germany
S 38 (1913) 122
DIVERS, EDWARD, chemistry,
1837-1912, England
A 183 (1912) 598
L A88 (1913) viii-x
N 89 (1912) 170
N 90 (1912) 43
S 35 (1912) 652
DIVISCH, PROCOPIUS, physics,
1696-1765, Germany
P 42 (1892-1893) 356-361
DIXON, HAROLD BAILY, physics,
1852-1930, England
L A134 (1932) P i-xvii

N 92 (1913) 405-406
DIXON, SAMUEL GIBSON, bac-
teriology-hygiene, 1851-
1918, U.S.A.
S 47 (1918) 236
DOBBIE, SIR JAMES JOHNSTONE,
chemistry, 1852-1924,
Scotland
L A107 (1925) P vi-viii
DOBSON, GEORGE EDWARD, zoology,
1848-1895, Ireland
L 59 (1896) xv-xvii
S 2 (1895) 770, 848
DODGE, CHARLES KEENE, botany,
1844?-1918, U.S.A.
S 47 (1918) 437-438
DODGE, JACOB RICHARDS, agri-
culture-statistics, 1823-
1902, U.S.A.
S 16 (1902) 638
DODGE, WILLIAM EARL, commerce-
philanthropy, 1805?-1903,
U.S.A.
S 18 (1903) 221
DODGSON, CHARLES LUTWIDGE
("LEWIS CARROLL"), fiction-
mathematics, 1832-1898,
England
N 57 (1898) 279-280, 303
S 7 (1898) 92
DÖBEREINER, JOHANN WOLFGANG,
chemistry, 1780-1849,
Germany
A 58 (1849) 450
DOEBNER, OSKAR GUSTAV, chem-
istry, 1850-1907, Germany
S 25 (1905) 798
DÖLL, JOHANN CHRISTOF, botany,
1807?-1885, Germany
Sl 5 (1885) 472
DÖLLEN, JOHANN HEINRICH
WILHELM, astronomy, 1820-
1897, Estonia
S 5 (1897) 548
DOERFLINGER, AUGUSTUS, en-
gineering, 1844?-1899,
Germany
S 10 (1899) 822
DÖRING, AUGUST, philosophy,
1834-   , Germany
S 19 (1904) 477
DOHRMANN, A., mineralogy,   ,
A 132 (1886) 487
DOHRN, FELIX ANTON, zoology,
1840-1909, Germany
N 58 (1898) 428

S 19 (1904) 773
DUCHENNE, GUILLAUME BENJAMIN
AMAND, medicine-physics,
1806-1875, France
S 2 (1895) 624
DUCIE, EARL OF, horticulture,
1827-1921, England
L B93 (1922) P i-ii
DUCOS (DU HAURON), ARTHUR
LOUIS, photography, 1837-
1910, France
A 200 (1920) 474
DUCROTAY DE BLAINVILLE, H.M.--
see BLAINVILLE
DUDDELL, WILLIAM DU BOIS,
electricity, 1872-1917,
England
L A94 (1918) P xxxiv-xxxv
N 100 (1917) 207-208
S 46 (1917) 563
DUDGEON, PATRICK, mineralogy,
1817?-1895,
E 21 (1895-1897) 12
DUDLEY, CHARLES BENJAMIN,
chemistry-metallurgy,
1842-1909, U.S.A.
S 30 (1909) 966
S 34 (1911) 639-640
DUDLEY, WILLIAM H., medicine,
1810?-1886, U.S.A.
S1 8 (1886) 364
DUDLEY, WILLIAM LOFLAND,
chemistry, 1859-1914,
U.S.A.
A 188 (1914) 490
DUDLEY, WILLIAM RUSSEL, botany,
1849-1911, U.S.A.
A 182 (1911) 84
S 33 (1911) 925
S 34 (1911) 142-145
DÜNKELBERG, . . ., agriculture,
1819-   , Germany
S 29 (1909) 892
DUFET, HENRY, physics, 1849-
1905, France
S 21 (1905) 838
DUFF, JAMES S., agriculture,
1856?-1916, Canada
S 44 (1916) 782
DUFF, SIR M.E.G.--see GRANT
DUFF
DUFFERIN AND AVA, MARQUIS OF--
see BLACKWOOD, F.T.H.T.
DUFFIELD, JOHN THOMAS, mathe-
matics, 1823-1901, U.S.A.
S 13 (1901) 636

DUFFIELD, WILLIAM WARD,
geodesy,   , U.S.A.
S 44 (1916) 48
DUFOUR, CHARLES H., astronomy,
1827-1903, France
S 17 (1903) 399, 838
DUFOUR, GUILLAUME HENRI,
topography, 1787-1875,
Switzerland
S1 3 (1884) 799-800
DUFOUR, HENRI EVERT, physics,
1852-1910, France
S 31 (1910) 381
DUFOUR, JEAN, botany, 1861?-
1904, France
S 19 (1904) 157
DUFOUR, JEAN MARIE LÉON, en-
tomology, 1782?-1865, France
A 90 (1865) 140
DUFRÉNOY, OURS PIERRE ARMAND
PETIT-, geology-mineralogy,
1792-1857, France
A 74 (1857) 160
DUGNET, NICOLAS JEAN BAPTISTE,
medicine, 1837?-1914,
France
S 40 (1914) 163
DUHEM, PIERRE MAURICE MARIE,
physics, 1861-1916, France
A 192 (1916) 509
N 93 (1914) 317
N 98 (1916) 131-132
S 44 (1916) 528
DULONG, PIERRE LOUIS, chemis-
try-physics, 1785-1838,
France
L 4 (1837-1843) 97-98
PM III 14 (1839) 65-66
DUMAS, JEAN BAPTISTE ANDRÉ,
chemistry, 1800-1884,
France
A 128 (1884) 289-299
E 12 (1882-1884) 937-938
L 5 (1843-1850) 481-483
L 37 (1884) x-xxvii
N 21 (1880) P 305 (Special
Issue, 5 February)
N 27 (1882) 174-175,
P 227
N 30 (1884) 15-17
N 31 (1884) 109
P 18 (1880-1881) P fp 145,
257-261
P 21 (1882) 667-679
S1 3 (1884) 526, P 750-752
S 13 (1901) 556

EBERLE, JOHN, medicine, 1787-
1838, U.S.A.
A 38 (1839-1840) 154
EBERMAYER, WILHELM FERDINAND
ERNST, chemistry-meteorol-
ogy, 1829-1908, Germany
S 28 (1908) 404
S 30 (1909) 802
EBERS, GEORG MORITZ, archeol-
ogy, 1837-1898, Germany
N 58 (1898) 396
EBERTH, KARL JOSEPH, anatomy-
bacteriology, 1835-1926,
Germany
S 22 (1905) 475
S 42 (1915) 607
EBSTEIN, WILHLEM, medicine,
1836-1912, Germany
S 36 (1912) 784
ECHEGARAY Y EIZAGUIRRE, JOSÉ,
mathematics-physics, poetry,
1832-1916, Spain
S 44 (1916) 564
ECKHARDT, CONRAD, physiology,
1822-1905, Germany
S 21 (1905) 838
EDDY, MRS. IMOGEN W., mathe-
matics,   -1904, U.S.A.
S 20 (1904) 382
EDDY, WILLIAM ABNER, meteorol-
ogy-photography, 1850-1909
U.S.A.
S 31 (1910) 141
EDELMANN, MAX THOMAS, physics,
1845-1913, Germany
S 37 (1913) 862
EDGAR, ARTHUR, chemistry,
      -1913, U.S.A.
S 38 (1913) 738
EDGECOMB, DANIEL W., instru-
mentation, 1840?-1915,
U.S.A.
S 41 (1915) 722
EDGEWORTH, MICHAEL PAKENHAM,
biology, 1812?-1881,
A 127 (1884) 243
EDINGER, LUDWIG, medicine,
1855-1918, Germany
S 48 (1918) 137
EDISON, THOMAS ALVA, invention,
1847-1931, U.S.A.
N 52 (1895) 193-194
N 78 (1908) 122-123
N 97 (1916) 158
P 13 (1878) P fp 385, 487-
491

S1 6 (1885) P 145-148
S 3 (1896) 891-892
S 41 (1915) 813-815
EDMANDS, J. RAYNER, astronomy,
1850?-1910, U.S.A.
S 31 (1910) 535
EDSON, ARTHUR WOODBURY,
botany,   -1905, U.S.A.
S 22 (1905) 61-62
EDSON, CYRUS, sanitation,
1857?-1903, U.S.A.
S 18 (1903) 767
EDSON, GEORGE C., geology,
      -1909, U.S.A.
S 29 (1909) 893
EDWARD, THOMAS, zoology, 1814-
1886, England?
N 15 (1877) 349-351
P 10 (1876) 594-608, P 751
EDWARDS, A. MILNE and H. MILNE
--see MILNE-EDWARDS
EDWARDS, MISS AMELIA ANN
BLANDFORD, archeology-
writer, 1831-1892, England
S1 19 (1892) 271
EDWARDS, HENRY, entomology,
1830-1891, England
P 76 (1910) P 470-472
S1 18 (1891) 18
S1 19 (1892) 271
EDWARDS, THOMAS, biology,
      -1886, Scotland
S1 7 (1886) 458
EDWARDS, VINAL N., zoology,
      -1919, U.S.A.
S 50 (1919) 34-35
EDWARDS, WILLIAM HENRY, ento-
mology, 1822-1909, U.S.A.
P 76 (1910) P 470-472
S 29 (1909) 654
EDYE, JOSEPH, administration,
1791-1866, England
L 16 (1868) x-xi
EGAN, F.W., geology,   -1901,
Ireland
S 13 (1901) 198
EGERTON, SIR PHILIP DE MALPAS
GREY-, geology, 1806-1881,
L 33 (1882) xxii-xxiv
N 23 (1881) 579-580
EGGER, VICTOR ÉMILE, psychol-
ogy, 1848-1909, France
S 29 (1909) 451
EGGERT, HEINRICH KARL DANIEL,
botany, 1841-1904
P 74 (1909) 251-258

EGLESTON, THOMAS F.M., metal-
lurgy-mining, 1832-1900,
U.S.A.
A 159 (1900) 160
P 55 (1899) P fp 145, 256-
265
S 11 (1900) 117, 361-364
EGLI, JOHANN JAKOB, geography,
1825-1896, Switzerland
S 4 (1896) 404
EHLER, OTTO G., exploration,
1855-1895, Germany
S 2 (1895) 770
EHLERS, ERNST HEINRICH, zool-
ogy, 1835-1925, Germany
N 74 (1906) 50-51
S 22 (1905) 806
S 42 (1915) 825
EHLERT, REINHOLD, seismology,
-1899, Germany
S 9 (1899) 158
EHRENBERG, CHRISTIAN GOTTFRIED,
biology-microscopy, 1795-
1876, Germany
A 112 (1876) 244
A 113 (1877) 238
E 9 (1875-1878) 230-231
P 14 (1878-1879) P fp 553,
668-672
EHRENREICH, PAUL, ethnology,
1856?-1914, Germany
S 39 (1914) 684
EHRLICH, PAUL, bacteriology,
1854-1915, Germany
A 190 (1915) 448
E 36 (1915-1916) 26-27
L B92 (1921) i-vii
N 95 (1915) 707-708
P 83 (1913) P 414-416
S 35 (1912) 943-944
S 39 (1914) 502
S 41 (1915) 27-28
S 42 (1915) 304, 332-333
EICHBERG, JULIUS H., medicine,
-1916,
S 44 (1916) 707
EICHELBERGER, WILLIAM SNYDER,
astronomy, 1865-1951,
U.S.A.
P 68 (1906) P 189
EICHLER, AUGUST WILHELM,
botany, 1839-1887, Germany
A 133 (1887) 427
N 35 (1887) 493-494
EIFFEL, ALEXANDRE GUSTAVE,
engineering, 1832-1923,

France
S1 13 (1889) 406
EIMBECK, WILLIAM, geodesy-
mathematics, 1841-1909,
Germany
S 30 (1909) 48-50
EINSTEIN, ALBERT, physics,
1879-1955, Germany
S 50 (1919) 478
EINTHOVEN, WILLEM, physics-
physiology, 1860-1927, Java
L A117 (1928) P xxvi-xxix
L B102 (1928) P v-viii
EISENGREIN, G.A., botany,
-1858, Germany
A 77 (1859) 443
EISENLOHR, FRIEDRICH, mathe-
matics, 1831-1904, Germany
S 20 (1904) 287
EKLUND, ADAM WILHELM, physics,
1796-1885, Sweden
S1 6 (1885) 260
EKSTRAND, EMIL VICTOR, botany,
-1884, Sweden
S1 5 (1885) 122
ELBERT, THEODORE, geology,
1857?-1899, Germany
S 10 (1899) 463
ELD, HENRY, exploration,
-1850, U.S.A.
A 60 (1850) 137
ELDER, GEORGE, commerce, 1816-
1897, Scotland
E 22 (1897-1899) 5-6
ELDER, JOHN MUNRO, surgery,
1858-1922, Canada
P 12 (1877-1878) P 537
ELDER, WILLIAM, chemistry-
1843-1903, Nova Scotia
S 18 (1903) 30
ELDON, . . ., the Earl of, law,
-1838,
L 4 (1837-1843) 94
ELDRIDGE, GEORGE, hydrography,
1828?-1900, U.S.A.
S 12 (1900) 348
ELDRIDGE, GEORGE HOMANS,
geology, 1854-1905, U.S.A.
S 22 (1905) 62
ELGAR, FRANCIS, naval archi-
tecture, 1845-1909, England
L A83 (1909-1910) viii-xi
N 54 (1896) 10
N 79 (1909) 372-373
ELIAS, NEY, geophysics, 1844-
1897, England

mathematics, 1848-1904,
U.S.A.
  S   20 (1904) 895
ELY, JOHN SLADE, medicine,
  1860-1906, U.S.A.
  S   23 (1906) 279
ELY, THEODORE NEWEL, engineer-
  ing, 1846-1916, U.S.A.
  S   44 (1916) 672
EMERSON, BENJAMIN KENDALL,
  geology, 1843-1932, Bahamas
  P   51 (1897) 217
EMERSON, GEORGE H., chemistry,
  1837-1864, U.S.A.
  A   89 (1865) 373-374
EMERSON, JAMES, invention,
        -1896,
  S   4 (1896) 76
EMERY, CHARLES EDWARD, en-
  gineering, 1838-1898,
  U.S.A.
  S   7 (1898) 799
EMIL, OSKAR, physics, 1835?-
  1909, Germany
  S   29 (1909) 893
EMINSON, A.F., biology,
        -1916, England
  S   44 (1916) 461
EMMERICH, RUDOLF, hygiene,
  1852?-1914, Germany
  S   40 (1914) 812
EMMERLING, FRIEDRICH CARL
  JULIUS AUGUST ADOLPH,
  chemistry, 1842-1906,
  Germany
  S   23 (1906) 599
EMMET, JOHN PATTEN, chemistry,
  1797-1842, Ireland
  A   43 (1842) 404
EMMINGHAUS, HERMANN, psychia-
  try, 1845-1904, Germany
  S   19 (1904) 559
EMMONS, EBENEZER, geology-
  medicine, 1799-1863, U.S.A.
  A   87 (1864) 151
  P   48 (1895-1896) P fp 289,
        406-411
  Sl   5 (1885) P 456-458
EMMONS, SAMUEL FRANKLIN,
  geology, 1841-1911, U.S.A.
  A 181 (1911) 467-468
  A 189 (1915) 229
  S   35 (1910) 522, 601-604
ENCKE, JOHANN FRANZ, astronomy,
  1791-1865, Germany
  A   90 (1865) 396

A   93 (1867) 10-15
E   5 (1862-1866) 469-470
L   3 (1830-1837) 221
L   15 (1867) xliv-xlvi
N   1 (1870) 479-480
ENDLICHER, STEPHAN LADISLAUS,
  botany, 1804-1849, Hungary
  A   58 (1849) 299-300
  N   63 (1901) 248
  S   10 (1899) 822
ENGEL, CHRISTIAN GOTTLIEB
  FERDINAND, mathematics,
  1805-1866, Germany
  A   95 (1868) 282-284
ENGEL, CHRISTIAN LORENZ ERNST,
  statistics, 1821-1896,
  Germany
  S   4 (1896) 941
ENGELBRECHT, ALBERT, chemistry,
        -1905, Germany
  S   22 (1905) 686
ENGELMANN, GEORGE, botany,
  1809-1884, Germany
  A 127 (1884) 244
  A 128 (1884) 61-67
  P   29 (1886) P fp 145, 260-
        265
  P   74 (1909) 124-133
  Sl   3 (1884) 238, 405-408,
        P 639
ENGELMANN, GEORGE JULIUS,
  gynecology, 1847-1903,
  U.S.A.
  S   18 (1903) 703
ENGLEMANN, THEODOR WILHELM,
  botany-physiology, 1843-
  1909, Germany
  N   29 (1884) 599
  S   29 (1909) 931
ENGELSTAD, . . ., meteorology,
        -1909, Norway
  S   30 (1909) 203
ENGLÄNDER, R., engineering,
  1850?-1909, Austria
  S   29 (1909) 179
ENGLEFIELD, HENRY CHARLES,
  astronomy, 1752-1822,
  PM   32 (1808) P fr
ENGLER, EDMUND ARTHUR, mathe-
  matics, 1836-1918, U.S.A.
  S   47 (1918) 217
ENGLER, HEINRICH GUSTAV ADOLF,
  botany, 1844-1930, Germany
  N   70 (1904) 418
  S   39 (1914) 388, 603
ENGLISCH, JOSEF, surgery,

L   A93 (1917) liv-lvii
N   97 (1916) 547
S   44 (1916) 421
ESTLANDER, KARL GUSTAV,
    esthetics, 1834?-1910,
    Sweden
    S   32 (1910) 374
ESTY, WILLIAM COLE, astronomy-
    mathematics, 1838-1916,
    U.S.A.
    S   44 (1916) 165
ETHERIDGE, ROBERT, geology,
    1819-1903, England
    L   75 (1905) 258-261
    N   69 (1903) 181-182
von ETTINGHAUSEN, ANDREAS,
    Baron, physics, 1796-1878,
    Germany
    A   116 (1878) 164
    N   18 (1878) 197
von ETTINGHAUSEN, CONSTANTIN,
    Baron, botany-paleontology,
    1826-1897, Austria
    S   5 (1897) 270
EUCLID, mathematics, fl. 323-
    285 B.C., Greece
    N   97 (1916) 98-99
    S   29 (1909) 974-977
EUDES-DESLONGCHAMPS--see
    DESLONGCHAMPS, E.E.
EUDOXOS, science, c.408-c.355
    B.C., Greece
    N   30 (1884) 315-316
EUING, WILLIAM, commerce,
    1788-1874, Scotland
    E   8 (1872-1875) 491-496
EULENBERG, HERMANN, psychiatry,
    1813?-1902, Germany
    S   16 (1902) 755
EULENBURG, ALBERT, neurology,
    1840-1917, Germany
    S   42 (1915) 305
EULER, LEONHARD, mathematics,
    1707-1783, Switzerland
    A   178 (1909) 88
    S   6 (1897) 767
    S   30 (1909) 10-12
    S   34 (1911) 717-718
EUSTACIO, BARTOLOMEO, anatomy,
    1524-1574, Italy
    S   38 (1913) 300
EUSTIS, HENRY LAWRENCE, en-
    gineering, 1819-1885,
    U.S.A.
    Sl   5 (1885) 62
EVANS, SIR ARTHUR JOHN,

archeology, 1851-1941,
England
N   64 (1901) 36
EVANS, SIR FREDERICK JOHN
    OWEN, hydrography, 1815-
    1885, England
    L   40 (1886) i-viii
    N   33 (1886) 246-248
EVANS, HENRY, zoology, 1831-
    1904,
    N   70 (1904) 327-328
EVANS, HENRY BROWN, astronomy-
    mathematics, 1871-   ,
    U.S.A.
    S   14 (1901) 335-336
EVANS, J. FENTON, pathology,
    -1899,
    S   9 (1899) 495
EVANS, JOHN, geology, 1812-
    1861, U.S.A.
    A   82 (1861) 311-318
EVANS, SIR JOHN, archeology,
    1823-1908, England
    L   B80 (1908) l-lvi
    N   78 (1908) 131-132
    S   27 (1908) 966
EVANS, OLIVER, invention,
    1755-1819, U.S.A.
    P   12 (1877-1878) 454
EVANS, THOMAS, chemistry,
    1863-1907, U.S.A.
    S   26 (1907) 29-30
EVEREST, SIR GEORGE, explora-
    tion, 1790-1866, England
    L   16 (1868) xi-xiv
EVERETT, HARRY DAY, forestry,
    1880?-1908, U.S.A.
    S   28 (1908) 338
EVERETT, JOSEPH DAVID, mathe-
    matics-physics, 1831-1904,
    England
    A   168 (1904) 320
    L   75 (1905) 377-380
    N   70 (1904) 372, 397
    S   20 (1904) 286-287
EVERHART, BENJAMIN MATLACK,
    botany-micology, 1818-1904,
    U.S.A.
    S   20 (1904) 476
EVERHART, ISAIAH FAWKES,
    philanthropy, 1840?-1911,
    U.S.A.
    S   33 (1911) 959
EWALD, KARL ANTON, medicine,
    1845-1915, Germany
    S   42 (1915) 608

EWART, JAMES COSSAR, zoology,
1851-1933, Scotland
E 22 (1897-1899) 731-732
N 48 (1893) 9
EWELL, ERVIN EDGAR, chemistry,
1867-1904, U.S.A.
S 19 (1904) 741
EWEN, DONALD, metallurgy,
-1915, Scotland
S 42 (1915) 794
EWING, FAYETTE CLAY, JR.,
engineering, 1886?-1914,
U.S.A.
S 40 (1914) 930
EWING, SIR JAMES ALFRED,
engineering-physics, 1855-
1935, Scotland
N 36 (1887) 5
N 53 (1895) 114
EYKMAN, JOHANN FREDERIK, chem-
istry, 1851-1915, Germany
S 42 (1915) 242
von EYTH, EDUARD FRIEDRICH
MAXIMILIAN, engineering,
1836-1906, Germany
S 24 (1906) 382
von FABER DU FAUR, ADOLPH
FRIEDRICH, engineering,
1826-1918, Germany
S 48 (1918) 219
FABRE, JEAN HENRI CASIMIR,
entomology, 1823-1915
France
A 190 (1915) 524
N 94 (1914) 85-86
N 96 (1915) 204-205
S 42 (1915) 567
FABRICIUS, GUILELMUS, surgery,
1560-   , Germany
S 30 (1909) 965
FABRITIUS, WILHELM, astronomy,
1845-1895, Finland
S 2 (1895) 340
FAGNANO, GIULIO CARLO DE'
TOSCHI DI (also, DE
FAGNANI), mathematics,
1682-1766, Senegal
N 90 (1913) 590
FAHLBERG, CHARLES, chemistry,
-1910,
S 32 (1910) 272
FAHRENHEIT, DANIEL GABRIEL,
physics, 1686-1736, Germany
N 64 (1901) 25-26
FAIRBAIRN, SIR WILLIAM, en-
gineering, 1789-1874,

Scotland
N 15 (1877) 370-372
FAIRCHILD, GEORGE THOMPSON,
education, 1838-1901
U.S.A.
S 13 (1901) 516
FAIRFAX, SIR HENRY, explora-
tion, 1837?-1900, England
S 11 (1900) 518
FAIRLEY, THOMAS, chemistry,
1843-1919, Scotland
E 40 (1919-1920) 3-4
FALCONER, HUGH, botany-
paleontology, 1808-1865,
Scotland
A 89 (1865) 236
A 91 (1866) 264
L 15 (1867) xiv-xx
von FALKE, JAKOB, curator,
1825-1897, Germany
S 5 (1897) 950
FALKENER, EDWARD, archeology,
1813?-1896, England
S 5 (1897) 56
FALLOWS, FEARON, astronomy,
-1831,
L 3 (1830-1837) 82-83
FALSHAW, SIR JAMES, engineer-
ing, 1810-1889, Scotland
E 17 (1889-1890) xxvi-
xxviii
FARABEUF, LOUIS HUBERT,
anatomy, 1841-1910, France
S 32 (1910) 339, 662
FARADAY, MICHAEL, chemistry-
physics, 1791-1867, England
A 94 (1867) 293
A 95 (1868) 145-173
A 96 (1868) 34-51, 180-201
A 118 (1879) 241-242
A 197 (1919) 230-231
E 6 (1866-1869) 192-196
L 3 (1830-1837) 156-157
L 4 (1837-1843) 100-101
L 5 (1843-1850) 635
L 17 (1869) i-lxviii
N 1 (1870) 384, 401-403
N 3 (1870) 51-52
N 6 (1872) 410-413
N 8 (1873) P 397-399
N 44 (1891) 178-180, 230-
231
N 60 (1899) 123-124
N 61 (1900) 337-340
N 83 (1910) 95
N 89 (1912) 514

S   44 (1916) 782
FERGUSON, ROBERT M'NAIR, edu-
cation-physics, 1828-1912,
Scotland
E   33 (1912-1913) 342-345
E   34 (1913-1914) 6
FERGUSSON, JAMES, architecture,
1808-1886, Scotland
P   31 (1887) P fr, 118-122
FERNET, ÉMILE, physics, 1829-
1905, France
S   21 (1905) 478
de FERRANTI, SEBASTIAN ZIANI,
engineering, 1864-1930,
England
L   A127 (1930) P xix-xxi
FERRARI, ANDREW, chemistry,
1839?-1915, U.S.A.
S   42 (1915) 641
FARRARIS, GALILEO, physics,
1847-1897, Italy
N   67 (1903) 460
N   69 (1904) 246
S   5 (1897) 304, 511-512
FERREL, WILLIAM, meteorology,
1817-1891, U.S.A.
A   142 (1891) 358
P   40 (1891-1892) P fp 577,
686-695
Sl   18 (1891) 270-274
S   45 (1917) 448
FERRERO, ANNIBALE, geodesy-
mathematics, 1840-1902,
Italy
S   16 (1902) 399
FERRERO, GUGLIELMO, sociology,
1872?-1942, Italy
P   52 (1897-1898) P 759
FERRERS, NORMAN MACLEOD,
mathematics, 1829-1903,
England
L   75 (1905) 273-276
S   17 (1903) 318
FERRI, ENRICO, criminology,
1856-1929, Italy
P   52 (1897-1898) P 748
FERRI, LUIGI, philosophy,
1826-1895, Italy
S   1 (1895) 446
S   3 (1896) 510
FERRIER, SIR DAVID, neurology-
physiology, 1843-1928,
Scotland
L   B103 (1928) P viii-xvi
N   43 (1890) 136
FERRINI, RINALDO EUGENIO

DOMENICO TRANQUILLINO,
physics, 1831-1908, Italy
S   27 (1908) 397
FERRIS, . . ., medicine,
-1831,
L   3 (1830-1837) 84
FERRY, JOHN FARWELL, orni-
thology, 1877-1910, U.S.A.
S   31 (1910) 411
FESTING, E.R., physics, 1839-
1912, England
N   89 (1912) 299
S   35 (1912) 958
FEUILLEAUBOIS, PIERRE VICTOR
ALFRED, botany,   -1899,
S   9 (1899) 525
FEULARD, HENRI, dermatology,
-1897, France
S   5 (1897) 839
FEWKES, JESSE WALTER, ethnol-
ogy-geology, 1850-1930
U.S.A.
P   41 (1892) 301
P   55 (1899) 464
S   47 (1918) 163
FICHTE, JOHANN GOTTLIEB,
philosophy, 1762-1814,
Germany
P   65 (1904) P 84
FICINUS, HEINRICH DAVID AUGUST,
biology-medicine, 1782-
1857, Netherlands
A   75 (1858) 293
FICK, ADOLF GASTON EUGEN,
physiology, 1829-1901,
Germany
N   66 (1902) 180-182
S   14 (1901) 422
FIEDLER, OTTO WILHELM   ,
mathematics, 1832-1912,
Germany
S   35 (1912) 731
S   36 (1912) 862
S   37 (1913) 16
FIELD, JOSHUA, engineering,
1787-1863, England
L   13 (1864) iii
FIELD, MARTIN, chemistry-
mineralogy, 1773?-1833,
U.S.A.
A   26 (1834) 204-205
FIELD, ROGERS, engineering,
1831?-1900, England
S   11 (1900) 635
FIELDE, MISS ADELE MARION,
biology, 1839-1916, U.S.A.

N   49 (1894) 296
FISCHER, RUDOLF, biology,
        -1915, Germany
S   41 (1915) 204
FISCHER, WILLIAM LEWIS FERDI-
    NAND, physics,   -1890?,
    Germany
N   43 (1890) 134
FISCHER VON WALDHEIM,
    ALEKSANDR, botany,
        , Russia
N   95 (1915) 544
S   42 (1915) 185
FISCHER VON WALDHEIM,
    ALEKSANDR GRIGORIEVICH,
    botany,   -1884, Russia
S1   4 (1884) 409
FISCHER VON WALDHEIM, GOTTHELF
    FRIEDRICH, geology, 1771-
    1853, Germany
A   70 (1855) 393
FISHER, ALEXANDER METCALF,
    mathematics-physics, 1794-
    1822, U.S.A.
A   5 (1822) P fr, 367-376
FISHER, OSMOND, geology, 1817-
    1914, England
A   188 (1914) 370
N   93 (1914) 535-536
S   40 (1914) 205
FISHER, W.R., forestry, 1846-
    1910, Australia
N   85 (1910) 113-114
FISKE, JOHN, biology, 1842-
    1901, U.S.A.
S   14 (1901) 76-77
FISON, LORIMER, ethnology,
    1832?-1907, Australia
S   27 (1908) 198
FISSORE, GIUSEPPE, pathology,
    1815?-1897, Italy
S   6 (1897) 167
FITCH, ASA, entomology, 1809-
    1879, U.S.A.
P   16 (1879-1880) P fr,
    116-120
P   76 (1910) P 474-475
FITCH, JOHN, invention, 1743-
    1798, U.S.A.
S   15 (1902) 917
FITCH, SIR JOSHUA G., educa-
    tion, 1824?-1903, England
S   18 (1903) 158
FITCH, ROBERT, genealogy,
    1802?-1895, England
S   1 (1895) 530

FITCH, WALTER HOOD, botany,
    1817-1892, Scotland
N   45 (1892) 302
FITTIG, RUDOLF, chemistry,
    1835-1910, Germany
N   75 (1906) 133
S   32 (1910) 915
FITTIGE, BERNHARD, chemistry,
    1850?-1912, Germany
S   35 (1912) 861
FITTON, WILLIAM HENRY, geology,
    1780-1861, Ireland
L   12 (1863) iv-vi
FITZ, HENRY, optics, 1808-
    1863, U.S.A.
A   87 (1864) 149-151
FITZ, REGINALD HEBER, anatomy-
    medicine, 1843-1913, U.S.A.
S   38 (1913) 507
FITZCLARENCE, GEORGE, Earl of
    Munster, orientalia, 1794-
    1842, •
L   4 (1837-1843) 414-415
FITZGERALD, GEORGE FRANCIS,
    physics, 1851-1901, Ireland
A   161 (1901) 402
A   166 (1903) 106
L   75 (1905) P 152-160
N   63 (1901) 445-447
P   63 (1903) P 470-473
S   14 (1901) 1021-1022
S   18 (1903) 366-368
S   38 (1913) 417-418
FITZGERALD AND VESEY, WILLIAM
    VESEY,   ,   -1843,
L   5 (1843-1850) 485
FITZINGER, LEOPOLD JOSEPH
    FRANZ JOHANN, curator,
        -1884, Austria
S1   5 (1885) 19
FITZROY, ROBERT, meteorology,
    1805-1865, England
A   90 (1865) 140
L   15 (1867) xxi-xxiii
FIXLMILLNER, PLACIDUS, astron-
    omy, 1721-1791, Austria
PM IV 34 (1867) 409-437
FIZEAU, ARMAND HIPPOLYTE LOUIS,
    physics, 1819-1896, France
A   152 (1896) 398
A   174 (1907) 498
N   54 (1896) 523-524
N   55 (1896) 112
N   97 (1916) 540-541
FLACHAT, EUGÈNE, metallurgy,
    1802-1873, France

S 8 (1898) 14-15

FLAMSTEED, JOHN, astronomy,
1646-1719, England
PM III 8 (1836) 139-147,
211-226
S1 2 (1883) 666

FLANERY, DAVID, astronomy,
-1900, U.S.A.
S 12 (1900) 453

von FLEISCHL MARXOW, G.,
physiology, 1846-1891,
Austria
S 8 (1898) 744

FLEMING, JAMES SIMPSON, law,
1828-1899, Scotland
E 23 (1899-1901) 8-9

FLEMING, JOHN, biology, 1785-
1857, Scotland
E 4 (1857-1862) 14-17

FLEMING, JOHN GIBSON, medicine, 1809-1879, Scotland
E 10 (1878-1880) 346-348

FLEMING, SIR SANDFORD, en-
gineering, 1827-1915,
Scotland
N 95 (1915) 596

FLEMING, MRS. WILLIAMINA PATON
STEVENS, astronomy, 1857-
1911, Scotland
A 182 (1911) 84
N 86 (1911) 453-454
S 33 (1911) 849, 987-988

FLETCHER, ALICE CUNNINGHAM,
anthropology-ethnology,
1838-1923, Cuba
P 41 (1892) P 304

FLETCHER, ARNOLD LOCKWOOD,
geology, -1917, Ireland
S 45 (1917) 611

FLETCHER, HORACE, dietetics,
1849-1919, U.S.A.
S 49 (1919) 89

FLETCHER, JAMES, botany-
entomology, 1852-1908,
Canada
P 76 (1910) P 474-477
S 28 (1908) 752, 916-917
S 29 (1909) 876

FLETCHER, SIR LAZARUS,
mineralogy, 1854-1921,
England
L A99 (1921) P ix-xii

FLETT, JOHN S., geology,   ,
E 24 (1901-1903) 590-593

FLEXNER, SIMON, bacteriology-
pathology, 1863-1946,

U.S.A.
P 81 (1912) P 616

FLIGHT, WALTHER, mineralogy,
1841-1885, England
N 33 (1885) 85

FLINT, AUSTIN, medicine,
1812-1886, U.S.A.
P 9 (1876) 103-105
S1 7 (1886) 263

FLINT, AUSTIN, JR., medicine,
1836-1915, U.S.A.
P 9 (1876) P 103-105
S 42 (1915) 449, 607-608

FLINT, ROBERT, theology,
1837-1910, Scotland
E 31 (1910-1911) 689-692

FLINT, WESTON, anthropology-
law, 1835-1906, U.S.A.
S 23 (1906) 599

FLOOD-PAGE, SAMUEL, electricity, 1834?-1915,
S 41 (1914) 678

FLOURENS, MARIE JEAN PIERRE,
biology-physiology, 1794-
1867, France
E 7 (1869-1872) 10-11
L 18 (1870) xxvii-xxviii

FLOWER, SIR WILLIAM HENRY,
medicine-zoology, 1831-
1899, England
A 158 (1899) 238
L 75 (1905) P 72-89
N 60 (1899) 252-255
N 70 (1904) 97-98
N 76 (1907) 611-612
P 65 (1904) P 380-382
S 10 (1899) 62-63, 90-91
S 18 (1903) 61, 249-250
S 20 (1904) 342-343

FLÜGEL, EWALD, philology,
1863?-1914, Germany
S 40 (1914) 849

FOAKES, W.J.E., engineering,
-1917?, England
S 47 (1918) 68

FÖRSTER, RICHARD, ophthalmology, -1902, Germany
S 16 (1902) 198

FÖRSTER, WILHELM JULIUS,
astronomy, 1832-1921,
Germany
S 16 (1902) 754
S 17 (1903) 159

FOKKER, ABRAHAM (PETER?),
bacteriology, 1840?-1906,
Germany

FOSTER, SIR CLEMENT LE NEVE,
   geology-mining, 1841-1904,
   England
   A 168 (1904) 96
   L 75 (1905) 371-377
   N 46 (1892) 36
   N 69 (1904) 614
   S 19 (1904) 743
FOSTER, FRANK PIERCE, medi-
   cine, 1841-1911, U.S.A.
   S 34 (1911) 268-269
FOSTER, GEORGE CARY, physics,
   1835-1919, England
   L A96 (1920) xv-xviii
   S 49 (1919) 234
FOSTER, HENRY, geodesy,
      -1831,
   L 3 (1830-1837) 82
FOSTER, JOHN, physics, 1814?-
   1897, U.S.A.
   S 6 (1897) 660
FOSTER, JOHN WELLS, geology,
   1815-1873, U.S.A.
   A 106 (1873) 159-160
   P 3 (1873) 508
   S 10 (1899) P fp 705, 707
FOSTER, SIR MICHAEL GEORGE,
   histology-physiology, 1836-
   1907, England
   A 173 (1907) 244
   L B80 (1908) P lxxi-lxxx
   N 75 (1907) 345-347
   P 56 (1899-1900) P 14
   S 25 (1907) 236
FOSTER, PETER LE NEVE, photog-
   raphy, 1809-1879, England
   N 19 (1879) 385-386
FOSTER, WINTHROP D., zoology,
   1880?-1918, U.S.A.
   S 48 (1918) 544
FOUCAULT, JEAN BERNARD LÉON,
   physics, 1819 - 1868, France
   L 6 (1850-1854) 65-68
   L 17 (1869) lxxxiii-lxxxiv
von FOULLON-NORBECK, HEINRICH,
   Baron, geology, 1850-1896,
   Austria
   S 4 (1896) 652
   S 7 (1898) 385
FOUQUÉ, FERDINAND ANDRÉ, ge-
   ology, 1828-1904, France
   A 167 (1904) 410
   N 69 (1904) 492-493
   S 19 (1904) 517
de FOURCROY, ANTOINE FRANÇOIS,
   comte, chemistry, 1755-1809,

France
   PM 11 (1801) P fr, 376-377
FOUREAU, FERNAND, engineering-
   exploration, 1850-1914,
   France
   S 40 (1914) 267
FOURIER, JEAN BAPTISTE JOSEPH,
   Baron, matematics, 1768-
   1830, France
   A 20 (1831) 174
FOURNIER, ALFRED JEAN, derma-
   tology, 1832-1914, France
   S 31 (1915) 127
FOURNIER, EUGÈNE P., botany,
      -1884,
   Sl 4 (1884) 409
de FOVILLE, ALFRED, economics,
   1842-1913, France
   S 37 (1913) 862
FOWLER, SIR JOHN, engineering,
   1817-1898, England
   E 23 (1899-1901) 9
   S 8 (1898) 789
FOWLER, RICHARD, medicine,
   1765-1863, England
   L 13 (1864) iii-v
FOWNES, GEORGE, chemistry,
   1815-1849, England
   A 57 (1849) 452
   L 5 (1843-1850) 702, 882-
      883
FOX, CHARLES L., bacteriology,
      -1898, U.S.A
   S 8 (1898) 509
FOX, LANE--see Pitt-Rivers,
   A. H. L. F.
FOX, OSCAR CHAPMAN, adminis-
   tration, 1830-1902, U.S.A.
   S 15 (1902) 1037
FOX, ROBERT WERE, geology,
   1789-1877, England
   A 114 (1877) 248
FOX-STRANGWAYS, CHARLES EDWARD,
   geology, 1844?-1910, England
   S 31 (1910) 535
FRAAS, EBERHARD, paleontol-
   ogy, 1862-1915, Germany
   A 189 (1915) 686
   S 41 (1915) 571-572
FRACASTORO, GIROLAMO, medicine,
   1483-1553, Italy
   S 31 (1910) 500-502, 666
FRAIPONT, JULIEN, paleontol-
   ogy, 1857?-1910, Belgium
   A 179 (1910) 566
   S 31 (1910) 615

L 28 (1879) vii-x
N 17 (1878) 343
FRITH, ARTHUR J., engineering,
-1913, U.S.A.
S 36 (1912) 210
S 38 (1913) 738
von FRITSCH, KARL WILHELM GEORG,
geology, 1838-1906, Germany
S 23 (1906) 237
FRITZ, JOHN, invention-metal-
lurgy, 1822-1913, U.S.A.
S 16 (1902) 638, 754, 837
FRODISHAM, W. I., instrumen-
tation,
A 36 (1839) 195
FRÖLOCK, OSCAR, electricity,
1843-1909, Germany
S 30 (1909) 237
FROST, CARLETON PENNINGTON,
medicine, 1830?-1896, U.S.A.
S 3 (1896) 839
FROST, CARLES CHRISTOPHER,
cryptogamia, 1805-1880, U.S.A.
A 119 (1880) 493
A 127 (1884) 242
FROST, EDWIN BRANT, astro-
physics, 1866-1935, U.S.A.
N 89 (1912) 534
P 80 (1912) P 206
FROST, PERCIVAL, mathe-
matics, 1817-1898, England
L 64 (1899) vii-ix
N 58 (1898) 131
S 7 (1898) 858
FROUDE, ROBERT EDMUND, naval
architecture,
N 50 (1894) 55
FROUDE, SIR WILLIAM, engi-
neering-technology, 1810-
1879, England
L 29 (1879) ii-vi
N 20 (1879) 109-110,
148-150, 169-173
FRY, SIR EDWARD, botany, 1827-
1918, England
S 48 (1918) 617
FUCHS, CARL WILHELM, entomology,
1839?-1914, Germany
A 188 (1914) 370
S 40 (1914) 91-92
FUCHS, IMMANUEL LAZARUS, math-
ematics, 1833-1902, Ger-
many
N 66 (1902) 156-157
S 15 (1902) 797

von FUCHS, JOHANN NEPOMUKM
mineralogy, 1774-1856,
Germany
A 73 (1857) 95-101, 225-
233
FUCHS, SIGMUND, physiology,
-1903, Austria?
S 18 (1903) 286
FÜCKEL, LEOPOLD, mycology,
-1876,
A 113 (1877) 238
FUERTES, ESTEVAN ANTONIO, engi-
neering, 1838-1903, Puerto
Rico
A 165 (1903) 242
P 86 (1915) P 414
S 17 (1903) 198, 303-305
FULLARTON, J. HAMILTON, biology,
1856-1920, Scotland
E 40 (1919-1920) 191
FULLER, ANDREW S., botany,
1828-1896, U.S.A.
S 3 (1896) 737
FULLER, HOMER TAYLOR, geology,
1838-1908, U.S.A
S 28 (1908) 481
FULLERTON, GEORGE STUART, phi-
losophy, 1859-1925, Germany
P 49 (1896) P 452
FULMER, ELTON, chemistry,
1864-1916, U.S.A.
S 43 (1916) 423
S 44 (1916) 198
FULTON, HENRY, administration,
1846?-1901, U.S.A.
S 14 (1901) 1022
FULTON, ROBERT, invention,
1765-1815, U.S.A.
P 12 (1877-1878) P 451
P 75 (1909) P 315
von FUNKE, KARL WALTER, agri-
culture, -1900?, Ger-
many
S 13 (1901) 79
FURTWÄNGLER, JOHANN ADOLF
MICHAEL, archeology, 1854-
1907, Germany
S 26 (1907) 647
FUSS, . . .,
-1825,
A 15 (1829) 177
GABB, WILLIAM MORE, geog-
raphy-paleontology, 1839-
1878, U.S.A.
A 166 (1878) 164
N 18 (1878) 285

GAD, JOHANNES, physiology,
1842-   , Germany
S   36 (1912) 113
GADDESDEN, JOHN OF, medicine,
1280?-1361, England
N   91 (1913) 54-55
GADOLIN, AXEL WILHELMOVICH,
physics, 1828-1893, Finland
N   47 (1893) 232
GADOLIN, JOHANN, chemistry,
1760-1852, Finland
N   86 (1911) 48-49
GADOW, HANS FRIEDRICH, mor-
phology, 1855-1928, Germany
N   46 (1892) 36
GAEDE, WOLFGANG, physics,
1878-1945, Germany
A   187 (1914) 365
GÄTKE, HEINRICH, ornithol-
ogy, 1814-1897, Germany
S   5 (1897) 181
GAGE, SIMON HENRY, biology-
histology, 1851-1914,
U.S.A.
S   43 (1916) 813
GAGE, SUSANNA S. PHELPS (MRS.
SIMON HENRY), anatomy-embry-
ology, 1857-1915, U.S.A.
S   42 (1915) 523
S   45 (1917) 82-83
GAIRDNER, SIR WILLIAM TENNANT,
medicine, 1824-1907, Scot-
land
L   B80 (1908) xi-xix
N   48 (1893) 9
S   26 (1907) 95
GALCOTTI, H., botany, 1812?-
1858,
A   77 (1859) 443
GALE, LEONARD D., chemistry-
physics, 1799?-1883, U.S.A.
A   126 (1883) 490
GALE, THOMAS, surgery, 1507-
1587, England
S   12 (1900) 260
GALILEI, GALILEO, science, 1564-
1642,   Italy
A   188 (1914) 97-98
E   20 (1892-1895) 12-13
N   1 (1870) P 529-531
N   8 (1873) 329-330
N   9 (1874) 169-170
N   14 (1876) 226-229
N   17 (1878) 299-301
N   20 (1879) 261-263
N   21 (1879) 40-43, 58-61

N   39 (1889) 509
N   47 (1892) 82-83,
180-181
N   69 (1904) 505-507
N   94 (1914) 443-445
N   95 (1915) 426-427
P   66 (1904-1905) 265-266
343-356
P   67 (1905) 66-75, 127-142
P   78 (1911) P 328
S   1 (1895) 141-157
S   2 (1895) 415-416
S   37 (1913) 463-470
GALILEO, H. NEWTON,   ,

,
S   1 (1895) 141-157
S   2 (1895) 415-416
GALITZINE, GALITZIN, GALIZIN,
GALLITZIN--see GOLITZYN
GALLAUDET, EDWARD MINER, edu-
cation, 1837-1917, U.S.A.
S   16 (1902) 399
GALLAUDET, THOMAS, education,
1822-1902, U.S.A.
S   16 (1902) 399
GALLAUDET, THOMAS HOPKINS, edu-
cation, 1787-1851, U.S.A.
Sl   11 (1888) 106
S   16 (1902) 399
GALLE, JOHANN GOTTFRIED, as-
tronomy, 1812-1910, Germany
A   180 (1910) 160
N   84 (1910) 45-46
S   28 (1908) 45
S   30 (1909) 14
S   32 (1910) 109
GALLOWAY, THOMAS, astronomy-
physics, 1796-1851, England
L   5 (1843-1850) 772
L   6 (1850-1854) 120-121
GALOIS, EVARISTE, mathematics,
1811-1832, France
A   23 (1832-1833) 371
GALTON, SIR DOUGLAS STRUTT,
engineering-sanitation,
1822-1899, England
N   59 (1899) 512-513
S   9 (1899) 421
GALTON, SIR FRANCIS, an-
thropology-eugenics,
1822-1911, England
A   181 (1911) 248
L   B84 (1912) x-xvii
N   32 (1885) 174-175
N   39 (1889) 603-604

Switzerland
N 43 (1891) 518-519
GAY, H. F. FRANÇOIS, botany,
1858-1899, France
S 9 (1899) 188
GAY, JACQUES, botany, 1786?-
1863, Switzerland
A 87 (1864) 292
GAY, MARTIN, chemistry-medi-
cine, 1803-1850, U.S.A.
A 59 (1850) 305-306
GAYER, K., forestry, 1822-
, Germany
S 16 (1902) 754
GAY-LUSSAC, LOUIS JOSEPH,
chemistry-physics, 1778-1850,
France
A 12 (1827) 187
A 60 (1850) 137-138
A 74 (1857) 409
L 5 (1843-1850) 1009, 1013-
1023
GEDDES, A.C.B., science, 1892?-
1917, England
S 45 (1917) 499
GEGENBAUR, KARL, anatomy-zoology,
1826-1903, Germany
L 75 (1905) 309-312
N 55 (1896) 115
N 65 (1902) 316
S 17 (1903) 1019
GEIGEL, ROBERT, physics, 1856-
1910, Germany
S 32 (1910) 626
GEIGER, H. R., geology,
-1899,
S 10 (1899) 126-127
GEIKIE, SIR ARCHIBALD, geology,
1835-1924, Scotland
E 10 (1878-1880) 272-274
E 16 (1888-1889) 816-818
L A111 (1926) P xxiv-xxxix
L B99 (1926) P i-xvi
N 47 (1893) P 217-220
N 55 (1896) 115-117
N 64 (1901) 34-36
N 70 (1904) 76-78
P 43 (1893) P fp 145, 257-
264
P 73 (1908) P 572
S 43 (1916) 93
GEIKIE, JAMES, geology, 1839-
1915, Scotland
A 189 (1915) 486
E 12 (1882-1884) 565-566

E 36 (1915-1916) 1-17, 18-
25, P fp 30
L B91 (1920) xxxiii-xxxv
S 41 (1915) 385
GEINITZ, HANS BRONO, geology-
paleontology, 1814-1900,
Germany
A 159 (1900) 236
S 11 (1900) 317
GEISBURG, HEINRICH, archeology,
1817?-1895, Germany
S 1 (1895) 723
GEISSLER, EWALD ALBERT, chemis-
try, 1848?-1898, Germany
S 8 (1898) 866
GEISSLER, HEINRICH, physics,
1814-1879, Germany
N 19 (1879) 350, 372
GELL, SIR WILLIAM, archeology,
-1836,
L 3 (1830-1837) 438-439
GEMMELLARO, GAETANO GEORGIO,
geology, 1832-1904, Italy
S 19 (1904) 901
GEMMILL, JAMES FAIRLIE, biology,
1867-1926, Scotland
L B99 (1926) xlv-xlviii
GENOUD, ERNEST G., bacteriology,
1880?-1918, U.S.A.
S 48 (1918) 467
GENTH, FRIEDRICH AUGUSTUS LUDWIG
KARL WILHELM, chemistry-
mineralogy, 1820-1893,
Germany
A 145 (1893) 257-258
S 39 (1913) 943
GENTH, FREDERICK AUGUSTUS, JR.,
chemistry, 1855-1910, U.S.A.
S 32 (1910) 339
GEOFFROY SAINT-HILAIRE, ÉTIENNE,
zoology, 1772-1844, France
A 55 (1848) 138-139
P 24 (1883-1884) P fp 289,
403-408
GEOFFROY SAINT-HILAIRE, ISIDORE,
biology-zoology, 1805-1861,
France
A 83 (1862) 149
A 84 (1862) 122-123
GERARD, ERIC MARY, electricity,
1856-1916, Belgium
A 191 (1916) 472
S 43 (1916) 530
GERARD, JOHN, botany-medicine,
1545-1612, England

P   53 (1898) 395-398
GERHARDT, CARL JAKOB CHRISTIAN
   ADOLPH, medicine, 1833-1902,
   Germany
   S   16 (1902) 239
GERHARDT, CHARLES FRÉDÉRIC, chem-
   istry, 1816-1856, France
   A   73 (1857) 102-107
   A   74 (1857) 258
   N   63 (1901) 318-320
   S   45 (1917) 163
von GERLACH, JOSEPH, anatomy,
         -1897, Germany
   S   5 (1897) 103
GERNEZ, DÉSIRÉ JEAN BAPTISTE,
   bacteriology-chemistry, 1834-
   1910, France
   S   32 (1910) 755
GERSTÄCKER, CARL EDUARD ADOLF,
   zoology, 1828?-1895, Germany
   S   2 (1895) 233
GERVAIS, FRANÇOIS LOUIS PAUL,
   zoology, 1816-1879, France
   P   31 (1887) P fp 433, 550-
   553
von GESNER, KONRAD, biology-
   zoology, 1516-1565, Switzer-
   land
   A   118 (1879) 327
   P   47 (1895) 49-59
GEYER, KARL ANDREAS, botany,
   1809-1853, England
   P   74 (1909) 124-133
GIACOMINI, CARLO, anatomy, 1840-
   1898, Italy
   S   8 (1898) 263
GIARD, ALFRED MATHIERU, biology,
   1846-1908, France
   P   74 (1909) P 517-519
   S   29 (1909) 70-71
GIBBES, LEWIS R., biology, 1810-
   1894, U.S.A.
   A   149 (1895) 80
GIBBES, ROBERT WILSON, biology,
   1809-1866, U.S.A.
   A   92 (1866) 435
GIBBONS, ALFRED ST. HILL, geog-
   raphy,   -1916,
   S   44 (1916) 306
GIBBS, GEORGE, geology-mineral-
   ogy, 1776-1833, U.S.A.
   A   25 (1833-1834) 214-215
GIBBS, JOSIAH WILLARD, philology,
   1790-1861, U.S.A.
   A   81 (1861) 463

GIBBS, JOSIAH WILLARD, math-
   ematics-physics, 1839-1903,
   U.S.A.
   A   113 (1877) 380-383
   A   165 (1903) 492
   A   166 (1903) P 187-202
   A   173 (1907) 144-145
   L   75 (1905) P 280-296
   N   33 (1911) 808-809
   N   39 (1914) 943
   N   43 (1916) 586
   N   46 (1892) 245
   N   61 (1900) 414-415
   N   65 (1901) 107-108
   N   66 (1902) 291-292
   N   68 (1903) 11, 448
   N   75 (1907) 361-362
   P   63 (1903) P 188-189
   P   74 (1909) 470-484, 551-
   561
   P   75 (1909) 41-48, 191-
   203
   S   17 (1903) 718
GIBBS, MORRIS M., ornithol-
   ogy,   -1908, U.S.A.
   S   28 (1908) 441
GIBBS, OLIVER WOLCOTT, chem-
   istry-physics, 1822-1908,
   U.S.A.
   A   177 (1909) 100, 253-
   259
   A   188 (1914) 489
   P   57 (1900) P fp 115, 219
   P   74 (1909) 96-97
   P   82 (1913) P 617
   S   27 (1908) 970-978
   S   28 (1908) 875-876
   S   29 (1909) 101-103
   S   34 (1911) 864-868
   S   39 (1914) 943
GIBELI, CAMILLO G., botany,
         -1898, Italy
   S   8 (1898) 629
GIBSON, ALEXANDER, education,
         -1883, Scotland
   E   14 (1886-1887) 448
GIBSON, GEORGE ALEXANDER, medi-
   cine, 1854?-1913, Scotland
   E   34 (1913-1914) 6
GIBSON, JAMES A., anatomy, 1867?-
   1917, U.S.A.
   S   46 (1917) 408
GIBSON, JOHN, chemistry, 1855-
   1914, Scotland
   E   34 (1913-1914) 285-289

GIRARD, . . ., PÈRE, education,
, Switzerland
A 9 (1825) 185-186
GIRARD, ALFRED CLAUDE AIMÉ,
agriculture-chemistry,
S 7 (1898) 635
GIRARD, ANTOINE CHARLES, sur-
gery, 1849?-1916,
Switzerland
S 43 (1916) 423
GIRAUD, JACOB P., ornithology,
1811?-1870, U.S.A.
A 100 (1870) 293-294
GIRDWOOD, GILBERT PROUT, chem-
istry, 1832-1918, England
S 47 (1918) 68
GIROD, PAUL, botany, 1855?-
1911, France
S 34 (1911) 485
von GIZYCKL, GEORG, philosophy,
-1895, Germany
S 1 (1895) 364
GLADSTONE, JOHN HALL, chem-
istry-physics, 1827-1902,
England
A 164 (1902) 470
L 75 (1905) 188-192
N 57 (1897) P 109-111
N 66 (1902) 609-610
N 68 (1903) 447
S 16 (1902) 638, 974-975
GLAISHER, JAMES, meteorology,
1809-1903, England
N 67 (1903) 348, 447
N 68 (1903) 447-448
P 36 (1889-1890) P fp 433,
546-551
S 17 (1903) 318, 713
GLAISHER, JAMES WHITBREAD LEE,
mathematics, 1848-1928,
England
L A126 (1930) P i-xi
N 92 (1913) 405-406
GLAN, PAUL, physics, 1846-
1898, Germany
S 8 (1898) 367
GLATFELTER, NOAH MILLER,
botany, 1837-   , U.S.A.
P 74 (1909) P 256-258
GLAVE, EDWARD JAMES, explora-
tion, 1862-1895, England
S 2 (1895) 15
GLAZEBROOK, SIR RICHARD
TETLEY, physics, 1854-1935,
England
N 82 (1909) 135

S 50 (1919) 365-366
GLOGAU, G., philosophy, 1845?-
1895, Germany
S 1 (1895) 446
GLOVER, JOHN, chemistry,
-1902,
S 15 (1902) 838
GLOVER, TOWNEND, entomology,
1813-1883, Brazil
P 76 (1910) P fp 475,
475-477
GLUGE, GOTTLIEB, anatomy,
1813?-1899,
S 9 (1899) 229
von GNEIST, HEINRICH RUDOLF
HERMANN FRIEDRICH, law,
1816-1895, Germany
S 2 (1895) 188
GODDARD, LOUIS, aeronautics,
-1885,
Sl 5 (1885) 264
GODEFFROY, . . .   , biology-
philanthropy,   -1885?,
Germany
Sl 5 (1885) 303
GODET, CHARLES HENRY, botany,
1796?-1879, France
A 119 (1880) 158
GODFERNAUX, ÉMILE, engineering,
-1904, France
S 19 (1904) 838
GODFREY, THOMAS, physics,
1704-1749, U.S.A.
A 35 (1838) 389-390
GODMAN, FREDERICK DU CANE,
biology, 1834-1919, England
L B91 (1920) i-vi
S 49 (1919) 282, 328
S 50 (1919) 204-205
GODROP, DOMINIQUE ALEXANDRE,
botany, 1807-1880, France
A 123 (1882) 333
GODWIN-AUSTEN, ROBERT ALFRED
CLOYNE, geology, 1808-1884,
England
A 129 (1885) 268
L 38 (1885) ix-xiii
N 31 (1884) 104
Sl 5 (1885) 19
von GOEBEL, KARL F., botany,
1855?-1932, Germany
N 81 (1909) 12
GOELDI, EMIL AUGUST, ornithol-
ogy-sanitation, 1859-1917,
Brazil?
P 87 (1915) P 171

S   46 (1917) 450
GOEPPERT, JOHANN HEINRICH
  ROBERT, botany-paleontology,
  1800-1884, Germany
  A 129 (1885) 172
  Sl 4 (1884) 76
  Sl 6 (1885) 160
GÖRANSSON, G. F., metallurgy,
  1819?-1900, Sweden
  S 11 (1900) 958
GOESSMANN, CHARLES ANTHONY,
  chemistry, 1827-1910,
  Germany
  S 32 (1910) 339
von GOETHE, JOHANN WOLFGANG,
  literature-science, 1749-
  1832, Germany
  A   9 (1825) 184
  A 15 (1829) 171
  A 23 (1832-1833) 371
  N 26 (1882) 533-541
  N 75 (1906) 146-147
  N 80 (1909) 368
  P 82 (1913) 332-337
GÖTZE, WALTER, botany,
        -1899,
  S 11 (1900) 317
GOFF, EMMETT STULL, horti-
  culture, 1852-1902, U.S.A.
  S 15 (1902) 957
GOLDEN, . . ., mechanics,
  1860?-1918, U.S.A.
  S 49 (1919) 42
GOLDFUSS, GEORG AUGUST,
  paleontology, 1782-1848,
  Germany
  A 57 (1849) 143
GOLDIE, JOHN, botany, 1793-
  1886, England
  A 135 (1888) 260-261
GOLDMANN, EDWIN E., surgery,
  1862-1913, Germany
  S 38 (1913) 328
GOLDSCHMIDT, CARL WOLFGANG
  BENJAMIN, astronomy, 1807-
  1851, Germany
  A 61 (1859) 443-444
GOLDSCHMIDT, HERRMANN (HAYUM)
  MAYER SALOMAN, astronomy,
  1803-1866, France
  A 93 (1867) 89
GOLDSCHMIDT, VICTOR MORDECHAI,
  crystallography, 1853-1933,
  Germany
  S 28 (1908) 402-403
GOLDSCHMIEDT, GUIDO, chemistry,

1850-1915, Austria
  S 42 (1915) 335
GOLDSTEIN, EUGEN, physics,
  1850-1930, Germany
  N 79 (1908) 137
GOLDSTÜCKER, THEODOR, philolo-
  gy, 1821-1872, Germany
  N   5 (1872) 400-401
GOLGI, CAMILLO, anatomy-
  zoology, 1843-1926, Italy
  N 58 (1898) 428
  S 16 (1902) 877
  S 50 (1919) 158
GOLITZYN, (GALIZIN, GALITZINE),
  BORIS BORISOVICH, prince,
  physics-seismology, 1862-
  1916, Russia
  A 192 (1916) 372
  L A94 (1817-1818) xxv
  N 97 (1916) 424
  S 44 (1916) 130, 358
GOLL, FRIEDRICH, medicine,
  1829-1903, Switzerland
  S 19 (1904) 39
GOLOVKINSKI, NICOLAI ALEKSEVICH,
  geology, 1834-1897, Russia
  S   6 (1897) 252
von der GOLTZ, . . ., agri-
  culture, 1827?-1905, Germany
  S 22 (1905) 726
GOMEZ, R. S., anatomy,
        -1918?, Argentina
  S 49 (1919) 89
GÓMEZ OCAÑA, JOSÉ, physiology,
  1860?-1919, Spain
  S 50 (1919) 249
GOMME, SIR GEORGE LAURENCE,
  ethnology, 1853-1916,
  England
  N 97 (1916) 11
GOMPERTZ (COHEN), BENJAMIN,
  mathematics, 1779-1865,
  England
  L 15 (1867) xxiii-xxiv
GONZALES HERNÁNDES, JOSÉ,
  medicine,   -1919,
  Venezuela
  S 50 (1919) 208
GOODALE, GEORGE LINCOLN,
  botany, 1839-1923, U.S.A.
  P 39 (1891) P fp 577,
    691-694
  P 55 (1899) P 455
GOODCHILD, J. G., geology,
        -1906, England
  S 23 (1906) 519

GRANT, SIR ALEXANDER, educa-
tion, 1826-1884, U.S.A.
E   13 (1884-1886) 352-353
E   14 (1886-1887) 99-105
GRANT, GEORGE MONRO, education,
1835-1902, Canada
S   15 (1902) 878
GRANT, JAMES, theology, 1800-
1890, Scotland
E   17 (1889-1890) xxxii-
xxxv
E   18 (1890-1891) 4-6
GRANT, JAMES AUGUSTUS, explora-
tion, 1827-1892, Scotland
L   50 (1892) xiv-xv
GRANT, ROBERT, astronomy,
1814-1892, Scotland
L   57 (1895) i-iii
N   47 (1892) 36-37
GRANT, ROBERT EDMOND, medi-
cine, 1793-1874, Scotland
E   8 (1872-1875) 486-490
L   23 (1875) vi-x
GRANT DUFF, SIR MOUNTSTUART
ELPHINSTONE, botany, 1829-
1906, Scotland
N   70 (1904) 172-173
GRASHOF, FRANZ KARL, engineer-
ing, 1826-1893, Germany
S   4 (1896) 941
GRASSI, GIOVANNI BATTISTA,
zoology, 1854-1925, Italy
N   55 (1896) P 116-118
P   87 (1915) P 71
GRATACAP, LOUIS POPE, con-
chology-mineralogy, 1851-
1917, U.S.A.
S   46 (1917) 635
de GRATELOUP, JEAN PIERRE
SILVESTRE, conchology,
-1861, France
A   83 (1862) 149-150
GRATAROLO, GUGLIELMO, medi-
cine, 1516-1568, Italy
S   8 (1898) 170
GRATIOLET, LOUIS PIERRE,
zoology, 1815-1865, France
A   90 (1865) 140
GRATORIX, . . ., instrumenta-
tion,   ,
E   2 (1844-1850) 208
GRATTAROLA, GIUSEPPE,
mineralogy,   -1907,
Italy
S   26 (1907) 358
GRAVATT, WILLIAM, engineering,

1806-1866, England
L   16 (1868) xvi-xvii
GRAVES, CHARLES B., botany,
-1857, France
A   75 (1858) 293
GRAVES, CHARLES, Bishop of
Limerick, mathematics,
1812-1899, Ireland
L   75 (1905) 90-92
S   10 (1899) 157
GRAVES, HERBERT CORNELIUS,
hydrography, 1869-1919,
U.S.A.
S   50 (1919) 208
GRAVES, JOHN THOMAS, mathe-
matics, 1806-1870, Ireland
L   19 (1871) xxvii-xxviii
GRAWITZ, ERNST, medicine,
1860?-1911, Germany
S   34 (1911) 210
GRAY, A. E. PHILLIMORE, arche-
ology,   -1895, England
S   2 (1895) 891
GRAY, ANDREW, physics, 1847-
1925, Scotland
L   A110 (1926) P xvi-xix
N   54 (1896) 10
N   116 (1925) 618-619
GRAY, ASA, botany, 1810-1888,
U.S.A.
A   135 (1888) 181-203
A   136 (1888) Appendix,
Sept. and Oct. issues
A   138 (1889) 419-420
A   146 (1893) 483
E   17 (1889-1890) xx-xxiii
L   46 (1890) xv-xviii
N   37 (1888) 375-377, 594
N   41 (1890) 221-222
P   1 (1872) P 419-495
P   62 (1901-1902) P 332
P   70 (1907) 513
P   78 (1911) 414
S1   5 (1885) P 436-438
S1   6 (1885) 465, 477
S1   7 (1886) 98
S1   11 (1888) 50-51, 181-
182
S   10 (1899) 709-711
S   30 (1909) 175
GRAY, ELISHA, electricity-
invention, 1835-1901, U.S.A.
N   63 (1901) 378
P   14 (1878-1879) P fp 409,
523-528
S   13 (1901) 198

GRAY, GEORGE ROBERT, entomol-
ogy, 1808-1872, England
A 104 (1872) 160
GRAY, HENRY, anatomy, 1825?-
1861, England
L 12 (1863) xi
GRAY, JOHN, anthropology,
1854-1912, Scotland
N 89 (1912) 246
GRAY, JOHN EDWARD, biology-
zoology, 1800-1875, England
A 110 (1875) 78-80
A 111 (1876) 326
N 11 (1875) 368
GRAY, JOHN MACFARLANE, en-
gineering, 1832?-1908,
Scotland
N 77 (1908) 277
S 27 (1908) 238
GRAY, LANDON-CARTER, neurology,
1850?-1900, U.S.A.
S 11 (1900) 795
GRAY, MARIA EMMA (Mrs. J. E.),
botany, 1786?-1876,
A 115 (1878) 225
GRAY, ROBERT, ornithology,
1825-1887, Scotland
E 14 (1886-1887) 447
E 17 (1889-1890) xvi-xx
GRAY, ROBERT KAYE, engineer-
ing-physics, 1852?-1914,
England
A 187 (1914) 566
N 93 (1914) 246
S 39 (1914) 755
GRAY, THOMAS, engineering,
1850-1908, Scotland
S 29 (1909) 23
GREATOREX, THOMAS, music,
-1831,
L 3 (1830-1837) 83-84
GREAVES, JOHN, mathematics,
-1913, England
S 38 (1913) 507
GREELEY, ARTHUR WHITE, zoology,
1875-1904, U.S.A.
S 19 (1904) 517
GREEN, ALEXANDER HENRY, geol-
ogy, 1833-1896, England
A 152 (1896) 246
L 62 (1898) v-ix
N 54 (1896) 421-422
S 4 (1896) 267
GREEN, BERNARD RICHARDSON,
engineering, 1843-1914,
U.S.A.

S 40 (1914) 632
GREEN, CHARLES EDWARD, pub-
lishing, 1867?-1920,
Scotland
E 40 (1919-1920) 191-192
GREEN, CYRIL, ecology,
-1917, England
S 46 (1917) 635
GREEN, G. W., mathematics,
1857?-1902?, U.S.A.
S 17 (1903) 37
GREEN, GABRIEL MARCUS, mathe-
matics, 1891-1919, U.S.A.
S 49 (1919) 167, 534-535
GREEN, GEORGE, mathematics,
1793-1841, England
A 166 (1903) 392-393
N 58 (1898) 220-221
GREEN, JOHN RICHARD, history,
1837-1883, England
N 27 (1883) 462
GREEN, JOSEPH HENRY, surgery,
1791-1863, England
L 14 (1865) i-v
GREEN, JOSEPH REYNOLDS,
botany-physiology, 1880-
1914, England
L B88 (1915) xxxvi-xxxviii
N 52 (1895) 31-32
N 93 (1914) 379
S 39 (1914) 937
GREEN, NATHANIEL EVERETT, art-
astronomy,   -1899,
England
S 10 (1899) 979
GREEN, THOMAS HILL, philosophy,
1836-1882, England
Sl 12 (1888) 262
GREEN, TRAILL, chemistry-
medicine, 1813?-1897,
U.S.A.
S 5 (1897) 728
S 34 (1911) 12
GREENE, BENJAMIN D., botany,
1793-1862, U.S.A.
A 85 (1863) 449-450
GREENE, EDWARD LEE, botany,
1843-1915, U.S.A.
S 42 (1915) 722
GREENFIELD, WILLIAM SMITH,
pathology, 1846-1919,
Scotland
E 40 (1919-1920) 4
S 50 (1919) 303
GREENHILL, SIR ALFRED GEORGE,
mathematics, 1847-1927,

England
L A119 (1928) P i-iv
N 38 (1888) 11
N 75 (1906) 133
GREENLEAF, ROBERT A.,
  P 55 (1899) P 641
GREENOUGH, GEORGE BELLAS, ge-
  ology, 1778-1855, England
  A 70 (1855) 147
GREENWELL, WILLIAM, arche-
  ology, 1820-1918, England
  N 100 (1918) 428
  S 47 (1918) 189
GREG, ROBERT PHILIPS, astron-
  omy-mineralogy, 1826-1906,
  England
  S 24 (1906) 350
GREGORY, SIR CHARLES HUTTON,
  engineering, 1814?-1898,
  England
  S 7 (1898) 92
GREGORY, EMILY L., botany,
       -1897, U.S.A.
  S 5 (1897) 728
GREGORY, JOHN WALTER, geology,
  1864-1932, Scotland
  N 64 (1901) 36
GREGORY, REGINALD PHILIP,
  botany, 1879?-1918, Eng-
  land
  A 197 (1919) 148
GREGORY, WILLIAM, chemistry,
  1803-1858, Scotland
  A 76 (1858) 155
  E 4 (1857-1862) 121-122
GREHANT, NESTOR, histology-
  medicine, 1838-1910, France
  S 31 (1910) 901
GREINER, ADOLPHE, metallurgy,
  1842?-1915, Belgium
  N 96 (1915) 373
  S 43 (1916) 18
von GREINZ, . . ., zoology,
       -1915?, Germany
  S 41 (1915) 500
GRENET, EUGENE, engineering,
       -1909, France
  S 29 (1909) 967
GREINER, JEAN CHARLES MARIE,
  botany, 1807?-1876, France
  A 111 (1876) 326
GRESHOFF, MAURITS, botany,
  1863?-1910, Netherlands
  S 31 (1910) 141
GRESSLY, AMANZ, geology, 1814-
  1865, Switzerland

A 90 (1865) 140
GRESSWELL, GEORGE, physiology,
       -1914,
  S 40 (1914) 550
GREVILLE, ROBERT KAYE, algol-
  ogy-botany, 1794-1866,
  England
  A 92 (1866) 277
  E 6 (1866-1869) 25-27
GREY-EGERTON--see EGERTON
GRIEPENKERL, FRIEDRICH, agri-
  culture, 1827?-1900, Germany
  S 12 (1900) 533
GRIEVE, DAVID, anthropology-
  geology,   -1889,
  Scotland
  E 18 (1890-1891) 10
GRIFFIN, BRADNEY BEVERLEY,
  zoology, 1872?-1898, U.S.A.
  S 7 (1898) 523-524
GRIFFIN, THOMAS W., law, 1773-
  1837, U.S.A.
  A 38 (1893-1894) 156
GRIFFITH, GEORGE, education-
  science, 1834?-1902,
  England
  N 66 (1902) 64, 463
  S 15 (1902) 878
  S 16 (1902) 534, 557
GRIFFITH, JOHN W., micrography,
  1819?-1901, England
  S 13 (1901) 516
GRIFFITH, SIR RICHARD JOHN,
  engineering-geology, 1784-
  1878, Ireland
  E 10 (1878-1880) 17-20
  N 18 (1878) 627-628
GRIFFITHS, ERNST HOWARD,
  physics, 1851-1932, Wales
  N 52 (1895) 32
  N 77 (1907) 110-111
  N 129 (1932) 461-462
  S 26 (1907) 901-902
GRIFFITHS, MRS. . ., algology,
  1768?-1858,
  A 75 (1858) 294
GRIFFITHS, JOHN, mathematics,
  1837-1916, Wales
  S 43 (1916) 848
GRIGORIEF, A., geography,
       -1909?, Russia
  S 29 (1909) 179
GRIMAUX, LOUIS ÉDOUARD, chem-
  istry, 1835-1900, France
  S 8 (1898) 331-332
  S 11 (1900) 795

A 77 (1859) 443
GÜNTHER, ALBERT KARL LUDWIG
GOTTHILF, zoology, 1830-
1914, Germany
A 187 (1914) 366
E 34 (1913-1914) 269-277
E 35 (1914-1915) 3
L B88 (1915) P xi-xxvi
N 92 (1914) 664-666
S 39 (1914) 280
GÜSSEFELD, EMIL LOUIS
FERDINAND, horticulture,
fl. 1864, Germany
N 76 (1907) 658-659
GUETTARD, JEAN ÉTIENNE, geol-
ogy, 1715-1786, France
S 6 (1897) 925
GUILBEAU, BRAXTON H., zoology,
-1909, U.S.A.
S 29 (1909) 179
GUILLEMAUP, CONSTANTIN, geol-
ogy,   -1914, Germany
S 40 (1914) 812
GUILLEMIN, . . ., botany,
-1841, France
A 43 (1842) 214
GUILLEMIN, AMÉDÉE VICTOR,
physics, 1826-1893, France
N 48 (1893) 82
GUINAND, PIERRE LOUIS, physics,
c.1745-c.1825, Switzerland
A 9 (1825) 380-381
N 26 (1882) 350, 573
GUITARAS, RAMON, surgery,
1860?-1917, U.S.A.
S 46 (1917) 614
GULDBERG, CATO MAXIMILAN,
chemistry-mathematics,
1836-1902, Norway
S 15 (1902) 318
GULDBERG, GUSTAV A., anatomy,
-1908, Norway
S 27 (1908) 903
GULL, SIR WILLIAM WITHEY,
medicine, 1816-1890,
England
L 48 (1891) viii-xii
N 43 (1890) 134
GULLIVER, FREDERIC PUTNAM,
geology, 1865-1919, U.S.A.
S 49 (1919) 333
GUNDER, HENRY, mathematics,
1837?-1916, U.S.A.
S 44 (1916) 782
GUNDLACH, JOHANNES CHRISTOPH,
zoology, 1810-1896, Germany

P 50 (1896-1897) P fp 577,
691-697
S 3 (1896) 511
GUNN, JOHN, geology,
, England
N 44 (1891) 612
GUNN, RONALD CAMPBELL, botany,
1808-1881, South Africa
L 34 (1883) xiii-xv
GUNN, WILLIAM, geology, 1837?-
1902, England?
S 16 (1902) 839
GUNNING, JAN WILLEM, chemistry,
1827-1900, Netherlands
S 11 (1900) 277
GUNNING, ROBERT HALLIDAY,
medicine, 1818-1900,
Scotland
E 23 (1899-1901) 489-497
GUNNING, WILLIAM DICKEY,
biology, 1828-1888, U.S.A.
P 50 (1896-1897) P 526-530
GUNTER, EDMUND, astronomy-
mathematics, 1581-1626,
England
S 32 (1910) 666-668
GUPPY, HENRY BROUGHAM, botany-
geology, 1854-1926, England
L B101 (1927) P xxviii-
xxix
GUPPY, ROBERT JOHN LECHMERE,
geology, 1836?-1916, Eng-
land
S 44 (1916) 564
GURNEY, H. P., mathematics,
-1904, England
S 20 (1904) 319
GURNEY, HUDSON, literature,
1769?-1864?, England
L 14 (1865) v
GUSSENBAUER, CARL IGNATZ,
surgery, 1842?-1903, Austria
S 18 (1903) 61
GUSTAVSON, . . ., meteorology,
, Sweden
A 5 (1822) 178
GUTHE, KARL EUGEN, physics,
1866-1915, Germany
A 190 (1915) 448
P 74 (1909) P 205
S 42 (1915) 371, 685-686
S 46 (1917) 207-208
GUTHRIE, FRANCIS, botany-
mathematics, 1831?-1899,
S 10 (1899) 901
GUTHRIE, FREDERICK (Frederick

A 193 (1917) 497
A 194 (1917) 73-75
S 45 (1917) 476
HAGUE, JAMES DUNCAN, engineer-
ing, 1836-1908, U.S.A.
A 176 (1908) 242
S 28 (1908) 207
HAHN, EUGEN, surgery, 1840?-
1902, Germany
S 16 (1902) 840
HAHN, F. FELIX, paleontology,
-1914, Germany
S 40 (1914) 849
S 41 (1915) 284
HAHN, FRIEDRICH GUSTAV, geog-
raphy, 1852-1917, Germany
S 45 (1917) 257
HAHNSCHAFFE, FELIX, geology,
1861?-1914, Germany
S 39 (1914) 249
HAIDENHAIN, RUDOLPH PETER
HEINRICH, physiology, 1834-
1897, Germany
S   6 (1897) 628, 645-648
von HAIDINGER, WILHELM KARL,
optics-mineralogy, 1795-
1871, Austria
A 101 (1871) 392
E   7 (1869-1872) 537-538
L 20 (1872) xxv-xxvii
N   3 (1871) 450
HAILSTONE, JOHN, mineralogy-
theology, 1759-1847,
L   5 (1843-1850) 711
HALBERG, CARL SVANTE, phar-
macy, 1856?-1910,
S 32 (1910) 626
HALDANE, DANIEL RUTHERFORD,
medicine,   -1886?,
Scotland
E 14 (1886-1887) 163-165,
449
HALDANE, JOHN SCOTT, physiol-
ogy, 1860-1936, Scotland
N 56 (1897) 55
N 98 (1916) 278
HALDEMAN, SAMUEL STEHMAN,
biology-geology, 1812-1880,
U.S.A.
A 120 (1880) 352
P 21 (1882) P fp 289, 395-
401
HALDEMAN, SILAS S., entomol-
ogy,   ,
P 76 (1910) P 468-469
HALE, GEORGE ELLERY,

astrophysics, 1868-1938,
U.S.A.
N 83 (1910) P 97-99
N 132 (1933) 1-6
HALE, HORATIO EMMONS, ethnol-
ogy, 1817-1896, U.S.A.
P 51 (1897) P fp 289, 401-
410
S   5 (1897) 56, 216-217
HALE, WILLIAM HENRY, adminis-
tration, 1840-1919, U.S.A.
S 49 (1919) 469
HALES, STEPHEN, chemistry-
physiology, 1677-1761,
England
N 64 (1901) 417-421
HALFORD (orig. Vaughn), SIR
HENRY, 1766-1844, England
L   5 (1843-1850) 524
S   5 (1897) 690
HALIDAY, A. H., entomology,
1807?-1870, Ireland
A 100 (1870) 294
HALL, ASAPH, astronomy, 1829-
1907, U.S.A.
A 175 (1908) 90-91
A 177 (1909) 493
N 79 (1908) 80
P 45 (1894) P fp 721, 833-
838
P 61 (1902) P fp 195, 284
S 26 (1907) 805-806, 809-
812
HALL, BASIL, astronomy, 1788-
1844, Scotland
L   5 (1843-1850) 526-527
HALL, CHARLES MARTIN, electro-
chemistry-invention, 1863-
1914, U.S.A.
S 21 (1903) 881-882
HALL, EDWIN HERBERT, geology-
physics, 1855-1938, U.S.A.
P 64 (1903-1904) P 376
S 24 (1906) 29
HALL, ELIHU, botany, 1822?-
1882,
A 127 (1884) 242
HALL, F., mineralogy, 1783?-
1843,
A 45 (1843) 404
HALL, GRANVILLE STANLEY, psy-
chology, 1846?-1924, U.S.A.
S1 13 (1889) 463
HALL, SIR JAMES, geology,
1761-1832, England
L   3 (1830-1837) 146-147

HALL, JAMES, geology, 1811-
1898, U.S.A.
A 156 (1898) 284, 437-438
P 26 (1884-1885) P fr,
120-123
P 49 (1896) P 502
P 51 (1897) P 214
Sl 3 (1884) P 571-572
S 4 (1896) 697-717, P 704,
705
S 8 (1898) 218, 262
S 10 (1899) 671-672
S 38 (1913) 607
HALL, LYMAN, mathematics,
1859-1905, U.S.A.
S 22 (1905) 253
HALL, MARSHALL, physiology,
1790?-1857, Scotland
E 4 (1857-1862) 11-14
HALL, THOMAS SERGEANT, biol-
ogy, 1858?-1916, Australia
S 43 (1916) 423
HALL, WILFRED P.,   ,   ,
P 51 (1897) P 90-91
HALLAM, HENRY, history, 1777-
1859, England
L 10 (1860) xii-xviii
HALLARD, FREDERICK, law, 1821-
1882, Scotland
E 12 (1882-1884) 32-34
HALLAUER, OCTAVE RENÉ, engi-
neering, 1842-1884, France
Sl 4 (1884) P 306-308
HALLE, HANS, botany,   -1914,
Germany
S 40 (1914) 632
HALLEN, JAMES H. B., veteri-
nary medicine, c. 1830-1901,
Scotland
E 24 (1901-1903) 642-645
HALLER, ALBIN, chemistry,
1849-1925, France
L A118 (1928) i-iii
N 100 (1917) 277
von HALLER, ALBRECHT, medicine,
1708-1777, Switzerland
N 17 (1878) 223-224
N 79 (1908) P 38-40
P 73 (1908) P 383
S 14 (1901) 76
S 16 (1902) 75-77
HALLER, BÉLA, zoology, 1858?-
1914,
S 40 (1914) 408
HALLEY, EDMUND, astronomy-
physics, 1656-1742, England

N 54 (1896) 196-197
N 72 (1905) 374-376, 567
N 83 (1910) 372-373, 387-
388
P 76 (1910) P 5-22
S 22 (1905) 239-241
S 27 (1908) 512-513
S 29 (1909) 104
S 31 (1910) 459-461
HALLIBURTON, R. G., science,
1832?-1901, Canada
S 13 (1901) 476
HALLIBURTON, WILLIAM DOBINSON,
physiology, 1860-1931,
England
N 44 (1891) 16
HALLOCK WILLIAM, physics,
1857-1913, U.S.A.
S 37 (1914) 830
HALLOWELL, BENJAMIN, mathe-
matics, 1799-1877, U.S.A.
A 114 (1877) 432
HALLOWELL, MISS SUSAN MARIA,
botany, 1835-1911, U.S.A.
S 34 (1911) 911-912
HALLWACHS, WILHELM LUDWIG
FRANZ, physics, 1859-1922,
Germany
S 41 (1915) 943-944
HALM, JACOB E., astrophysics,
E 27 (1906-1907) 383-385
HALSTED, BYRON DAVID, botany,
1852-1918, U.S.A.
S 48 (1918) 244
HAMILTON, ALLAN McLANE, neurol-
ogy-psychiatry, 1848-1919,
U.S.A.
E 40 (1919-1920) 192-194
S 50 (1919) 565
HAMILTON, DAVID JAMES, pathol-
ogy, 1849-1909, Scotland
L B81 (1909) i-vi
S 29 (1909) 416
HAMILTON, JOHN B., medicine,
-1898, U.S.A.
S 9 (1899) 38
HAMILTON, SIR G. R.,
Sl 8 (1886) 639-640
HAMILTON, SIR WILLIAM, antiqui-
ty-mathematics, 1730-1803,
England
PM V 16 (1833) 66
HAMILTON, WILLIAM EDWIN, en-
gineering, 1842?-1902,
Ireland
S 15 (1902) 950

HAMILTON, SIR WILLIAM ROWAN,
mathematics-physics,
1805-1865, Ireland
A   90 (1865) 396
A   92 (1866) 293-302
E   5 (1862-1866) 473-475
N   28 (1883) 1-4
N   32 (1885) 619-623
N   40 (1889) 614-618
N   66 (1902) 478-480
N   87 (1911) 77, 111
N   99 (1917) 221-222
Sl   3 (1884) 19-23
S   13 (1901) 517
HAMLIN, CHARLES EDWARD, biol-
ogy, 1826?-1886, U.S.A.
Sl   7 (1886) 74
HAMMARSTEN, OLOF, chemistry,
1841-   , Sweden
S   24 (1906) 870-871
HAMMERL, HANS, hygiene,
-1915, Germany
S   41 (1915) 678
HAMMOND, JOHN HAYS, invention-
sociology, 1855-1936,
U.S.A.
P   82   (1913) P 205
HAMMOND, WILLIAM ALEXANDER,
medicine, 1828-1900, U.S.A.
S   11 (1900) 159
HAMPE, ERNST, bryology, 1775?-
1880, Germany
A 123 (1882) 333
A 127 (1884) 243
HAMPE, JOHANN FRIEDRICH
WILHELM, chemistry, 1841-
1899, Germany
S   9 (1899) 268
HAMPSON, THOMAS, editor,
-1888, U.S.A.
Sl 11 (1888) 205
HAMY, JULES THÉODORE ERNEST,
anthropology, 1842-1908,
France
S   29 (1909) 74
HAN, KARL, chemistry, 1834?-
1908, Hungary
S   28 (1908) 173
HANBURY, DANIEL, pharmacy,
1825-1875, England
A 109 (1875) 475-476
A 111 (1876) 326
L   24 (1876) ii-iii
N   11 (1875) 428-429
N   14 (1876) 366-367
HANCE, HENRY FLETCHER, botany,

1817?-1886, England
A 133 (1887) 165
HANCOCK, ALBANY, biology-
zoology, 1806-1873, England
N   9 (1873) 43-44
HANCOCK, EDWARD LEE, mechanics,
1873-1911, U.S.A.
S   34 (1911) 485
HANCOCK, JOHN, zoology, 1806-
1890, England
N   42 (1890) 616
HANDYSIDE, JOHN, philosophy,
1881?-1916, England
S   44 (1916) 782
HANDYSIDE, PETER DAVID, medi-
cine, 1808-1881, Scotland
E   11 (1880-1882) 329-333
HANKE, WILHELM, anatomy, 1834?-
1896, Germany
S   3 (1896) 899
HANKEL, WILHELM GOTTLIEB,
physics, 1814-1899, Germany
S   9 (1899) 461
HANKS, HENRY G., geology,
1826-1907, U.S.A.
S   25 (1907) 1015
von HANN, JULIUS FERDINAND,
physics, 1839-1921, Austria
S   28 (1908) 206
S   29 (1909) 609
S   39 (1914) 683
HANNACK, JOSEF, engineering,
1855?-1914, Austria
S   40 (1914) 267
HANOT, VICTOR CHARLES, medi-
cine, 1844-1896, France
S   4 (1896) 835
HANSCOM, JOHN FORSYTH, naval
architecture, 1842-1912,
U.S.A.
S   36 (1912) 473
HANSEN, EMIL CHRISTIAN, biol-
ogy, 1842-1909, Denmark
S   30 (1909) 305
HANSEN, GERHARD HENRIK ARMAUER,
bacteriology-medicine,
1841-1912, Norway
S   13 (1901) 515, 917
S   14 (1901) 117, 380
S   35 (1912) 369
HANSEN, PETER ANDREAS, astron-
omy, 1795-1874, Denmark
L   5 (1843-1850) 1009-1011
L   25 (1877) v-x
P   27 (1885) 340-344
HANSHOFER, KARL,

HARRINGTON, CHARLES, hygiene,
1856-1908, U.S.A.
S 28 (1908) 404
HARRINGTON, HERBERT HASTINGS,
ornithology, 1868-1916,
England, India?
S 44 (1916) 564
HARRINGTON, MARK WALROD, as-
tronomy, 1848-1926, U.S.A.
S 28 (1908) 792
HARRINGTON, NATHAN RUSSELL,
zoology, -1899, U.S.A.
S 10 (1899) 157
HARRINGTON, W. HAGUE, entomol-
ogy, 1852?-1918, Nova
Scotia
S 47 (1918) 458
HARRIOTT, THOMAS, astronomy-
mathematics, 1560-1621,
England
A 24 (1833) 204
HARRIS, DAVID, chemistry-com-
merce, 1842-1912, England
E 32 (1911-1912) 475-476
HARRIS, GEORGE H., entomology,
-1905, U.S.A.
S 21 (1905) 158
HARRIS, JOSEPH SMITH, astron-
omy-geodesy, 1836-1910,
U.S.A.
S 31 (1910) 947
HARRIS, ROLLIN ARTHUR, geodesy-
mathematics, 1863-1918,
U.S.A.
S 47 (1918) 140, 162
HARRIS, THADDEUS WILLIAM, edu-
cation-entomology, 1795-
1856, U.S.A.
A 71 (1856) 300-301
P 69 (1906) P 283-284
P 76 (1910) P 468-475
HARRIS, SIR WILLIAM SNOW,
physics, 1791-1867, England
L 3 (1830-1837) 349
L 16 (1868) xviii-xxii
HARRIS, WILLIAM TORREY, edu-
cation-psychology, 1835-
1909, U.S.A.
S 30 (1909) 671
HARRISON, C. A., engineering,
1848?-1916, England
S 44 (1916) 850
HARRISON, CHARLES CUSTIS, edu-
cation, 1844-1929, U.S.A.
P 49 (1896) P 442
HARRISON, JOSEPH H., engineering,

1810-1874, U.S.A.
A 103 (1872) 237
HART, CHARLES ARTHUR, entomol-
ogy, 1859-1918, U.S.A.
S 47 (1918) 236
HART, DAVID BERRY, medicine,
1851-1920, Scotland
E 40 (1919-1920) 185-186
HART, EDWARD, chemistry, 1854-
1931, U.S.A.
S 21 (1905) 877
HART, ERNEST ABRAHAM, medi-
cine, 1835-1898, England
N 57 (1898) 251-252
S 7 (1898) 60
HART, J. W., horticulture,
-1916, England
S 44 (1916) 782
HARTEL, HEINRICH, geodesy,
-1903, Austria
S 17 (1903) 838
HARTER, NOBLE, psychology,
-1907, U.S.A.
S 25 (1907) 517
HARTIG, KARL ERNST, engineer-
ing, 1836-1900, Germany
S 12 (1900) 66-67
HARTLAUB, KARL JOHANN GUSTAV,
ornithology, 1814-1900,
Germany
S 12 (1900) 1013
HARTLEY, ..., astronomy,
-1917, England
S 46 (1917) 614
HARTLEY, SIR CHARLES AUGUSTUS,
engineering, 1825-1915,
England
E 36 (1915-1916) 31
S 41 (1915) 356
HARTLEY, EDWARD, geology,
1847?-1870, U.S.A.
A 101 (1871) 74
HARTLEY, FRANK, surgery, 1856-
1913, U.S.A.
S 37 (1913) 976
HARTLEY, SIR WALTER NOEL,
chemistry-spectroscopy,
1846-1913, England
A 186 (1913) 576
E 34 (1913-1914) 8
L A90 (1914) vi-xiii
N 92 (1913) 102-103
HARTMAN, ROBERT NELSON, chem-
istry, -1903, U.S.A.
S 17 (1903) 799
von HARTMANN, KARL ROBERT

Ireland
L 5 (1843-1850) 884-885
HAUGHTON, SAMUEL, mathematics-
zoology, 1821-1897, Ireland
A 155 (1898) 80
L 62 (1898) xxix-xxxvii
N 57 (1897) 55-56, 79, 106
HAUKSBEE, FRANCIS, physics,
-c.1713, English
E 2 (1844-1850) 213-214
HAUPTFLEISCH, P., botany,
1863?-1906, Germany
S 24 (1906) 288
von HAUSCHKA, DOMENIK JOSEPH,
medicine, 1816?-1900,
Austria
S 11 (1900) 118
HAUSEN, EMIL CHRISTIAN, micro-
biology, 1842-1909, Denmark
N 81 (1909) 310
von HAUSHOFER, KARL, mineral-
ogy, 1839-1895, Germany
A 149 (1895) 248
HAUSKNECHT, HEINRICH KARL,
botany, -1903, Germany
S 18 (1903) 286
HAUSSMANN, JOHANN FRIEDRICH
LUDWIG, geology-mineralogy,
1782-1859, Germany
A 79 (1860) 304
E 6 (1866-1869) 21-22
HAUTEFEUILLE, PAUL GABRIEL,
chemistry-mineralogy, 1826-
1902, France
S 17 (1903) 37
HAVARD, FRANCIS T., metallurgy,
1878?-1913, U.S.A.
S 37 (1913) 904
HAVILAND, ALFRED, medicine,
1825?-1903, England
S 17 (1903) 1020
HAWES, GEORGE WESSON, mineral-
ogy, 1848-1882, U.S.A.
A 124 (1882) 80, 159-160
HAWKINS, BISSET, medicine,
1796-1894, England
L 57 (1895) xxiv-xxv
HAWKSHAW, SIR JOHN, engineer-
ing, 1811-1891, England
L 50 (1892) i-iv
HAWKSLEY, CHARLES, engineer-
ing, 1830?-1917, England
S 47 (1918) 19
HAWKSLEY, THOMAS, engineering,
1807-1893, England
L 55 (1894) xvi-xvii

HAWKSLEY, W. L., sanitation,
-1916, England
S 43 (1916) 710
HAY, ARTHUR, Marquis of
Tweeddale, zoology, 1824?-
1878, England
E 10 (1878-1880) 348-350
L 29 (1879) xxv-xxvii
N 19 (1879) 205-206
HAY, GEORGE, Marquis of
Tweeddale, agriculture,
1787-1876, England
E 9 (1875-1878) 225-227
HAY, SIR JOHN CHARLES DALRYMPLE,
naval science, 1822?-1912,
England
S 35 (1912) 299
HAYDEN, FERDINAND VANDIVEER,
geology, 1829-1887, U.S.A.
A 135 (1888) 88, 179-180
N 37 (1888) 325-327
Sl 11 (1888) 1-2
S 3 (1896) 405
HAYDEN, SIR HENRY HUBERT, ex-
ploration-geology, 1869-
1923,
L B96 (1924) xvii-xx
HAYDUCK, MICHAEL MAXIMILIAN,
chemistry, 1842-1899,
Germany
S 10 (1899) 702
HAYES, AUGUSTUS ALLEN, chem-
istry, 1806-1882, U.S.A.
A 124 (1882) 80
HAYES, CHARLES WILLARD, geol-
ogy, 1859?-1916, U.S.A.
A 191 (1916) 382
S 43 (1916) 235
S 44 (1916) 124-126
HAYES, EZEKIEL, publisher,
-1867, U.S.A.
A 94 (1867) 139
HAYMOND, RUFUS, zoology,
1805?-1886, U.S.A.
Sl 8 (1886) 123
von HAYNALD, LUDWIG, botany,
1816-1891, Hungary
N 44 (1891) 256
HAYNES, ARTHUR EDWIN, mathe-
matics, 1849-1915, U.S.A.
S 41 (1915) 606
HAYNES, HENRY WILLIAMSON,
archeology, 1831-1912,
U.S.A.
S 35 (1912) 299
HAYWARD, ROBERT BALDWIN,

HEMSLEY, WILLIAM BOTTING,
  botany, 1843-1924, England
  L B98 (1925) i-ix
HENCK, JOHN BENJAMIN, en-
  gineering, 1816-1903,
  U.S.A.
  P 63 (1903) P 477-478
  S 17 (1903) 159
HENDERSON, THOMAS, astronomy,
  1798-1844, Scotland
  E 2 (1844-1850) 35-45
  L 5 (1843-1850) 530-532
HENDRICKSON, W. F. (George
  M.?), pathology, 1876?-
  1902, U.S.A.
  S 16 (1902) 357
HENFREY, ARTHUR, botany,
  1819-1859, Scotland
  A 79 (1860) 441
  L 10 (1860) xviii-xix
HENLE, FRIEDRICH GUSTAV JACOB,
  anatomy-pathology, 1809-
  1885, Germany
  L 39 (1886) iii-viii
  Sl 6 (1885) 20
HENLEIN, PETER HELE, inven-
  tion, 1480-1542, Germany
  S 22 (1905) 286
HENNELL, HENRY
  chemistry,   -1842,
  England
  L 4 (1837-1843) 419
HENNESSEY, J. B. N., geog-
  raphy, 1830?-1910, England
  S 31 (1910) 901
HENNESSY, HENRY G., physics,
  1826-1901, Ireland
  L 75 (1905) 140-142
  S 14 (1901) 1022
HENNING, PAUL, botany,
      -1908, Germany
  S 28 (1908) 679
HENNINGER, ARTHUR RODOLPHE
  MARIE, chemistry, 1850-1884,
  France
  Sl 5 (1885) 62
HENOCH, EDUARD HEINRICH,
  pediatrics, 1820-1910,
  Germany
  S 32 (1910) 405
HÉNOCQUE, ALBERT WILLIAM LÉON,
  biophysics,   -1903,
  France
  S 17 (1903) 198
HENRICI, OLAUS MAGNUS
  FRIEDRICH ERDMANN,

  mathematics, 1840?-1918,
  England
  S 48 (1918) 341
HENRY, (The Navigator), Prince
  of Portugal, geography,
  1394-1460, Portugal
  N 49 (1894) 301, 433
  N 51 (1895) 532
HENRY, JOSEPH, physics, 1797-
  1878, U.S.A.
  A 110 (1875) 477-479
  A 115 (1878) 462-468
  A 116 (1878) 490
  A 131 (1886) 69
  A 133 (1887) 325-326
  N 18 (1878) 143-144
  N 38 (1888) 98-99
  N 53 (1896) P 257-261
  P 2 (1872-1873) P fp 641,
    741-744
  P 62 (1901-1902) P 328
  P 70 (1907) 298-300
  P 82 (1913) P 614
  PM V 36 (1893) 142-143
  Sl 16 (1890) 21
  S 10 (1899) 628-629
  S 15 (1902) 597
  S 37 (1913) 784
HENRY, MORRIS HENRY, surgery,
  1835-1895, England
  Sl 4 (1884) 480
  Sl 15 (1890) 273
  S 1 (1895) 641
HENRY, PAUL PIERRE, astronomy,
  1848-1905, France
  N 71 (1905) 302
  S 21 (1905) 237
HENRY, MATHIEU PROSPER, astron-
  omy, 1849-1903, France
  N 71 (1905) 302
  S 18 (1903) 253
HENRY, WILLIAM, chemistry,
  1774-1836, England
  A 32 (1837) 216
  L 3 (1830-1837) 439-440
HENRY, WILLIAM CHARLES, medi-
  cine, 1804-1892, England
  L 54 (1894) xix
HENSEN, VICTOR ANDREAS
  CHRISTIAN, pathology-
  physiology, 1835-1924,
  Germany
  S 21 (1905) 438
  S 41 (1915) 498
HENSHAW, MARSHALL, astronomy-
  physics,   -1900, U.S.A.

S 21 (1905) 934
HILGER, OTTO, optics,
    Germany
    N 67 (1903) 208, 230
    N 68 (1903) 447
HILL, CHARLES BARTON, geodesy,
    1863?-1910, U.S.A.
    S 32 (1910) 303
HILL, FRANK A., education,
    1841?-1903, U.S.A.
    S 18 (1903) 414
HILL, GEORGE ANTHONY, physics,
    1842?-1916, U.S.A.
    S 44 (1916) 270
HILL, GEORGE WILLIAM, astron-
    omy-mathematics, 1838-1914,
    U.S.A.
    A 187 (1914) 486
    E 35 (1914-1915) 4-5
    L A91 (1914-1915) xlii-li
    N 73 (1906) 409-410
    N 76 (1907) 635-636
    N 82 (1909) 134
    S 25 (1907) 933-936
    S 36 (1912) 422
    S 39 (1914) 641
HILL, H. C., forestry, 1852?-
    1902, England
    S 16 (1902) 959
HILL, HAMPDEN, chemistry,
    1886-1918, U.S.A.
    S 48 (1918) 392
HILL, HENRY BARKER, chemistry,
    1843-1903, U.S.A.
    A 165 (1903) 418
    P 64 (1903-1904) P 287-288
    S 17 (1903) 636, 841-843
HILL, LEONARD ERSKINE, physiol-
    ogy, 1866-1952, England
    N 62 (1900) 57
HILL, MICAIAH JOHN MULLER,
    mathematics, 1856-1929,
    India
    L A124 (1929) P i-v
    N 50 (1894) 55
HILL, SAMUEL ALEXANDER,
    meteorology, 1851-1890,
    Ireland
    N 42 (1890) 616
HILL, WALTER B., education,
        -1905, U.S.A.
    S 23 (1906) 39
HILLEBRAND, WILLIAM FRANCIS,
    chemistry, 1853-1886,
    Hawaii
    A 133 (1887) 164-165

HILLHOUSE, W., botany, 1850-
    1910, England
    S 31 (1910) 295
HILLS, E. H. GROVE--see GROVE-
    HILLS, E. H.
HINCKS, THOMAS, biology, 1818-
    1899, England
    L 75 (1905) 39-40
    N 59 (1899) 374
    S 9 (1899) 268
HIND, HENRY YOULE, geology,
    1823-1908, England
    S 28 (1908) 370
HIND, JOHN RUSSELL, astronomy,
    1823-1895, England
    N 53 (1896) 201-202
    S 3 (1896) 65-66
HIND, WHEELTON, zoology,
    E 30 (1909-1910) 589-590
HINDE, GEORGE JENNINGS, geol-
    ogy-paleontology, 1839?-
    1918, England
    A 195 (1918) 485
    N 54 (1896) 10-11
    S 48 (1918) 588-590
HINRICHSEN, FRIEDRICH WILLY,
    chemistry, 1877-1914,
    Germany
    S 41 (1915) 129
HINSDALE, BURKE AARON, educa-
    tion, 1837?-1900, U.S.A.
    S 12 (1900) 892-893
HINTON, CHARLES H., mathema-
    tics, 1844-1907, England
    S 25 (1907) 758
HIRN, GUSTAVE ADOLPHE, thermo-
    dynamics, 1815-1890, France
    N 41 (1890) 323-324
    Sl 15 (1890) 108
    Sl 19 (1892) 116
    Sl 21 (1893) 68
HIROTA, SHINOBU, seismology,
        , Japan
    N 90 (1912) 435
    S 37 (1913) 747
HIRSCH, ADOLPH, astronomy-
    meteorology, 1830-1901,
    Germany
    N 64 (1901) 18
    S 13 (1901) 755, 837
HIRSCH, JOSEPH, engineering,
    1836?-1901, France
    S 14 (1901) 191, 927-928
HIRSCHFELDT, WERNER, technol-
    ogy,   -1915, Germany
    S 41 (1915) 204

psychology, 1843-1931,
Switzerland
N 81 (1909) 12
HÖGYES, ANDREAS, pathology,
1846?-1906, Hungary
S 24 (1906) 478
HOEPFNER, S., chemistry,
-1900, Canada
S 12 (1900) 971
HÖRMANN, A., technology,
1835?-1906, Germany
S 24 (1906) 127
HÖRNES, MORIZ, mineralogy,
1814?-1868, Austria
A 97 (1869) 294
HÖRNES, RUDOLF, geology,
1850?-1912, Austria
A 184 (1912) 404
S 36 (1912) 370, 399
von HOFF, KARL ERNST ADOLF,
geology, 1771-1837, Germany
N 72 (1905) 123-124
HOFFMAN, ADOLF, geology, 1853?-
1913,
S 38 (1913) 738
HOFFMAN, WALTER J., ethnology,
1846?-1899, U.S.A.
S 10 (1899) 782
HOFFMANN, FRIEDRICH, pharmacy,
-1904, Germany
S 20 (1904) 933
HOFFMANN, GEORGE CHRISTIAN,
chemistry-mineralogy,
1837-1917, England
S 45 (1917) 330
HOFFMEYER, NIELS HENRIK
CORDULUS, meteorology,
1836-1884, Denmark
P 39 (1891) P fr, 115-120
von HOFMANN, AUGUST WILHELM,
chemistry, 1818-1892,
Germany
P 24 (1883-1884) P fp 721,
831-835
Sl 19 (1892) 314-316
S 15 (1902) 422-423
S 42 (1915) 458
HOFMEISTER, WILHELM FRIEDRICH
BENEDICT, botany, 1824-
1877, Germany
A 113 (1877) 238
A 115 (1878) 225
HOGDEN, JOHN T., surgery,
-1882, U.S.A.
S 25 (1907) 798
HOGG, A. D., botany,   -1902,

Scotland
S 16 (1902) 197-198
HOGG, JAMES, ophthalmology,
1817?-1899, England
S 9 (1899) 692
HOGG, ROBERT, horticulture,
-1897
S 5 (1897) 580
HOHENHACHER, RUDOLPH FRIEDRICH,
botany,   -1874, Germany
A 111 (1876) 326
von HOHENHEIM--see PARACELSUS
HOLBROOK, JOHN EDWARDS, zoolo-
gy, 1794-1871, U.S.A.
A 102 (1871) 389-390
HOLCOMB, AMASA, instrumenta-
tion-optics, 1787-1875,
U.S.A.
A 23 (1832-1833) 403
HOLDEN, EDWARD SINGLETON, as-
tronomy, 1846-1914, U.S.A.
A 187 (1914) 366
N 93 (1904) 89-90
P 30 (1886-1887) P fr,
114-120
S 39 (1914) 421
HOLDEN, HENRY CAPEL LOFFT,
physics,   ,
N 52 (1895) 32
HOLDEN, MISS RUTH, botany,
-1917, U.S.A.
S 45 (1917) 562
HOLDER, CHARLES FREDERICK,
archeology-zoology, 1851-
1915, U.S.A.
A 191 (1916) 152
S 42 (1915) 567-568, 823-
825
HOLDICH, SIR THOMAS HUNGERFORD,
geography, 1843-1929,
N 76 (1907) 189
HOLLAENDER, LUDWIG, anatomy,
-1897,
S 5 (1897) 652
HOLLAND, SIR HENRY, medicine-
science, 1788-1873, England
N 12 (1875) 181-182
HOLLOWAY, GEORGE T., metal-
lurgy, 1863?-1917,
S 46 (1917) 538
HOLM, I. C. L., medicine,
1846?-1919, Norway
S 49 (1919) 234
HOLM, JAMES, physics, 1869?-
1897, England
S 7 (1898) 60

HOLMAN, DAVID SHEPARD, micros-
copy,   -1901, U.S.A.
S 13 (1901) 838
HOLMAN, SILAS WHITCOMB,
physics, 1856-1900, U.S.A.
S 11 (1900) 556
S 13 (1901) 857-859
HOLMES, J. ARTHUR, geology,
1890-   , England
P 82 (1913) P 204
HOLMES, JOSEPH AUSTIN, geol-
ogy, 1859-1915, U.S.A.
A 190 (1915) 222
S 42 (1915) 156-157, 217
HOLMES, NATHANIEL, literature,
1815-1901, U.S.A.
P 52 (1897-1898) P 644-645
HOLMES, TIMOTHY, anatomy,
-1907, England
S 26 (1907) 423
HOLMES, W. P., botany-mineral-
ogy,   -1860, Canada
A 80 (1860) 424
HOLMES, WILLIAM HENRY, archeol-
ogy-anthropology, 1846-
1933, U.S.A.
P 76 (1910) P 205
S 44 (1916) 52, 913-914
HOLMGREN, ALARIK FRITHJOF,
physiology, 1831-1897,
Sweden
S 6 (1897) 519
HOLMGREN, HJALMAR, mathematics,
1822-1885, Sweden
Sl 6 (1885) 429
HOLT, JACOB FARNUM, anatomy,
-1908, U.S.A.
S 28 (1908) 338
HOLTHOUSE, CARSTEN, anatomy,
1810?-1901, England
S 14 (1901) 270
HOLTON, ISAAC F., botany,
1812?-1873, U.S.A.
A 107 (1874) 240
HOLTON, MISS NINA, botany,
-1908, U.S.A.
S 27 (1908) 798
HOLUB, EMIL, exploration,
1847-1902, Austria
S 15 (1902) 438
HOLZAPFEL, GUSTAV HERMANN
EDUARD, geology, 1853-1913,
A 186 (1913) 186
HOME, SIR ANTHONY, surgery,
1826-1914, England
S 40 (1914) 376

HOME, DAVID MILNE, geology-
meteorology, 1805-1890,
Scotland
E 18 (1890-1891) 8-9
HOME, SIR EVERARD, medicine,
1756-1832, England
PM III 2 (1833) 136-137
L 3 (1830-1837) 145-146
HOME-DRUMMOND, GEORGE STIRLING,
antiquity, 1813-1876,
E 9 (1875-1878) 218-219
von HOMEYER, EUGENE FERDINAND,
ornithology, 1809-1889,
Germany
Sl 13 (1889) 501
HOMMAIRE de HELL,. . ., biology,
1815?-1849, France
A 57 (1849) 451
HOOD, OZNI PORTER, engineer-
ing, 1865-1937, U.S.A.
P 84 (1914) P 202
HOOGEWERFF, SEBASTIAN, chem-
istry, 1847-   , Germany
S 46 (1917) 383-384
HOOKE, ROBERT, physics, 1635-
1703, England
E 2 (1844-1850) 209-210
N 50 (1894) 351-352
HOOKER, CHARLES W., entomol-
ogy, 1883?-1913, U.S.A.
S 37 (1913) 368
HOOKER, MRS. HENSLOW, botany,
-1874, England
A 109 (1875) 68
HOOKER, J. D., astronomy,
1838?-1911, U.S.A.
S 34 (1911) 74
HOOKER, SIR JOSEPH DALTON,
botany-exploration, 1817-
1911, England
A 114 (1877) 498-499
A 131 (1866) 77-78
A 183 (1912) 72
A 200 (1920) 78
L B85 (1912) P i-xxv
N 16 (1877) P 537-539
N 37 (1887) 117-118
N 47 (1892) 111
N 88 (1911) 249-254
N 91 (1913) 12
N 97 (1916) P 58
P 4 (1873-1874) P 237-240
P 80 (1912) P 102-104
P 83 (1913) P 100
S 20 (1904) 158
S 26 (1907) 93, 229

S   30 (1909) 109
S   34 (1911) 836
S   49 (1919) 525-530
HOOKER, SIR WILLIAM JACKSON,
  botany, 1785-1865, England
  A   90 (1865) 288
  A   91 (1866) 1-10, 265
  E   5 (1862-1866) 471-473
  L   15 (1867) xxv-xxx
  N   67 (1903) 404
  S   49 (1919) 525
HOOPER, FRANKLIN WILLIAM,
  geology-zoology, 1851-1914,
  U.S.A.
  A 188 (1914) 370
  S   40 (1914) 205
HOOPER, WILLIAM LESLIE, en-
  gineering, 1855-1918, Nova
  Scotia
  S   48 (1918) 442-443
HOOPES, JOSHUA, botany, 1788?-
  1874, U.S.A.
  A 107 (1874) 600-601
HOPE, THOMAS, writer,   -1831,
  L   3 (1830-1837) 84
HOPE, THOMAS CHARLES, chem-
  istry, 1766-1844,
  L   5 (1843-1850) 525
  PM III   27 (1845) 138-139
HOPKINS, CYRIL GEORGE, agron-
  omy-chemistry, 1866-1919,
  U.S.A.
  A 198 (1919) 478
  S   50 (1919) 387-388
HOPKINS, SIR FREDERICK GOWLAND,
  biochemistry, 1861-1947,
  England
  N 141 (1938) P 989-993
HOPKINS, GEORGE M., writer,
  1842?-1902, U.S.A.
  S   16 (1902) 357
HOPKINSON, BERTRAM, physics,
  1874-1918, England
  L A95 (1919) xxvi-xxxvi
  S   48 (1918) 341
HOPKINSON, JOHN, engineering-
  physics, 1849-1898, England
  L   64 (1899) xvii-xxiv
  N   43 (1890) 136
  N   58 (1898) 419-420
  N   70 (1904) 169-172
  S   8 (1898) 331
HOPPE, REINHOLD, mathematics,
  1816?-1900, Germany
  S   12 (1900) 39
HOPPE-SEYLER, ERNST FELIX

IMMANUEL, physiology,
  1825-1895, Germany
  N   52 (1895) 575-576, 623-
    625
  P   53 (1898) P fp 433, 542-
    552
  S   2 (1895) 341
HORN, GEORGE HENRY, entomol-
  ogy-medicine, 1840-1897,
  U.S.A.
  N   57 (1897) 156
  P   76 (1910) P 468-469
  S   6 (1897) 839, 875
  S   7 (1898) 73-77
HORNE, JOHN, geology, 1848-
  1928, Scotland
  E   20 (1892-1895) 512
  L B104 (1929) P i-vii
  N   62 (1900) 57
HORNER, LEONARD, geology,
  1785-1864, Scotland
  E   5 (1862-1866) 294-298
  L   14 (1865) v-x
HORNER, WILLIAM GEORGE,
  mathematics, 1786-1837,
  England
  PM III 11 (1837) 459-460
HORNSCHUCH, ..., muscology,
    -1851,
  A   63 (1852) 45
HORNUNG, CHRISTIAN, astronomy-
  mathematics, 1845-1918,
  U.S.A.
  S   47 (1918) 236
HORROCKS, JEREMIAH, astronomy,
  1617-1641, England
  N   8 (1873) 117-118, 137-
    138
  N   10 (1874) 190
  N   13 (1875) 112
  N   62 (1900) 357-358
HORSBRUGH, BOYD ROBERT, orni-
  thology, 1871-1916,
  S   44 (1916) 564
HORSBURGH, JAMES, hydrography,
    -1836,
  L   3 (1830-1837) 436-437
HORSFIELD, THOMAS, biology,
  1773-1859, U.S.A.
  A   78 (1895) 444
  A   79 (1860) 441
  L   10 (1860) xix-xxi
HORSFORD, EBEN NORTON, chem-
  istry, 1818-1893, U.S.A.
  S   21 (1905) 877-878
HORSFORD, N. S., chemistry,

U.S.A.
S 8 (1898) 203
HORSLEY, SIR VICTOR ALEXANDER
HADEN, neurology-pathology,
1857-1916, England
L B91 (1920) xliv-xlviii
N 97 (1916) 447
S 4 (1896) 223-224
S 44 (1916) 130
HORSTMAN y CANTOS, FEDERICO,
anatomy,   -1901, Cuba
S 14 (1901) 941
HORTON, WILLIAM, mineralogy,
-1845, U.S.A.
A 51 (1846) 152
HORWITZ, ORVILLE, surgery,
1858?-1913, U.S.A.
S 37 (1913) 250
HOSACK, DAVID, botany-medicine,
1769-1835, U.S.A.
A 29 (1835-1836) 395-396
L 3 (1830-1837) 437
P 47 (1895) P fp 721,
834-842
S 12 (1900) 161
HOSIUS, AUGUST, mineralogy,
1825-1896, Germany
S 3 (1896) 899
HOSKINS, THOMAS H., agricul-
ture-anatomy, 1828?-1902,
U.S.A.
S 16 (1902) 158
HOSPITALIER, EDOUARD, elec-
tricity, 1853?-1907, France
S 25 (1907) 599
HOTCHKISS, JED, geology, 1828?-
1899, U.S.A.
S 9 (1899) 158
HOUGH, GEORGE WASHINGTON, as-
tronomy, 1836-1909, U.S.A.
A 177 (1909) 196
S 29 (1909) 73, 690-693
HOUGH, SYDNEY SAMUEL, astron-
omy, 1870-1923, England
L A107 (1925) P i-v
HOUGH, THEODORE, biology,
1865-1924, U.S.A.
P 84 (1914) P 205
HOUGH, WALTER, ethnology,
1859-1935, U.S.A.
P 66 (1904-1905) P 388
HOUGH, WILLISTON SAMUEL,
philosophy, 1868-1912,
U.S.A.
S 36 (1912) 399
HOUGHTON, DOUGLAS, chemistry-

geology, 1801 (1809?)-1845
(1846?), U.S.A.
A 51 (1846) 150-152
A 55 (1848) 217
HOUGHTON, SAMUEL, biology-
geology, 1821?-1897, U.S.A.
S 6 (1897) 839
HOUSTON, EDWIN JAMES, engi-
neering, 1847-1914, U.S.A.
S 39 (1914) 390
HOUSTON, JOHN, chemistry-
engineering,   -1896,
Scotland
S 4 (1896) 355
HOUZEAU, AUGUSTE, agriculture-
chemistry, 1829-1911, France
S 33 (1911) 686
HOUZEAU de LAHAIE, JEAN
CHARLES, geology-geography,
1820-1888, Belgium
N 41 (1890) 20
P 38 (1890-1891) P fp
433, 544-552
HOVELACQUE, MAURICE, geology,
-1898, France
S 7 (1898) 771
HOVEY, HORACE CARTER, biology,
1833-1914, U.S.A.
A 51 (1846) 150-152
A 55 (1848) 217
A 188 (1914) 370
S 40 (1914) 205
HOWARD, J. L., physics,
c.1866-c.1899,
PM V 49 (1900) 160
HOWARD, LUKE, meteorology,
1772-1864, England
L 14 (1865) x-xii
HOWARD, LELAND OSSIAN, ento-
mology, 1857-1950, U.S.A.
P 66 (1904-1905) P 391
HOWE, CHARLES SUMNER, astron-
omy, 1858-   , U.S.A.
P 66 (1904-1905) P 390
P 80 (1912) P 206
HOWELL, EDWIN EUGENE, geology,
1845-1911, U.S.A.
A 181 (1911) 468
S 33 (1911) 720-721
HOWELL, THOMAS JEFFERSON,
botany, 1842-1913, U.S.A.
S 37 (1913) 96
HOWELL, WILLIAM HENRY, physi-
ology, 1860-1945, U.S.A.
P 74 (1909) P 206
HOWES, THOMAS GEORGE BOND,

A   127 (1884) 160
Sl   3 (1884) 476-477
HYMPHREYS, JOSHUA, naval archi-
  tecture, 1751-1838, U.S.A.
A   38 (1839-1840) 153
HUMPHRY, SIR GEORGE MURRAY,
  anatomy, 1820-1896, England
L   75 (1905) 128-130
S   4 (1896) 568
HUNICKE, HENRY AUGUST, chemistry,
  1861-1909, U.S.A.
S   29 (1909) 696
HUNT, EDWARD B., physics, 1823-
  1863, U.S.A.
A   86 (1863) 450-451
HUNT, ROBERT, medicine-metallurgy,
  1807-1887, England
L   47 (1890) i-ii
N   37 (1887) 14
HUNT, THOMAS STERRY, chemistry-
  geology, 1826-1892, U.S.A.
A 143 (1892) 246-248
L   51 (1892) xxiv-xxvii
N   45 (1892) 400-401
P   8 (1875-1876) P 486-488
S   10 (1899) 708-709
S   21 (1905) 876
S   39 (1914) 943
HUNTER, ADAM, medicine, 1791-
  1870, Scotland
E   7 (1869-1872) 240-242
HUNTER, JOHN, anatomy, 1728-1793,
  Scotland
N   33 (1886) 233, 275-276
N   50 (1894) 169-170
N   57 (1897) 194-195
S   12 (1900) 259-261
S   21 (1905) 403-405
HUNTER, JOHN, chemistry, 1843-
  1872, Ireland
E   8 (1872-1875) 322-324
HUNTER, WILLIAM, anatomy,
  1718-1783, Scotland
N   50 (1894) 169-170
HUNTER, WILLIAM, medicine,
  1885?-1909,
S   30 (1909) 175
HUPPERT, HUGO, physiology,
  1841?-1904, Germany
S   20 (1904) 695
HURST, ..., archeology, 1842?-
  1895,
S   2 (1895) 663
HURST, C. HERBERT, zoology,
      -1898, Ireland

S   7 (1898) 799
HURTER, F., chemistry-physics,
      -1898, England
S   7 (1898) 458
HUSTED, ALBERT N., mathematics,
  1833-1912, U.S.A.
S   36 (1912) 627-628
HUSSEY, RICHARD, LORD VIVIAN,
  soldier,   -1842, England
L   4 (1837-1843) 415
HUTCHINSON, SIR JONATHAN, surgery,
  1828-1923, England
L B91 (1920) xli-xliii
N   91 (1913) 429
P   83 (1913) P 206
S   38 (1913) 22
HUTCHINSON, T. NEVILLE, science,
  1826?-1899,
S   9 (1899) 789
HUTTON, CHARLES, mathematics,
  1732-1823, England
PM   21 (1805) P fr, 62-67
PM   61 (1823) 70
HUTTON, FREDERICK REMSEN, engi-
  neering, 1853-1918, U.S.A.
S   47 (1918) 533
HUTTON, FREDERICK WOLLASTON,
  biology-geology, 1836-1905,
  England
L B79 (1907) xli-xliv
N   46 (1892) 36
N   73 (1905) 32-33
N   79 (1909) P 432-433
S   22 (1905) 645
HUTTON, JAMES, geology, 1726-
  1797, Scotland
E   12 (1882-1884) 460-462
E   22 (1897-1899) 3
S   6 (1897) 925
HUTTON, WILLIAM RICH, engineer-
  ing, 1826?-1901,
S   14 (1901) 981
HUXLEY, THOMAS HENRY, biology-
  physiology, 1825-1895, England
A 150 (1895) 177-183
A 151 (1896) 249-250
E   21 (1895-1897) 14-15
L   6 (1850-1854) 244
N   9 (1874) P 257-258
N   10 (1874) 455-457
N   49 (1894) 310-311
N   52 (1895) 226-229, 248-
  249, 318-320
N   53 (1895) 110, 183-187
N   58 (1898) 613-614

N   61 (1900) 440-441
N   62 (1900) 10-12, 363, 495-496
N   63 (1900) 92-96, 116-119, 127,
        184-185
N   64 (1901) 76, 145-151
N   65 (1902) 366
N   66 (1902) 121-123, 241-242,
        P 658
N   76 (1907) 75-76
P   4 (1873-1874) P 739-743
P   47 (1895) 776-783
P   48 (1895-1896) 326-335
P   61 (1902) 558-559
P   58 (1900-1901) 337-359
Sl 17 (1891) 340
S   2 (1895) 14, 85-87, 131, 339,
        421-422, 483, 621, 796-799
S   3 (1896) 147-154, 253-263
S   4 (1896) 139, 267, 453
S   7 (1898) 674, 859
S   11 (1900) 818-821
S   16 (1902) 678, 755, 804-805,
        850
S   45 (1917) 445-446
HUXLEY, MRS. T. H.,
        -1914?, England
S   39 (1914) 604-605
HUYGENS (HUYGHENS) van ZUYLICHEM,
    CHRISTIAAN, physics, 1629-1695,
    Netherlands
N   38 (1888) 193-194
N   40 (1889) 591-592
N   43 (1891) 433-434
N   45 (1892) 434-436
N   58 (1898) 361-362
N   60 (1899) 457-458
N   72 (1905) 362-363
N   75 (1907) 509
N   76 (1907) 381
N   77 (1908) 247
N   80 (1909) 307
N   89 (1912) 436-437
N 116 (1925) 741-742
P   28 (1885-1886) P fp 721,
        835-839
P   78 (1911) P 329-332
S   2 (1895) 415-416
HYATT, ALPHEUS, biology-paleontol-
    ogy, 1838-1902, U.S.A.
A 163 (1902) 164
P   28 (1885-1886) P fp 145,
        261-267
P   55 (1899) P 451
P   78 (1911) P 128-146
S   15 (1902) 158, 300-302

HYATT, JAMES,   ,
        ,
A 167 (1904) 410
HYATT, JOHN WESLEY, invention,
    1837-1920, U.S.A.
S   21 (1905) 880
HYATT, JONATHAN, microscopy,
    1826?-1912, U.S.A.
S   37 (1913) 172
HYDE, JAMES NEVINS, dermatol-
    ogy, 1840-1910, U.S.A.
S   32 (1910) 405
HYLAND, JOHN SHEARSON, mineral-
    ogy, 1866?-1898, England
S   7 (1898) 674
IBBETSON, SIR DENZIL CHARLES
    JELF, ethnology, 1847-1908,
S   27 (1908) 518
IDDINGS, JOSEPH PAXSON, petrol-
    ogy, 1857-1920, U.S.A.
A 200 (1920) 316
P   72 (1908) P 191
INCHLEY, WILLIAM, engineering,
    1884?-1915, England
S   43 (1916) 236
INGALS, EPHRAIM FLETCHER, medi-
    cine, 1848-1918, U.S.A.
S   47 (1918) 458
S   49 (1919) 118
INGEN-HOUSZ (INGENHOUSZ), JAN,
    botany-physics, 1730-1799,
    Netherlands
N   75 (1906) 3-4
INGHIRAMI, GIOVANNI, geography,
    1779-1851, Italy
A   64 (1852) 450
INGLIS, JOHN, law, 1810-1891,
    Scotland
E   19 (1891-1892) 9-11,
        xiii-xxii
INGLIS, JOHN W., engineering,
    1838-1914, Scotland
E   35 (1914-1915) 9
INNES, COSMO, antiquity-law,
    1798-1874, Scotland
E   8 (1872-1875) 453-460
INOSEMZEFF, FEDOR, surgery, 1802-
    1869, Russia
S   15 (1902) 917
IORNS, M. J., horticulture,
    1909, U.S.A.
S   29 (1909) 893
IRBY, L. H. L., ornithology,
    1836?-1905, England
S   21 (1905) 870

IRMISCH, THILO, botany-morphol-
ogy, 1815?-1879, Germany
A 119 (1880) 77
IRONS, DAVID, philosophy-psy-
chology, 1870-1907, Scotland
S 25 (1907) 198
IRVINE, ALEXANDER FORBES, law,
1818-1892, Scotland
E 19 (1891-1892) xxiii-xxxiii
E 20 (1892-1895) 9
IRVINE, ROBERT, oceanography,
E 21 (1895-1897) 521-522
IRVING, JOHN DUER, geology-mining,
1874-1918, U.S.A.
A 196 (1918) 550
S 48 (1918) 136-137, 255-256
IRVING, ROLAND DUER, geology,
1847-1888, U.S.A.
A 136 (1888) 80
S1 11 (1888) 288
von ISAKOVITZ, ALOIS, chemistry,
1870-1917, Bohemia
S 46 (1917) 58
ISTRATI, CONSTANTIN I., chemistry-
medicine, 1850-1918, Roumania
S 47 (1918) 342
ITO, KEISUKE, Baron, botany,
1803-1901, Japan
S 13 (1901) 556
ITZIGSOHN, HERMANN, cryptogamia,
1814?-1879, Germany
A 119 (1880) 77
IVES, ELI, botany, 1799?-1861,
U.S.A.
A 82 (1861) 455
IVORY, SIR JAMES, mathematics-
physics, 1765-1842, Scotland
L 3 (1830-1837) 220
L 4 (1837-1843) 172-173,
406-412
PM III 22 (1843) 142-148
IVORY, JAMES, law, 1792-1866,
Scotland
E 6 (1866-1869) 20-21
JACKMAN, WILBUR SAMUEL, educa-
tion, 1855-1907, U.S.A.
S 25 (1907) 237-238
JACKSON, ARTHUR, medicine,
-1911, England
S 34 (1911) 796
JACKSON, CHARLES THOMAS, chem-
istry-geology, 1805-1880,
U.S.A.
A 120 (1880) 351-352
P 19 (1881) P fp 289, 404-
407
S 21 (1905) 875

JACKSON, GEORGE THOMAS, derma-
tology, 1852-1916, U.S.A.
S 43 (1916) 95
JACKSON, SIR JOHN, engineering,
1851-1919, England
E 40 (1919-1920) 182-184
JACKSON, SIR HENRY BRADWARDINE,
electricity, 1855-1929,
England
L A127 (1930) P vi-ix
N 64 (1901) 37
JACKSON, HENRY WILLIAM, anthro-
pology-astronomy, 1832?-
1899, England
S 9 (1899) 756
JACKSON, JOHN HUGHLINGS, neurol-
ogy-physiology, 1835-1911,
England
L B84 (1912) xviii-xxv
N 87 (1911) 524
JACOBI, ANDREAS, botany, 1801-
1875, Germany
A 111 (1876) 326
JACOBI, ABRAHAM, pediatrics,
1830-1919, Germany
S 31 (1910) 696
S 41 (1915) 572
S 45 (1917) 477
S 47 (1918) 559
S 50 (1919) 62, 102-104
JACOBI, CARL GUSTAV JACOB, math-
ematics, 1804-1851, Germany
A 52 (1846) 291
A 62 (1859) 148-149
S 18 (1903) 220
JACOBI, MARY PUTNAM (MRS. ABRAHAM),
medicine, 1843?-1906, U.S.A.
S 23 (1906) 959
S 25 (1907) 917
JACOBSEN, JENS PETER, writer,
1847-1885, Denmark
S1 6 (1855) 20
JACOBUS, DAVID SCHENCK, engineer-
ing-physics, 1862-   , U.S.A.
P 66 (1904-1905) P 383
JACQUIN, JR., ..., botany,
1839, Hungary
A 40 (1840-1841) 219
JAEGER, GUSTAV, medicine,

A 155 (1898) 160
JAFFÉ, MAX, biochemistry-phar-
macology, 1841-1911, Germany
S 34 (1911) 178, 709
JAGO, JAMES, medicine, 1815-
1893, England
L 54 (1894) i-iii

Scotland
S 22 (1905) 286
KEITH, PATRICK, botany, 1768?-
1839,
A 40 (1840-1841) 219
KEITH, THOMAS, medicine, 1826?-
1895, England
S 2 (1895) 586
KEKULÉ von STRADONITZ, FRIEDRICH
AUGUST, chemistry, 1829-1896,
Germany
A 152 (1896) 314
N 46 (1892) 205-206
N 54 (1896) 297
N 55 (1896) 112
N 57 (1897-1898) 180, 395
P 54 (1898-1899) P fp 289,
401-408
S 4 (1896) 111
KELLAND, PHILIP, mathematics,
1808-1879, England
E 10 (1878-1880) 208-211,
321-329
L 29 (1879) vii-x
KELLAS, ARTHUR, psychiatry,
-1915, England
S 42 (1915) 373
KELLEHER, S. B., mathematics,
-1917, Ireland
S 46 (1917) 286
KELLER, HELEN ADAMS, communica-
tion, 1880-1968, U.S.A.
Sl 12 (1888) 89-91, 160-161
S 3 (1896) 925
KELLER, P. H., physics, 1836?-
1903,
S 18 (1903) 125
KELLERMAN, WILLIAM ASHBROOK,
mycology, 1850-1908, U.S.A.
S 27 (1908) 118, 479, 858
KELLICOTT, D. S., zoology,
-1898, U.S.A.
S 7 (1898) 596
KELLICOTT, WILLIAM ERSKINE,
biology, 1878-1919, U.S.A.
S 49 (1919) 146, 322-323
KELLNER, OSKAR, agriculture,
1851-1911, Germany
S 34 (1911) 509
KELLOGG, ALBERT, botany-medicine,
1813-1887, U.S.A.
A 135 (1888) 261-262
Sl 9 (1887) 391-392, 514
KELLY, ALOYSIUS OLIVER JOSEPH,
medicine, 1870-1911, U.S.A.
S 33 (1911) 368

KELLY, WILLIAM, invention, 1811-
1888, U.S.A.
S 21 (1905) 875
KELVIN, LORD--SEE THOMSON, WILLIAM
KEMPE, SIR ALFRED BRAY, law-math-
ematics, 1849-1922, England
L A102 (1923) P i-x
L B94 (1923) P i-x
KENDALL, E. OTIS, mathematics,
1818?-1899, U.S.A.
S 9 (1899) 78
KENNEDY, SIR ALEXANDER BLACKIE
WILLIAM, engineering, 1847-
1928, England
N 36 (1887) 6
KENNEDY, ALFRED L., metallurgy,
1810?-1896, U.S.A.
S 3 (1896) 200
KENNEDY, FRANCIS, philosophy,
1875?-1901, U.S.A.
S 13 (1901) 356-357
KENNEDY, HORACE T., geology,
-1917, Ireland
A 194 (1917) 160
S 46 (1917) 35
KENNELLY, ARTHUR EDWIN, physics,
1861-1939, India
N 74 (1907) 463-464
KENNGOTT, GUSTAV ADOLF, mineral-
ogy, 1813-1897, Germany
S 5 (1897) 652
KENNICOTT, ROBERT, biology-ex-
ploration, 1835-1866, U.S.A.
A 92 (1866) 435-436
KENSIT, E. G., botany,
-1916,
S 44 (1916) 564
KEPLER (KEPPLER), JOHANN, astron-
omy-optics, 1571-1630, Germany
N 34 (1886) 189-190
N 54 (1896) 186
P 78 (1911) P 323-327
KEPPEL, HERBERT GOVERT, mathemat-
ics, 1866-1918, U.S.A.
S 48 (1918) 415
KERL, GEORG HEINRICH BRUNO, metal-
lurgy, 1824-1905, Germany
S 21 (1905) 718
KERNOT, WILLIAM CHARLES, engineer-
ing, 1845-1909, England
S 29 (1909) 575
KERR, JOHN, mathematics-physics,
1824-1907, Scotland
L A82 (1909) i-v
N 42 (1890) 15
N 59 (1898) 138-139

N 86 (1907) 575-576
S 26 (1907) 326
KERR, JOHN GRAHAM, biology,
    , Scotland
E 25 (1903-1905) 1184-1185
KERR, WASHINGTON CARUTHERS,
geology, 1827-1885, U.S.A.
A 130 (1885) 248
KERRY, R. E., bacteriology,
1862?-1896,
S 4 (1896) 721
KERSCHNER, LUDWIG, histology,
1859?-1911, Austria
S 33 (1911) 959
KETTELER, EDUARD, physics,
1836-1900, Germany
S 13 (1901) 79
KEY, SIR ASTLEY COOPER, naval
science, 1821-1888,
England
L 43 (1888) ix-xi
KEY, THOMAS, medicine, 1803-
1880, Scotland
E 11 (1880-1882) 95-96
KEY, THOMAS HEWITT, mathemat-
ics, 1799-1875, England
L 24 (1876) x-xv
KEYSER, CARL JOHAN, mathemat-
ics, 1821-   , Germany
P 74 (1909) P 205
KEYSER, PETER D., ophthal-
mology,   -1897, U.S.A.
S 5 (1897) 473
KHANG-HI (KHANG-HSI), science,
1653-1722?, China
N 25 (1881) 82-84
KIDDER, JEROME, surgery,
    , U.S.A.
S 41 (1915) 749
KIDSTON, ROBERT, botany-
paleontology, 1852-1924,
Scotland
E 17 (1889-1890) 419-420
E 18 (1890-1891) 16-17
L B98 (1925) P xiv-xxii
KIENER, . . ., pathology,
    -1895, France
S 2 (1895) 232
KIEPERT, HEINRICH, geography,
1818-1899, Germany
S 9 (1899) 629
KIERNAN, FRANCIS, anatomy,
1800-1874, Ireland
L 3 (1830-1837) 442-443
N 11 (1875) 193
von KIESENWETTER, ERNST

AUGUST HELMUTH, entomology,
1820-1880, Germany
N 21 (1880) 538
von KIESER, D. G., botany,
1779?-1862, Germany
A 85 (1863) 449
KIESERITSKI, GUSTAV, mathe-
matics, 1829?-1896, Russia
S 4 (1896) 616
KIESSELBACH, W., otology,
    -1902, Germany
S 16 (1902) 198
KIKUCHI, DAIROKU, Baron,
mathematics-seismology,
1855-1917, Japan
N 100 (1917) 227-228
KIMBALL, ALONZO S., physics,
1843?-1897?, U.S.A.
S 6 (1897) 876
S 7 (1898) 54-56
KIMBALL, EDWIN A., mechanics,
1834?-1898, U.S.A.
S 8 (1898) 744
KIMBALL, RODNEY G., mathemat-
ics,   -1900, U.S.A.
S 11 (1900) 717
KING, ALBERT FREEMAN AFRICANUS,
medicine, 1841-1914,
England
P 87 (1915) P 175
KING, ANDREW, chemistry,
    -1919, Scotland
E 40 (1919-1920) 5
KING, CHARLES, microscopy,
N 37 (1887) 152
KING, CLARENCE, geology, 1842-
1901, U.S.A.
A 163 (1902) 163, 224-237
S 15 (1902) 37, 113
KING, SIR GEORGE, botany,
1840-1909, Scotland
L B81 (1909) xi-xxviii
N 36 (1887) 6
N 79 (1909) 493-494
S 29 (1909) 381, 416
KING, VERNON, entomology,
    -1918, U.S.A.
S 48 (1918) 67
KING, WILLIAM, geology,
    -1900, England
S 13 (1901) 78
KING, WILLIAM FREDERICK,
astronomy, 1854-1916,
England
S 43 (1919) 639-640
KINGSLEY, GEORGE HENRY,

zoology, 1827-1892, England
N   62 (1900) 5
KINGSLEY, MARY HENRIETTA,
  botany-exploration, 1862-
  1900, England
S   11 (1900) 958
S   12 (1900) 39
KINKELIN, GEORGE FRIEDRICH,
  geology, 1836-1913, Germany
S   38 (1913) 440
KINNEAR, ALEXANDER SMITH, law,
  1833-1917, Scotland
E   39 (1918-1919) 13-14
KINNICUTT, LEONARD PARKER,
  chemistry, 1854-1911,
  U.S.A.
P   66 (1904-1905) P 382
S   33 (1911) 248, 649-651
KIPPING, FREDERIC STANLEY,
  chemistry, 1863-1949,
  England
N   56 (1897) 56
KIRBY, WILLIAM, botany, 1759-
  1850
L   5 (1843-1850) 1023-1026
KIRBY, WILLIAM FORSELL, en-
  tomology, 1844-1912,
  England
A   185 (1913) 120
N   90 (1912) 364
S   36 (1912) 822
KIRCHER, ATHANASIUS, mathe-
  matics-physics, 1602-1680,
  Germany
S   31 (1910) 263-264, 666,
  857-859
KIRCHHOFF, GUSTAV ROBERT,
  physics, 1824-1887, Germany
A   134 (1887) 496
L   46 (1890) vi-ix
N   36 (1887) 606-607
N   65 (1902) 587-590
P   33 (1888) P fr, 120-124
KIRCHOFF, ALFRED, geography,
  1838-1907, Germany
S   14 (1901) 302
S   25 (1907) 439
KIRCHOFF, CHARLES WILLIAM
  HENRY, metallurgy-mining,
  1853-1916, U.S.A.
S   44 (1916) 130
KIRK, . . ., botany,   -1898,
  New Zealand
S   7 (1898) 458
KIRK, SIR JOHN, zoology, 1832-
  1922, Scotland

L   B94 (1923) xi-xxx
N   36 (1887) 6
KIRKALDY, GEORGE WILLIS, en-
  tomology, 1873-1910, U.S.A.
S   31 (1910) 454
KIRKMAN, THOMAS PENYNGTON,
  mathematics, 1806-1895,
  England
N   99 (1917) 221-222
KIRKWOOD, DANIEL, astronomy,
  1814-1895, U.S.A.
S   1 (1895) 694
KIRMAN, THOMAS HARDY, corpu-
  lence, 1821-   ,
L   3 (1830-1837) 176-177
KIRNALDY, DAVID, engineering
  1821?-1897,
S   5 (1897) 304
KIRSCH, P. H., ichthyology,
        -1900?, U.S.A.
S   13 (1901) 38
KIRTLAND, JARED POTTER, biology,
  1793-1877, U.S.A.
A   115 (1878) 80
KIRWAN, RICHARD, geology,
  1735-1812, Ireland
PM   14 (1802) P fr, 353-355
KITTL, ERNST, geology, 1854-
  1913, Austria
S   37 (1913) 830
KJELDAHL, JOHANN GUSTAV
  CHRISTOFFER, chemistry,
  1849-1900, Denmark
S   12 (1900) 277, 533
KJELLMAN, FRANZ, botany, 1846?-
  1907, Sweden
S   25 (1907) 718
KJERULF, THEODOR, geology,
  1825-1888, Norway
A   137 (1889) 422
KLAATSCH, HERMANN, anthro-
  pology, 1863-1916, Germany
S   43 (1916) 309
KLAPROTH, HEINRICH JULIUS,
  magnetism, 1783-1835,
  Germany
A   40 (1840-1841) 242
KLATT, F. W., botany,   -1897,
S   5 (1897) 652
KLEBS, EDWIN THEODOR ALBRECHT,
  physiology, 1834-1913,
  Germany
S   19 (1904) 438
S   38 (1914) 738, 920-921
KLEBS, RICHARD HERMANN AUGUST,
  geology, 1850-1911, Germany

KOCH, CHARLES RUDOLPH EDWARD,
dentistry, 1844?-1916,
U.S.A.
S 44 (1916) 165-166
KOCH, GUILLAUME DANIEL JOSEPH,
botany, 1771-1849, Germany
A 63 (1852) 45
KOCH, KARL HEINRICH EMIL,
botany-dendrology, 1809-
1879, Germany
A 119 (1880) 78
N 20 (1879) 173
KOCH, ROBERT, medicine-micro-
biology, 1843-1910, Germany
L B83 (1911) xviii-xxiv
N 43 (1910) 402-404
P 36 (1889-1890) P fp 145,
259-263
P 68 (1906) 91-93
P 77 (1910) P 102-103
S 19 (1904) 116
S 20 (1905) 476
S 31 (1910) 854
KOCH, WALDEMAR, pharmacology,
1875-1912, Germany
S 35 (1912) 214
KOCHER, EMIL THEODOR, surgery,
1841-1917, Switzerland
S 46 (1917) 159, 432
KOCHS, W., physiology,
-1898, Germany
S 8 (1898) 668
von KOELLIKER, RUDOLPH ALBRECHT,
anatomy-zoology, 1817-1905,
Switzerland
N 57 (1897) 109
N 58 (1898) P 1-4
N 62 (1900) 169-170
N 65 (1901) 76-77
N 68 (1903) 414
P 67 (1905) P 118
S 5 (1897) 340
S 22 (1905) 684
KÖNIG, ARTHUR, physiology,
1856-1901, Germany
S 14 (1901) 863, 1022
KÖNIG, FRANZ, surgery, 1832?-
1910, Germany
S 33 (1911) 22
KÖNIG, FREDERICK, surgery,
-1914, Germany
S 40 (1914) 667, 812
KOENIG, GEORGE AUGUSTUS, chem-
istry, 1844-1913, Germany
A 185 (1913) 204
S 37 (1913) 145

KÖNIG, KARL, mineralogy, 1774?-
1851, England?
A 62 (1851) 446
KOENIG, KARL RUDOLPH, physics,
1832-1901, Germany
A 162 (1901) 474
N 43 (1891) 224-227
N 64 (1901) 630-633
P 37 (1890) P fp 433,
545-550
S 14 (1901) 660, 724-727,
993-994
KÖNIGS, WILHELM, chemistry,
1851-1906, Germany
S 25 (1907) 158
KOENIGSBERGER, LEO, mathemat-
ics, 1837-1921, Poland
S 36 (1912) 668
KÖRÖSY, JOSEPH, demography,
-1906, Hungary
S 24 (1906) 159
KOESTER, KARL, pathology,
-1904?, Germany
S 21 (1905) 38
KÖTTER, FRITZ, mathematics,
1851?-1912, Germany
S 36 (1912) 370
KOETTLITZ, REGINALD, medicine,
-1916,
S 43 (1916) 236
KOHLENBERG, LOUIS, chemistry,
P 74 (1909) P 205
KOHLRAUSCH, FRIEDRICH WILHELM
GEORG, physics, 1840-1910,
Germany
L A85 (1911) xi-xiii
N 82 (1910) 402-403
N 83 (1910) 216-217
N 87 (1911) 509-510
KOHLRAUSCH, FRITZ LUDWIG,
physics,   -1914, Germany
S 40 (1914) 930
KOHLSTOCK, P., hygiene,
-1901, Germany
S 13 (1901) 676
von KOKEN, ERNST, geology-
mineralogy, 1860?-1912?,
Germany
A 185 (1913) 204
S 37 (1913) 16
KOKSHAROV, NICOLAS, mineralogy,
-1893, Russia
A 145 (1893) 362
KOLBE, ADOLPH WILHELM HERMANN,
chemistry, 1818-1884,
Germany

N 73 (1905) 97-98
LAHUSEN, JOSEPH, paleontology,
1845?-1911, Russia?
S 33 (1911) 608
LAIDLAY, JOHN WATSON, oriental-
ism, 1808-1885, Scotland
E 14 (1886-1887) 120-122
LAING, ALEXANDER GORDON, ex-
ploration, 1793-1826,
England?
S 33 (1911) 248
LAING, GEORGE, theology,
1831-1916, Scotland
E 37 (1916-1917) 15
LALLEMAND, CLAUDE FRANÇOIS,
surgery, 1790-1854, France
A 68 (1854) 431
LAMANSKI, S., astronomy-
physics,   -1901, Russia
S 13 (1901) 755
de LAMARCK, JEAN BAPTISTE
PIERRE ANTOINE de MONET,
biology, 1744-1829, France
A 118 (1879) 340-341
N 26 (1882) 533-541
N 66 (1902) 169-170
N 94 (1915) 639-640
P 24 (1883-1884) P fr,
105-111
P 60 (1901-1902) 263-264
S 6 (1897) 995-997
S 15 (1902) 988-989
S 20 (1904) 811-812
S 25 (1907) 795
S 26 (1907) 502
S 27 (1908) 151-153, 377
S 31 (1910) 394
S 35 (1912) 110-111
LAMB, GEORGE, medicine, 1869?-
1911, Scotland
N 86 (1911) 249
S 33 (1911) 686
LAMB, SIR HORACE, mathematics-
physics, 1849-1934, England
N 53 (1895) 49-50
N 67 (1902) 109
N 70 (1904) 236, 373
P 65 (1904) 509, P 561
S 22 (1905) 221
LAMB, SIR JOHN CAMERON, en-
gineering, 1846?-1915,
England
S 41 (1915) 528
LAMBE, LAWRENCE M., paleontol-
ogy, 1863-1919, Canada
A 197 (1919) 454

S 49 (1919) 563
LAMBERT, AYLMER BOURKE,
botany, 1761-1842,
L 4 (1837-1843) 412-413
LAMBERT, JOHANN HEINRICH,
mathematics-physics, 1728-
1777, Germany
PM 18 (1804) 333-340
LAMBTON, WILLIAM, astronomy-
geodesy, 1756-1823, England
PM 62 (1823) 77-78
de LA MÉTHERIE, JEAN CLAUDE,
editor, 1743-1817, France
PM 20 (1804) P fr
von LAMONT, JOHANN, astronomy,
1805-1879, Scotland
E 10 (1878-1880) 358-359
N 20 (1879) 425
LAMP, JOHANNES, geodesy,
-1901, Germany
S 14 (1901) 117-118
LAMPLUGH, GEORGE WILLIAM,
geology, 1859-1926,
L B101 (1927) P xii-xiv
LANCASTER, ALBERT BENÔIT
MARIE, astronomy, 1849-
1908, Belgium
N 78 (1908) 33-34
S 27 (1908) 319
LANDOIS, HERMANN, zoology,
1835?-1905, Germany
S 14 (1901) 117-118
S 21 (1905) 358
LANDOIS, LEONARD, physiology,
1837-1902, Germany
S 17 (1903) 159
LANDOLT, HANS HEINRICH, chem-
istry, 1831-1910,
Switzerland
A 179 (1910) 566
N 83 (1910) 194-195
S 31 (1910) 499
LANDOUZY, LOUIS THÉOPHILE
JOSEPH, medicine, 1845-1917,
France
S 45 (1917) 562
LANE, ALBERT GRANNIS, edu-
cation, 1841-1906, U.S.A.
S 24 (1906) 287
LANE, ALFRED CHURCH, geology,
1863-1948, U.S.A.
P 70 (1907) P 185
LANE, JONATHAN HOMER, physics,
1819-1880, U.S.A.
S1 21 (1893) 291
LANE-FOX--see PITT-RIVERS

1904, France
S 19 (1904) 399

de LAUNAY, CHARLES EUGÈNE,
astronomy-physics, 1816-
1872, France
A 104 (1872) 332
L 24 (1876) vii-ix
S 14 (1901) 3

LAURENT, HERMANN, mathematics,
1841-1908, Luxembourg
S 27 (1905) 479

LAURENT, ÉMILE, botany, 1861-
1904, Belgium
S 19 (1904) 638

LAURIE, S. H., education,
1830?-1909, Scotland
S 29 (1909) 498

LAUSSÉDAT, AIMÉ, astronomy-
geodesy, 1819-1907, France
S 25 (1907) 758

LAUTH, ..., egyptology,
1822?-1895, Germany
S 1 (1895) 304

de LAVAL, CARL GUSTAF PATRIK,
engineering, 1845-1913,
Sweden
S 37 (1913) 302

LAVALLÉE, ALPHONSE, botany,
1835?-1884, France
A 128 (1884) 75-76
A 132 (1886) 326
Sl 3 (1884) 698
Sl 4 (1884) 10

de LA VALLÉE-POUSSIN, CHARLES
LOUIS JOSEPH XAVIER,
mineralogy, 1827-1903,
Belgium
S 17 (1903) 1020

LAVERAN, CHARLES LOUIS ALPHONSE,
medicine-parasitology, 1845-
1922, France
L B94 (1923) P xlix-liii
P 87 (1915) P 73

LAVERRIÈRE, JULES, agriculture,
-1895, France
S 2 (1895) 409

de LAVOISIER, ANTOINE LAURENT,
chemistry, 1743-1794,
France
A 52 (1846) 291-292
A 82 (1861) 98-101
A 85 (1863) 262
A 91 (1866) 105-106
N 9 (1874) 185
N 27 (1882) 8-11, 53,
100-101, 147

N 42 (1890) 313-314, 449-
454
N 43 (1890) 1-3
N 62 (1900) P 390-391
N 95 (1914) 356
P 35 (1889) P fp 433, 548-
553
P 58 (1900-1901) P fp 115
PM 1 (1798) P fr
PM 9 (1801) P 78-85
S 4 (1896) 355

LAW, MISS ANNIE E., conchology,
-1889, Malta
A 137 (1889) 422

LAW, JAMES, medicine, 1838-
1921, Scotland
S 37 (1913) 367

LAWES, SIR JOHN BENNETT,
agriculture-chemistry,
1814-1900, England
L 75 (1905) 228-236, 242-
245
N 93 (1914) 164
P 28 (1885-1886) P fp 577,
694-698
S 12 (1900) 380

LAWRENCE, GEORGE NEWBOLD, or-
nithology, 1806-1895,
U.S.A.
S 1 (1895) 268-269

LAWRENCE, SIR THOMAS, art,
1769-1830, England
A 20 (1821) 308
L 3 (1830-1837) 10-11

LAWRENCE, SIR TREVOR, horti-
culture, 1831?-1913, England
A 187 (1914) 208
N 92 (1914) 506

LAWRENCE, SIR WILLIAM, ophthal-
mology-surgery, 1783-1867,
England
L 16 (1868) xxv-xxx
N 56 (1897) P 200-201

LAWS, JOHN BENNET, botany,
N 48 (1893) 327-329
N 62 (1900) 467-468

LAWSON, A. ANSTRUTHER, botany,
E 39 (1918-1919) 255

LAWSON, GEORGE, botany, 1827-
1895, Scotland
A 151 (1896) 78
S 2 (1895) 768

LAWTON, GEORGE K., astronomy,
-1901, U.S.A.
S 14 (1901) 191, 215-216

LAX, WILLIAM, astronomy-

mathematics, -1836,
L 3 (1830-1837) 438
LAYARD, EDGAR LEOPOLD, or-
nithology, 1824-1900, Italy
S 12 (1900) 157-158
LAYCOCK, THOMAS, medicine,
1812-1876, England
E 9 (1875-1878) 223-225
LAYET, ALEXANDRE, hygiene,
-1916, France
S 44 (1916) 306
LAZARUS, MORITZ, philosophy-
psychology, 1824-1903,
Germany
S 17 (1903) 718
LAZEAR, JESSE WILLIAM, medi-
cine, 1866-1900, U.S.A.
P 87 (1915) P 178
S 13 (1901) 1038
S 14 (1901) 225
S 15 (1902) 718
LAZENBY, WILLIAM RANE, horti-
culture, 1850-1916, U.S.A.
S 44 (1916) 912-913
LEA, ARTHUR SHERIDAN, chem-
istry-physiology, 1853-1915,
U.S.A.
A 189 (1915) 612
L B89 (1917) xxv-xxvii
S 41 (1915) 606
LEA, ISAAC, conchology-mala-
cology, 1792-1886, U.S.A.
A 131 (1886) 239-240
A 133 (1887) 85-86
P 31 (1887) P fp 289, 404-
411
Sl 8 (1886) P 556-558
Sl 9 (1887) 88
S 10 (1899) P fp 665, 675-
676
LEA, MATHEW CAREY, chemistry,
1823-1897, U.S.A.
A 153 (1897) 428
S 39 (1914) 943
LEACH, FRANK A., biology,
-1905,
S 21 (1905) 158
LEACH, WILLIAM ELFORD, biol-
ogy, -1836,
L 3 (1830-1837) 439
LEAF, CECIL HUNTINGTON, medi-
cine, 1864-1910, England
S 32 (1910) 626
LEAKE, WILLIAM MARTIN, ex-
ploration, 1777-1860,
England

L 11 (1862) vii-ix
LEAMING, EDWARD, photography-
physics, 1861-1916, U.S.A.
S 43 (1816) 710
LEAVENWORTH, MELINS, C.,
botany, -1863, U.S.A.
A 85 (1863) 306, 451
LEAVITT, ERASMUS DARWIN, en-
gineering, 1836-1916,
U.S.A.
S 43 (1916) 423
LE BARON, WILLIAM, entomology,
1814-1876, U.S.A.
P 76 (1910) P 474-476
LEBEDEV, PIOTR NIKOLAYEVICH,
physics, 1866-1911, Russia
A 183 (1912) 598
S 35 (1912) 616
LE BEL, JOSEPH ACHILLE, chem-
istry, 1846-1930, France
L A130 (1931) P xxviii-xxx
LEBOUR, GEORGE ALEXANDER LOUIS,
geology, 1847-1918, England
A 195 (1918) 424
N 100 (1914) 487
S 47 (1918) 342
LE CHATELIER, HENRY LOUIS,
chemistry, 1850-1936,
France
N 98 (1916) 278
LECONTE, FELIX, mathematics-
physics, 1865?-1915, Belgium
S 42 (1915) 688
LE CONTE, JOHN, physics, 1818-
1891, U.S.A.
A 141 (1891) 525-526
P 36 (1889-1890) P fr,
112-120
S 17 (1891) 257
S 21 (1905) 878-879
LE CONTE, JOHN E., biology,
1784-1860, U.S.A.
A 81 (1861) 303, 462-463
LE CONTE, JOHN LAWRENCE, biol-
ogy-entomology, 1825-1883,
U.S.A.
A 126 (1883) 490
N 29 (1883) 128
P 5 (1874) P 622-623
P 76 (1910) P 468-469
Sl 2 (1883) 696, 783-786,
P 808-809
Sl 17 (1891) 257
S 10 (1899) 761-762
LE CONTE, JOSEPH, chemistry-
geology, 1823-1901, U.S.A.

A   81 (1861) 461
von LEIBNIZ (LEIBNITZ),
    GOTTFRIED WILHELM, Baron,
    mathematics-physics, 1646-
    1716, Germany
    A   52 (1846) 292-293
    P   64 (1903-1904) P 415-
        425, P 528
    Sl 14 (1889) 197
    S   50 (1919) 41-43
von LEICH, JOHANN, medicine,
    1813?-1897, Austria
    S   6 (1897) 211
LEIDIE, . . ., chemistry,
        -1904, France
    S   19 (1904) 807
LEIDY, JOSEPH, anatomy-
    zoology, 1823-1891, U.S.A.
    A 141 (1891) 523-525
    A 171 (1906) 338
    N   44 (1891) 63
    P   17 (1880) P fp 577, 684-
        691
    P   70 (1807) P 311-314
    P   72 (1908) 94-96
    Sl 17 (1891) 757
    Sl 18 (1891) 274-276
    S   1 (1895) 724
    S   23 (1906) 198
    S   26 (1907) 812-815
    S   35 (1912) 778-779
    S   37 (1913) 809-814
LEISHMAN, SIR WILLIAM BOOG,
    pathology, 1863-1926,
    Scotland
    L B102 (1928) P ix-xvii
LEJEAN, GUILLAUME, geography,
    1828-1871, France
    A 101 (1871) 392
LEJEUNE, A. L. S., botany,
        -1858, Belgium
    A   79 (1860) 441
LELOIR, HENRI CAMILLE
    CHRYSOSTÔME, dermatology,
    1855-1896, France
    S   4 (1896) 75
LEMBERG, JOHAN, mineralogy,
        -1903?, Estonia
    S   17 (1903) 119
LÉMERY, NICOLAS, chemistry,
    1645-1715, France
    S   14 (1901) 165
LEMOINE, VICTOR, paleontology,
        -1897, France
    S   5 (1897) 728
    S   8 (1890) 219

LeMONNIER, PIERRE CHARLES,
    astronomy, 1715-1799, France
    PM   6 (1800) 180-183
LEMOULT, PAUL, chemistry,
        -1916, France
    S   43 (1916) 924
LEMSTRÖM, KARL SELIM, physics,
    1838-1904, Finland
    N   71 (1904) 129
    S   20 (1904) 653
von LENARD, PHILIPP EDUARD
    ANTON, physics, 1862-1947,
    Czechoslovakia
    N   55 (1896) P 116-117
LENCH, . . ., astronomy,
        -1899, Switzerland
    S   9 (1899) 301
von LENDERFELD, ROBERT,
    zoology, 1857?-1913, Germany
    S   38 (1913) 152
LENGEMANN, . . ., mining,
        -1904, Germany
    S   19 (1904) 901
LENGYEL, BELA, chemistry,
    1854?-1913, Hungary
    S   37 (1913) 598
LENNON, WILLIAM H., science,
    1838-1913, U.S.A.
    S   37 (1913) 443
LENOIR, PAUL ÉTIENNE MARIE,
    instrumentation, 1776-1827,
    PM 63 (1824) 252-259
LENORMAND, SEBASTIAN RENÉ,
    algology, 1795?-1871, France
    A 103 (1872) 154
LENORMANT, FRANÇOIS, archeol-
    ogy-history, 1837-1883,
    France
    Sl   3 (1884) 339
LÉON, L. G., astronomy, 1866?-
    1913, Mexico
    S   37 (1913) 937
LEONARD, CHARLES LESTER,
    roentgenology, 1861?-1913,
    U.S.A.
    S   38 (1913) 476
LEONARDO da VINCI, art-science,
    1452-1519, Italy
    A   19 (1830-1831) 397-398
    A 118 (1879) 327
von LEONHARD, CARL CÄSAR,
    geology, 1779-1862, Germany
    A   83 (1862) 453
    A   86 (1863) 278
LEONHARD, GUSTAV, mineralogy,
    1816-1878, Germany

N   67 (1902) 108-109, 154-
    155
N   75 (1907) 564-565
N   82 (1910) 451-452
N   88 (1912) 556-560
N   90 (1912-1913) 254-255,
    499-505
N   91 (1913) 559-560
N   92 (1914) 523-524, 595
N   95 (1915) 160-166
N   97 (1916) P 58
N 100 (1914) 501-502
P   52 (1897-1898) P fp 577,
    693-698
P   70 (1907) P 565-566
P   80 (1912) P 310-312
S   5 (1897) 579
S   21 (1905) 797
S   25 (1907) 477, 717
S   35 (1912) 264, 329, 541-
    542, 614
S   47 (1918) 563-565
LISTER, JOSEPH JACKSON, zoolo-
    gy, 1857-1927,
    L B102 (1928) P i-v
LISTER, MARTIN, conchology,
    1638-1712, England
    A 37 (1839) 136-138
LISTING, JOHANN BENEDICT,
    physics, 1808-1882, Germany
    N 27 (1883) 316-317
LITTLE, ARCHIBALD J., geography,
    -1908,
    S 28 (1908) 752
LITTLE, JAMES, medicine, 1837?-
    1916, Ireland
    S 45 (1917) 112
LITTON, ABRAM, chemistry,
    1814?-1901, U.S.A.
    S 14 (1901) 542
LITTRÉ, MAXIMILIEN PAUL ÉMILE,
    medicine-philology, 1801-
    1881, France
    P 21 (1882) 667-679
von LITTROW, JOSEPH JOHANN,
    astronomy-physics, 1781-
    1840, Bohemia
    A 40 (1840-1841) 220
LIVEING, GEORGE DOWNING, spec-
    troscopy, 1827-1924,
    England
    L A109 (1925) P xxviii-
       xxix
    N 65 (1901) 108
    N 97 (1916) 377-378
    N 115 (1925) 25, 127-129

LIVERSIDGE, ARCHIBALD, chem-
    istry-mineralogy, 1847-
    1927, Australia
    L A126 (1930) P xii-xiv
LIVINGSTONE, DAVID, biology-
    exploration, 1813-1873,
    Scotland
    A 95 (1868) 14-16, 141
    N   9 (1874) 486
    N 23 (1887) 238-240
    N 91 (1913) 89-90
    P   2 (1872-1873) P fp 257,
        327-343
    S 11 (1900) 998
    S 36 (1912) 513, 822
    S 37 (1913) 923-929
LLOYD, HUMPHREY, physics,
    1800-1881, Ireland
    L 31 (1881) xxi-xxvi
    N 23 (1881) 292-293
    N 25 (1881) 115
    N 66 (1902) 478
LOBACHEVSKI, NIKOLAI IVANOVICH,
    mathematics, 1793-1856,
    Russia
    N 48 (1893) 296
    S1 21 (1893) 246-247
    S   1 (1895) 356-358
    S   2 (1895) 842-843
    S   4 (1896) 268
    S   9 (1899) 813-817
    S 10 (1899) 545-547
    S 12 (1900) 842-846
    S 13 (1901) 462-465
    S 35 (1912) 736-737
LO BIANCO, SALVATORI, zoology,
    1860?-1910, Italy
    S 31 (1910) 901
LOCK, ROBERT HEATH, botany-
    genetics, 1879-1915,
    England
    S 42 (1915) 119, 157
LOCKE, JOHN, philosophy, 1632-
    1704, England
    P 66 (1904-1905) P 189-
       191
    S 20 (1904) 614, 694
LOCKE, JOHN, botany-physics,
    1792-1856, U.S.A.
    A 72 (1856) 301-302
LOCKE, JOSEPH, engineering,
    1806-1860, England
    L 11 (1862) ix-x
LOCKINGTON, WILLIAM NEALE,
    zoology, 1842?-1902,
    England

von LOMMEL, E., physics, 1837?-
1899, Germany
S 10 (1899) 92
LOMONOSOV, MIKHAIL VASILIEVICH,
chemistry, c.1711-1765,
Russia
S 35 (1912) 121-129
LONG, CRAWFORD WILLIAMSON,
surgery, 1815-1878, U.S.A.
P 80 (1912) P 616-617
LONG, JOHN HARPER, chemistry,
1856-1918, U.S.A.
S 47 (1918) 635
S 49 (1919) 31-38
LONG, WILLIAM J., biology,
1867-1904?, U.S.A.
S 19 (1904) 347-350, 387-
389, 667-675, 760-767
LONGSTRETH, MORRIS, anatomy,
1846-1914, U.S.A.
S 40 (1914) 478
de LONGUININE, WALDEMAR, chem-
istry, 1834?-1911,
S 34 (1911) 870
LOOMIS, EBEN JENKS, astronomy,
1828-1912, U.S.A.
A 185 (1913) 120
S 36 (1912) 822
LOOMIS, ELIAS, meteorology-
mathematics, 1811-1889,
U.S.A.
A 138 (1889) 256
A 139 (1890) P 427-455,
(appendix of June issue,
i-xii)
N 33 (1885) 49-51
N 36 (1887) 1-3
P 40 (1891-1892) P fp 289,
405-412
Sl 14 (1889) 131
S 24 (1906) 871
LOOS, HERMANN A., chemistry,
1876?-1900, U.S.A.
S 12 (1900) 277
LOPER, SAMUEL WARD, paleontol-
ogy, 1835-1910, U.S.A.
A 179 (1910) 464
S 31 (1910) 535
LORBERG, HERMANN, physics,
1831-1906, Germany
S 23 (1906) 558, 639
LORD, NATHANIEL WRIGHT, metal-
lurgy, 1854-1911, U.S.A.
S 33 (1911) 849
LORD, WILLIAM ROGERS, orni-
thology, 1847-1916, U.S.A.

S 46 (1917) 450
LORENTZ, HENDRIK ANTOON,
physics, 1853-1928,
Netherlands
L A121 (1928) P xx-xxviii
N 79 (1908) 136
N 111 (1923) P 1-6
LORENTZ, PAUL GUNTHER, biology,
1829?-1881
A 127 (1884) 243
LORENTZEN, L. R., medicine,
1853?-1916, Denmark
S 43 (1916) 236
LORENZ, LUDWIG VALENTIN,
physics, 1829-1891, Denmark
N 61 (1900) 465-466
N 70 (1904) 528
LORENZ, T. H., mineralogy,
1875?-1909, Germany
S 30 (1909) 146
LORIMER, JAMES, law,   -1890,
E 17 (1889-1890) 408-409
LORTET, LOUIS, archeology,
1836-1909, France
S 31 (1910) 105
LOSCHMIDT, JOSEF, physics,
1821-1895, Austria
S 2 (1895) 163
LOSSEN, WILHELM CLEMENS, chem-
istry, 1838-1906, Germany
S 24 (1906) 789
LOTHIAN, MAURICE, law, 1795?-
1880,
E 11 (1880-1882) 99
LOTHROP, HENRY W., entomology,
1844?-1904, U.S.A.
S 19 (1904) 117
LOTZE, RUDOLF HERMANN, philos-
ophy, 1817-1881, Germany
S 36 (1912) 346
LOUDON, MRS. J. C., botany,
    -1858, England
A 77 (1859) 443
LOVE, AUGUSTUS EDWARD HOUGH,
mathematics-physics, 1863-
1940, England
N 50 (1894) 56
N 82 (1909) 134
LOVELL, SIR FRANCIS HENRY,
medicine,   -1916, England
S 43 (1916) 167
LOVÉN, OTTO CHRISTIAN, physiol-
ogy,   -1904, Sweden
S 20 (1904) 190
LOVÉN, SVEN LUDVIG, zoology,
1809-1895, Sweden

S 33 (1911) 421

MACNAMARA, FRANCIS M., chemistry, 1842?-1899,
S 9 (1899) 461

MACNEE, SIR DANIEL, art, 1806-
1882, Scotland
E 12 (1882-1884) 24-27

MACOUN, JAMES M., biology,
1862?-1920, Canada?
A 199 (1920) 455

MACPHERSON, HUGH ALEXANDER,
zoology, 1858?-1901,
England
S 15 (1902) 79

MACVICAR, J. G., physics,
1801-1884?, England
S1 3 (1884) 425

MADAN, HENRY GEORGE, chemistry,
-1901, England
S 15 (1902) 79

MADDEN, EDWARD, botany,
-1856,
E 3 (1850-1857) 410-412

MADSEN, ANDREAS PETER, archeology, 1822-   , Denmark
P 47 (1895) P 23

MADVIG, JOHAN NICOLAI, philology, 1804-1886, Denmark
E 16 (1889-1890) iii-vi

von MÄDLER, JOHANN HEINRICH,
astronomy, 1794-1874,
Germany
A 107 (1874) 608
P 27 (1885) 340-344
PM IV47 (1874) 320

MAERCKER, MAX, agriculture-
chemistry, 1842?-1901,
Germany
S 14 (1901) 741, 780, 821

MAGEE, ..., theology,
-1831,
L 3 (1830-1837) 84

MAGENDIE, FRANÇOIS, physiology,
1783-1855, France
A 71 (1856) 117

MAGGI, LEOPOLD, anatomy,
-1905, Italy
S 21 (1905) 718

MAGIE, WILLIAM FRANCIS, physics,
1858-1943, U.S.A.
P 66 (1904-1905) P 384

MAGNAN, A., psychiatry,
-1916, France
S 44 (1916) 564, 672

MAGNENTIOS OF FULDA, RABANUS
MAURUS, botany-mathematics,

c.775-856, Germany
P 20 (1881-1882) 523-527

MAGNIN, AMI JACQUES, surgery,
-1917, France
S 46 (1917) 614

MAGNUS, HEINRICH GUSTAV, chem-
istry, 1802-1870, Germany
A 99 (1870) 442
L 20 (1872) xxvii-xxix
N 1 (1870) 607
N 2 (1870) P 143-145

MAGOWAN, CHARLES S., engineering,   -1907, U.S.A.
S 26 (1907) 767

MAGRUDER, ERNEST P., medicine,
-1915, U.S.A.
S 41 (1915) 606

MAIDEN, JOSEPH HENRY, botany,
1859-1925, England
L B100 (1926) P viii-xi

MAIN, PHILIP THOMAS, astronomy-
chemistry,   -1899, England
S 9 (1899) 756

MAIN, ROBERT, astronomy, 1808-
1878, England
N 18 (1878) 72-73

MAIN, WILLIAM, chemistry,
1844?-1918, U.S.A.
S 48 (1918) 467

MAINE, THOMAS, engineering,
-1896, U.S.A.
S 3 (1896) 839

MAITLAND, EDWARD FRANCIS, Lord
Barcaple, law, 1808-1870,
Scotland
E 7 (1869-1872) 242-245

MAITLAND, SAMUEL ROFFEY,
author, 1792-1866, England
L 16 (1868) xxxi-xxxiii

MAJOR, CHARLES IMMANUEL FORSYTH,
paleontology, 1844-1923,
Scotland
L B95 (1924) P liv-lv

MALAGUTI, FAUSTINO JOVITA
MARIANUS, chemistry, 1802-
1878, Italy
N 18 (1878) 15

MALCOLM, SIR CHARLES, geography,
1783?-1852,
A 64 (1852) 450

MALCOLM, SIR JOHN, diplomacy-
history, 1769-1833,
L 3 (1830-1837) 224-226

MALERBA, P., chemistry,
-1917, Italy
S 46 (1917) 563

A   59 (1850) 304
A   65 (1853) 147-150
L   5 (1843-1850) 872
L   6 (1850-1854) 252-256
MAPES, CHARLES VICTOR, chem-
istry, 1836-1916, U.S.A.
S   43 (1916) 131
MAPLES, CHAUNCY, anthropology,
, England
N   61 (1900) 294
de MARBAIX, ADOLPHE, bac-
teriology-zoology,
-1899,
S   5 (1897) 728
S   10 (1899) 302
MARBE, THEODORE, zoology,
1816?-1896, Hungary
S   4 (1896) 652
MARBLE, ALBERT PRESCOTT,
education, 1838?-1906,
U.S.A.
S   23 (1906) 519
MARBLE, CHARLES C., ornithol-
ogy,   -1900,
S   12 (1900) 814
MARCET, ALEXANDRE, chemistry-
medicine, 1770-1822, Switzer-
land
A   17 (1829-1830) 363-364
MARCET, WILLIAM, medicine,
1828-1900, Switzerland
L   75 (1905) P 165-169
N   61 (1900) 497
S   11 (1900) 476
MARCGRAVE (MARCGRAF), GEORGE,
biology, 1610-1644,
England
P   81 (1912) 250-274
S   40 (1914) 507-509
MARCH, FRANCIS ANDREW, philol-
ogy, 1825-1911, U.S.A.
S   22 (1905) 605
S   34 (1911) 343
MARCHOUX, D., sanitation,
P   87 (1915) P 76
MARCONI, GUGLIELMO, physics,
1874-1937, Italy
N   70 (1904) 235
MARCOU, JULES, geology, 1824-
1898, France
A   155 (1898) 398
S   5 (1897) 11
S   7 (1898) 566
MARCY, OLIVER, geology, 1820-
1899, U.S.A.
S   9 (1899) 495

MARÈS, HENRI PIERRE LOUIS,
agriculture-chemistry,
1820-1901, France
S   13 (1901) 997
MAREY, ÉTIENNE JULES, physiol-
ogy, 1830-1904, France
N   65 (1902) P 349
N   70 (1904) 57-58
S   19 (1904) 838
MARGETS, GEORGE, instrumenta-
tion, 1748-1804,
PM   23 (1806) 76-79
MARGO, THEODORE, zoology,
1816?-1896, Hungary
S   4 (1896) 529
MARIÉ-DAVY, EDME HIPPOLYTE,
physics, 1820-1893, France
N   48 (1893) 351
de MARIGNAC, JEAN CHARLES
GALISSARD, chemistry,
1817-1894, Switzerland
N   67 (1902) 146-147, 607
N   76 (1907) 465-466
S   15 (1902) 422
von MARILAUN, ANTON KERNER,
botany, 1831-1898, Austria
N   58 (1898) 251-252
MARINDIN, HENRY LOUIS FRANÇOIS,
hydrography, 1843-1904,
Switzerland
S   19 (1904) 598
MARINGER, JULES, medicine,
-1899, France
S   10 (1899) 192
MARK, EDWARD LAURENS, anatomy-
zoology, 1847-   , U.S.A.
N   71 (1904) 169-170
P   64 (1903-1904) P 379
S   19 (1904) 455
MARK, LUDWIG, agriculture,
1840?-1896, Germany
S   3 (1896) 899
MARKHAM, SIR CLEMENTS ROBERT,
anthropology-geography,
1830-1916, England
A   191 (1916) 382
N   76 (1907) 189
N   96 (1916) 627-628
N   100 (1918) 383
S   43 (1916) 167, 559-562
S   44 (1916) 351-352
MARKOE, FRANCIS H., surgery,
1855?-1907, U.S.A.
S   26 (1907) 390
MARKOE, GEORGE F. H., chemistry,
-1896, U.S.A.

E   34 (1913-1914) 6
MARTIN, ARTEMAS, geodesy,
   1835-1918, U.S.A.
   S   48 (1918) 508
MARTIN, CHARLES H., biology,
   1882?-1915, England
   S   41 (1915) 819
MARTIN, CHARLES JAMES, phys-
   iology,   ,
   N   64 (1901) 37
MARTIN, DOUGLAS S., electricity,
             -1914, U.S.A.
   S   40 (1914) 812
MARTIN, GEORGE A. agriculture,
   1831?-1904, U.S.A.
   S   19 (1904) 743
MARTIN, HENRY NEWELL, phys-
   iology, 1848-1896, Ireland
   L   60 (1897) xx-xxiii
   N   54 (1896) 147-148
   N   55 (1896) 56-57
   S   4 (1896) 721-722
MARTIN, SIR JAMES RANALD,
   medicine, 1793-1874,
   Scotland
   N   57 (1898) 462
MARTIN, JOSEPH BIDDULPH,
   statistics,   -1897,
   England
   S   5 (1897) 580
MARTIN, NICHOLAS HENRY,
   pharmacy, 1847-1916,
   England
   E   37 (1916-1917) 15
MARTIN, PIERRE ÉMILE, engi-
   neering-metallurgy, 1824-
   1915, France
   S   41 (1915) 938
MARTIN, SIDNEY HARRIS COX,
   medicine, 1860-1924, Jamaica
   L   B99 (1926) xliv-xlv
   N   52 (1895) 32
MARTIN, VIVIAN S., geography,
             -1897,
   S   5 (1897) 103
MARTINDALE, WILLIAM, pharmacy,
   1841?-1902, England
   S   15 (1902) 396
MARTINEAU, JAMES, philosophy,
   1805-1900, England
   S   11 (1900) 159
MARTINI, ..., invention,
             -1897,
   S   5 (1897) 270
von MARTIUS, KARL FRIEDRICH
   PHILIPP, botany, 1794-1868,

Germany
   A   97 (1869) 288-291
   E   7 (1869-1872) 20-22
   L   18 (1870) vi-xi
MARVIN, CHARLES FREDERICK,
   meteorology, 1858-1943,
   U.S.A.
   P   83 (1913) P 311
MARVIN, FRANK OLIN, engineer-
   ing, 1852-1915, U.S.A.
   S   41 (1915) 600-601
MARVIN, JAMES, education,
   1820?-1901, U.S.A.
   S   14 (1901) 158
MARVINE, ARCHIBALD, R., geology,
   1848-1876, U.S.A.
   A   111 (1876) 424
MARYE, GEORGES, curator,
             -1900,
   S   12 (1900) 197
MASCARI, ANTONINO, astronomy,
   1862-1906, Italy
   N   75 (1907) 373-374
   S   25 (1907) 78
MASCART, ÉLEUTHÈRE ÉLIE NICOLAS,
   physics, 1837-1908, France
   A   176 (1908) 404
   L   A83 (1909-1910) i-ii
   N   78 (1908) 446-448
   S   28 (1908) 404
MASCHKE, HEINRICH, mathematics,
   1853-1908, Germany
   P   66 (1904-1905) P 9
   S   27 (1908) 871
MASKELL, WILLIAM MILES, ento-
   mology, 1840-1898, England
   S   7 (1898) 829
MASKELYNE, ANTHONY MERVYN REEVE,
   law, 1791-1879, England
   L   29 (1879) xx-xxi
MASKELYNE, M.H. NEVIL STORY--
   see Story-Maskelyne
MASKELYNE, NEVIL, astronomy,
   1732-1811, England
   PM   42 (1813) 3-14
de MAS-LATRE, ..., count,
   paleontology,   -1897,
   S   5 (1897) 103
MASON, AMOS LAWRENCE, medicine,
   1842?-1914, U.S.A.
   S   39 (1914) 867
MASON, EBENEZER PORTER, astron-
   omy, 1819-1840, U.S.A.
   A   40 (1840-1841) 407-408
MASON, JAMES WEIR, mathematics,
   1836-1905, U.S.A.

S 21 (1905) 117

MASON, OTIS TUFTON, anthro-
pology-ethnology, 1838-
1908, U.S.A.
P 41 (1892) P 299-303
P 74 (1909) P 96-100
S 28 (1908) 722, 746-748

MASON, W.C., entomology, 1884?-
1917, England
S 47 (1918) 92

de MASOUTY, ..., astronomy,
1815?-1895, France
S 1 (1895) 390

MASPERO, GASTON CAMILLE CHARLES,
egyptology, 1846-1916,
France
N 97 (1916) 405-406
S 44 (1916) 130

MASSEE, GEORGE, mycology,
1851?-1917, England
A 193 (1917) 497
N 99 (1917) 9-10
S 45 (1917) 257, 307

MASSINGER, ADAM, astronomy,
-1915, Germany
S 41 (1915) 322

MASTERMAN, ARTHUR T., zoology,
E 25 (1903-1905) 1170-1171

MASTERMAN, STILLMAN, astronomy,
1831-1863, U.S.A.
A 86 (1863) 314, 448-450

MASTERS, MAXWELL TYLDEN, botany-
horticulture, 1833-1907,
England
N 76 (1907) 157
S 25 (1907) 982
S 26 (1907) 260

MATHER, ..., mineralogy,
-1900, France
S 11 (1900) 198

MATHER, FREDERIC, ichthyology,
1833-1900, U.S.A.
S 11 (1900) 556-557

MATHER, WILLIAM WILLIAMS,
geology, 1804-1859, U.S.A.
A 77 (1859) 452
P 49 (1896) P fp 433,
550-555

MATHERS, GEORGE SCHRADER, medicine, 1887?-1918, U.S.A.
S 48 (1918) 443, 507-508

MATHESON, GEORGE, literature,
1842-1906, Scotland
E 26 (1905-1906) 550-551

MATHESON, SIR JAMES, commerce,
1796-1879?, Scotland?

L 29 (1879) xxi-xxii

MATHEWS, GEORGE BALLARD,
mathematics, 1861-1922,
England
L A101 (1922) x-xiv
N 56 (1897) 56

MATHISON, G. C. M., physiology,
-1915, England
S 42 (1915) 119

MATTEI, CESARE, count, medicine,
1809-1896, Italy
S 7 (1898) 398-402
S 12 (1900) 693

MATTEUCCI, VITTORIO RAFFAELE,
seismology, 1866-1909, Italy
S 30 (1909) 111

MATTEUCCI, CARLO, medicine-
physics, 1811-1868, Italy
A 96 (1868) 285
L 5 (1843-1850) 522

MATTHEWS, CHARLES P., electricity, 1867-1907, U.S.A.
S 26 (1907) 842-843

MATTHEWS, DUNCAN, biology,
-1890, Scotland
E 19 (1891-1892) 7

MATTHEWS, JAMES DUNCAN,
zoology, 1831?-1870,
Scotland
E 17 (1889-1890) xxxviii-
xliii

MATTHEWS, WASHINGTON, anthropology-ethnology, 1843-
1905, Ireland
S 22 (1905) 126

MATTHEY, GEORGE, metallurgy,
1826?-1913, England
N 90 (1913) 679
S 37 (1913) 443

MATTHIESEN, AUGUSTUS, chem-
istry, 1831-1870, England
A 100 (1870) 437
A 101 (1871) 73-74

MATTHIESSEN, HEINRICH FRIED-
RICH LUDWIG, physics, 1830-
1906, Germany
S 21 (1905) 717

MATZKE, JOHN ERNST, language,
1862-1910, Germany
S 32 (1910) 505

MAUDSLAY, HENRY, engineering,
1771-1831, England
P 6 (1874-1875) P 612-613

MAUDSLEY, HENRY, psychology-
physiology, 1835-1918,
England

McCALL, JAMES, medicine,
1834?-1915, Scotland
S 42 (1915) 794
McCALLA, ALBERT, commerce-
microscopy, 1846-1918,
U.S.A.
S 48 (1918) 9
McCALLEY, HENRY, geology,
1852-1904, U.S.A.
S 20 (1904) 773-774
McCHEENEY, ..., geology,
-1876, U.S.A.
A 112 (1876) 244
McCLEAN, FRANK, astrophysics,
1837-1904, Ireland
L A78 (1907) xix-xxiii
N 52 (1895) 32
N 71 (1904) 58-59
N 72 (1905) 372
S 20 (1904) 734, 892
McCLELLAN, E. B., astronomy,
1862?-1907, England
S 25 (1907) 318
McCLELLAN, GEORGE, anatomy-
surgery, 1849-1913, U.S.A.
S 37 (1913) 556
McCLELLAND, JOHN ALEXANDER,
physics, 1870-1920,
L A106 (1924) P v-ix
McCLINTIC, T. B., sanitation,
1873?-1912, U.S.A.
S 36 (1912) 238
McCLINTOCK, SIR FRANCIS
LEOPOLD, exploration-geog-
raphy, 1819-1907, England
L A80 (1908) xxiii-xxix
N 77 (1907) 61-62
S 26 (1907) 886
McCLINTOCK, THOMAS W., medi-
cine,   ,
S 39 (1914) 323
McCLOSKEY, ALICE GERTRUDE,
education,   -1915, U.S.A.
S 42 (1915) 641
McCLURE, EDGAR, geology,
-1897, U.S.A.
S 6 (1897) 211
McCOLLOM, JOHN HILDRETH,
medicine, 1843-1915, U.S.A.
S 41 (1915) 937
McCONNELL, J. C., anatomy,
-1904, U.S.A.
S 20 (1904) 188
McCOOK, HENRY CHRISTOPHER,
entomology, 1837-1911,
U.S.A.

S 34 (1911) 680
McCORMICK, LEANDER JAMES
astronomy, 1819-1900,
U.S.A.
S 11 (1900) 357
McCORMICK, WILLIAM SYMINGTON,
education, 1859-1930,
Scotland
L A130 (1931) P xv-xxiii
McCOSH, ANDREW JAMES, surgery,
1858-1908, Ireland
S 28 (1908) 836
McCOY, SIR FREDERICK, geology,
1823-1899, Ireland
L 75 (1905) 43-45
N 60 (1899) 83
S 9 (1899) 789
McCRAE, JOHN, pathology-poetry,
1875-1918, Canada
N 60 (1899) 83
N 100 (1918) 487-488
S 47 (1918) 266
McCURDY, GEORGE GRANT, anthro-
pology, 1863-   ,
P 68 (1906) P 191
McDONALD, CHARLES, mathematics,
-1901, Canada
S 13 (1901) 476
McDONALD, MARSHALL, ichthyol-
ogy, 1835?-1895, U.S.A.
S 2 (1895) 341
McELROY, GEORGE B., mathemat-
ics, 1821?-1907, U.S.A.
S 25 (1907) 238
McFARLAND, ROBERT WHITE, en-
gineering-mathematics,
1825-1910, U.S.A.
S 32 (1910) 626
McFARLANE, LAUGHTON, surgery,
1842?-1896, Canada
S 3 (1896) 352
McGEE, D. W., literature,
-1895,
S 2 (1895) 133
McGEE, WILLIAM JOHN, anthro-
pology-geology, 1853-1912,
U.S.A.
A 184 (1912) 404, 496
S 36 (1912) 341, 348-350
McGREGOR, H. H., chemistry,
-1915, Canada
S 42 (1915) 449
McGREGOR, SIR WILLIAM, ethnol-
ogy, 1847?-1919, England
S 50 (1919) 109
McHARDY, M. M., ophthalmology,

1853?-1913, England
S 37 (1913) 443
S 50 (1919) 109
McHATTON, HENRY, medicine,
1856?-1917, U.S.A.
S 45 (1917) 458
McHENRY, A., geology, -1919,
Ireland
S 49 (1919) 493
McINTOSH, DONALD, medicine,
-1915, U.S.A.
S 42 (1915) 373
McIVER, CHARLES DUNCAN, edu-
cation, 1860-1906, U.S.A.
P 67 (1905) P 380
McKAY, CHARLES LESLIE, ichthyol-
ogy, -1883, U.S.A.
S1 2 (1883) 635
McKAY, JOHN S., mathematics-
physics, 1850?-1917, U.S.A.
S 45 (1917) 289
McKEAN, THOMAS, philanthropy,
-1898,
S 7 (1898) 421
McKENDRICK, JOHN GRAY, zoology,
1841-1926, Scotland
L B100 (1926) xiv-xviii
N 81 (1909) P 488
McKINLEY, WILLIAM, government,
1843-1901, U.S.A.
S 14 (1901) fp 425
McKINNEY, ROBERT CHRISTIAN,
topography, 1856?-1918,
U.S.A.
S 48 (1918) 341
McKREADY, KELVIN (pseud. of
Edgar Gardner Murphy),
astronomy, 1869-1913
U.S.A.
S 38 (1913) 507
McLACHLAN, ROBERT, entomology,
1837-1904, England
L 75 (1905) 367-370
N 70 (1904) 106
S 19 (1904) 933
McLANE, JAMES WOODS, obstetrics,
1839-1912, U.S.A.
S 36 (1912) 784
McLAREN, SAMUEL BRUCE, mathe-
matics, 1876-1916, Japan
N 97 (1916) 547
McLAUGHLIN, HUGH C., linguis-
tics, 1811?-1896, U.S.A.
S 4 (1896) 140
McLEOD, CLEMENT HENRY, astron-
omy, 1851?-1917, Canada

S 47 (1918) 19
McLEOD, HERBERT, chemistry,
1841-1923, England
L A105 (1924) x-xi
McLEOD, JOHN JAMES RICKARD,
physiology, 1876-1935,
Scotland
P 82 (1913) P 205
McMAHON, CHARLES ALEXANDER,
geology, 1830-1904,
Ireland
L 75 (1905) 363-366
N 58 (1898) 33
N 69 (1904) 419-420
S 19 (1904) 439
McMURRAY, WILLIAM JOSIAH,
hygiene, 1842-1905, U.S.A.
S 22 (1905) 807
McMURTIE, WILLIAM, chemistry,
1851-1913, U.S.A.
S 37 (1913) 830
S 38 (1913) 185-187
McNAB, JAMES, botany, 1809?-
1878, Scotland
A 117 (1879) 179
N 19 (1878) 85
McNAB, WILLIAM RAMSAY, botany,
1844-1889, Scotland
N 41 (1889) 159-160
McNAIR, FRED WALTER, educa-
tion-engineering, 1862-
1924, U.S.A.
P 68 (1906) P 189
McNAMARA, WILLIAM HENRY,
surgery, 1844?-1915,
England
S 41 (1915) 163
McNEILL, BEDFORD, engineering-
mining, 1861?-1916, England
N 98 (1916) 94
McNEILL, SIR JOHN, surgery,
1795-1883, Scotland
E 14 (1886-1887) 129-130
McPHERSON, WILLIAM, chemistry,
1864-1951, U.S.A.
P 76 (1910) P 204
M'CULLOCH, JOHN, finance,
1807-1882, Scotland
E 12 (1882-1884) 28-29
McVAIL, SIR DAVID C., medi-
cine, 1845?-1917, Scotland
S 46 (1917) 563
MEAD, SAMUEL B., botany,
-1880, U.S.A.
A 123 (1882) 333
A 127 (1884) 242

MEADE, WILLIAM, geology,
-1833, Ireland
A 25 (1833-1834) 215-216
A 26 (1834) 209
MEADE-WALDO, GEOFFREY,
entomology, -1916,
England
S 43 (1916) 530
MEARS, LEVERETT, chemistry,
1850-1917, U.S.A.
S 45 (1917) 657
MÉCHAIN, PIERRE FRANÇOIS
ANDRÉ, astronomy, 1744-
1804, France
PM 20 (1804) 89.
MECKEL, JOHN FREDERICK,
anatomy, 1783?-1833,
Germany
L 3 (1830-1837) 232-233
MECZNIKOV, ELIAS, biology-
zoology, 1845-1916,
L B89 (1917) li-lix
MEDLICOTT, HENRT BENEDICT,
geology, 1829-1905,
Ireland
A 169 (1905) 473
L B79 (1907) xix-xxvi
N 71 (1905) 612-613
S 21 (1905) 677
MEEHAN, THOMAS, botany,
1826-1901, England
A 163 (1902) 164
N 65 (1901) 132
S 14 (1901) 863
MEEK, FIELDING BRADFORD,
paleontology, 1817-1876,
U.S.A.
A 113 (1877) 88, 169-171
MEEK, SETH EUGENE, zoology,
1859-1914, U.S.A.
A 188 (1914) 370
S 40 (1914) 95
MEIER, EDWARD DANIEL, engi-
neering, -1914, U.S.A.
S 40 (1914) 930
MEIGS, ARTHUR VINCENT,
medicine, 1850-1912, U.S.A.
S 35 (1912) 58
MEIKLEJOHN, JOHN M. D.,
education, -1902,
Scotland
S 15 (1902) 597
MEININGER, HEINRICH, physics,
1821?-1905, Germany
S 22 (1905) 886

MEISSEL, DANIEL FRIEDRICH
ERNST, mathematics, 1826-
1895, Germany
S 1 (1895) 500
MEISSL, EMERICH, agriculture,
-1905, Austria
S 21 (1905) 557, 677-678
MEISSNER, C.F., botany,
-1874, Switzerland
A 108 (1874) 72
MEISSNER, GEORG, physiology,
1829-1905, Germany
S 21 (1905) 678
MEISSNER, MAXIMILLIAN, zoology,
1861?-1908, Germany
S 27 (1908) 358
MELDE, FRANZ EMIL, physics,
1832-1901, Germany
S 13 (1901) 636
MELDOLA, RAPHAEL, chemistry,
1849-1915, England
A 190 (1915) 670
L A93 (1917) P xxix-
xxxvii
N 92 (1913) 405
N 96 (1915) 345-347
N 98 (1916) 125
S 42 (1915) 762
MELDRUM, CHARLES, mathe-
matics-meteorology, 1821-
1901, Scotland
L 75 (1905) 151-152
N 65 (1901) 9-11
S 14 (1901) 463, 780,
1022
MELL, PATRICK HUES, botany-
geology, 1850-1918, U.S.A.
S 48 (1918) 513
MELLONI, MACEDONIO, physics,
1798-1854, Italy
A 68 (1854) 431
A 69 (1855) 414-415
A 70 (1855) 143
MELLOR, CLIVE,
1876- ,
P 59 (1901) P 7
MELSHEIMER, FRIEDRICH
VALENTIN, entomology-
theology, 1749-1814,
Germany
P 76 (1910) 469
MELVILL, THOMAS, physics,
1726-1753, Scotland
N 94 (1914) 263
MELVILLE, GEORGE WALLACE,

exploration-naval archi-
tecture, 1841-1912, U.S.A.
P 64 (1903-1904) P 182-186
S 35 (1912) 447
MELVIN, ALONZO DORUS, medicine,
1862-1917, U.S.A.
S 46 (1917) 585
MENAULT, ERNEST, agriculture,
1831?-1903, France
S 18 (1903) 253
MENDEL, GREGOR JOHANN, biology,
1822-1884, Austria
A 174 (1907) 508
N 74 (1906) 640-641
S 32 (1910) 551
MENDELEYEV, DMITRI IVANOVICH,
chemistry, 1834-1907,
Russia
A 173 (1907) 244
L A84 (1910-1911) xvii-xxi
N 40 (1889) P 193-197
N 73 (1905) 130-131
N 75 (1907) 371-373
N 82 (1910) 412-417
P 40 (1891-1892) P fp
145, 261-266
P 69 (1906) P 285-286
S 25 (1907) 236
MENDENHALL, THOMAS CORWIN,
meteorology-physics,
1841-1924, U.S.A.
P 37 (1890) P fp 577,
690-695
P 85 (1914) P 517
MENDONÇA, A., bacteriology,
-1916, Brazil
S 43 (1916) 236
MENDOZA, A., microphotography,
-1918, Spain
S 48 (1918) 392
MENEGHINI, GIUSEPPE, zoology,
1811-1889, Italy
A 137 (1889) 422
A 138 (1889) 336
MENKE, . . ., exploration,
-1901, Germany
S 13 (1901) 667
MENOCAL, ANICETO GARCIA, en-
gineering, 1836-1908,
Cuba
S 28 (1908) 173
MENSCH, P. CALVIN, biology,
-1901, U.S.A.
S 14 (1901) 228
MENSCHUTKIN, NICOLAI ALEKSAN-
DROVICH, chemistry, 1842-

-1907, Russia
N 75 (1907) 397
S 25 (1907) 398
MERCALLI, GIUSEPPI, vul-
canology, 1850?-1914,
Italy
A 187 (1914) 336
S 39 (1914) 461
MERCATOR, GERARDUS (GERHARD
KREMER), geography-mathe-
matics, 1512-1594, Belgium
P 16 (1879-1880) P 494
P 29 (1886) P fp 289,
404-410
MERCER, JOHN, chemistry,
1791-1866, England
N 35 (1886) 145-147
MERCIER, CHARLES ANTHONY,
psychiatry, 1852-1919,
England
S 50 (1919) 303
MERCUR, JAMES, engineering,
-1896, U.S.A.
S 3 (1896) 703
MERCURIALIS, . . ., medicine,
1530-1607, Italy
S 31 (1910) 263-264, 666
MERGENTHALER, OTTMAR, invention,
1854-1899, Germany
S 10 (1899) 742
MERIAN, PETER, chemistry-
physics, 1795-1883,
Switzerland
Sl 1 (1883) 155-156
MÉRICOURT, LEROY, hygiene,
1826?-1901, France
S 14 (1901) 380
MERITENS, D., electricity,
-1898, France
S 8 (1898) 902
MERIVALE, J.H., engineering,
1851?-1916, England
S 44 (1916) 889
MERKEL, G., medicine, 1835-
, Germany
S 22 (1905) 157
MERLE, WALTER, meteorology,
fl.1340   ,
Sl 17 (1891) 257
MERRIAM, CLINTON HART, biology,
1855-1942, U.S.A.
P 66 (1904-1905) P 386
MERRIFIELD, CHARLES WATKINS,
mathematics, 1827-1884,
England
L 36 (1884) i-iii

S   40 (1914) 889
MICHAELSON, HENRY, forestry,
     -1904, U.S.A.
  S   19 (1904) 439
MICHAUX, ANDRÉ, botany,
  1746-1802, France
  P   73 (1904) 488-493
MICHAUX, FRANCOIS ANDRÉ,
  arboriculture-botany,
  1770-1855, France
  A   74 (1857) 161-177
  A   132 (1886) 466-473
von MICHEL, JULIUS, opthal-
  mology, 1843-1911, Germany
  S   34 (1911) 635
MICHELET, MME. JULES, biology,
     -1899, France
  S   9 (1899) 558
MICHELI, MARC, botany, 1845?-
  1902, Switzerland
  S   16 (1902) 437-438
MICHEL-LÉVY, AUGUSTE, geol-
  ogy-mineralogy, 1847?-1911,
  France
  A   182 (1911) 480
  N   87 (1911) 524-525
  S   34 (1911) 558
MICHELSON, ALBERT ABRAHAM,
  physics, 1852-1931, Germany
  A   145 (1893) 248-249
  A   177 (1909) 338
  N   77 (1907) 109-110
  N   117 (1926) P 1-6
  P   51 (1897) P 788
  P   72 (1908) P 283-284
  P   76 (1910) P 202
  S1   13 (1889) 463-464
  S   26 (1907) 898-899
MICHENER, EZRA, botany, 1794-
  1887, U.S.A.
  A   135 (1888) 263
MICHIE, PETER SMITH, philos-
  ophy-physics, 1839-1901,
  Scotland
  S   13 (1901) 316
von MICKWITZ, KARL AUGUST,
  paleontology, 1849-1910,
  Russia
  A   180 (1910) 96
  S   31 (1910) 854
MIDDLETON, JOHN HENRY, art,
  1847?-1896, England
  S   4 (1896) 75
MIERS, SIR HENRY ALEXANDER,
  crystallography-mineralogy,
  1858-1942, Brazil

N   54 (1896) 11
  S   48 (1918) 434-436
MIERS, JOHN, botany-engineering,
  1789-1879, England
  L   29 (1879) xxii-xxiii
  N   20 (1879) 614
  N   21 (1879) 11
MIERZEJEVSKI, J. L., psychiatry,
  1869-1908, Russia
  S   27 (1908) 677
MIESCHER, FRIEDERICH, phys-
  iology, 1844-1895,
  Switzerland
  S   2 (1895) 409
MIETSCHKE, . . ., entomology,
     -1897, Germany
  S   6 (1897) 700
MIK, JOSEPH, dipterology,
  1838?-1900, Austria
  S   12 (1900) 771
de MIKLUCHO-MAKLAY, NIKOLAI
  NIKOLAIVICH, Baron, geography,
  1846-1888, Russia
  N   27 (1883) 137, 184,
  371
MILDE, JULIUS, botany,
     -1871, Germany
  A   103 (1872) 153
MILES, MANLY, agriculture,
  1826-1898, U.S.A.
  P   54 (1898-1899) P fp 721,
  834-841
MILL, H. R., geography,
          ,
  E   20 (1892-1895) 511-512
MILL, JOHN STUART, philosophy-
  sociology, 1806-1873,
  England
  E   8 (1872-1875) 259-273
  N   8 (1873) 47
  P   3 (1873) P 367-388
  P   14 (1878-1879) 697-714
  P   15 (1879) 327-345, 750-
  759
  P   16 (1879-1880) 25-35,
  311-318, 501-507
  P   69 (1906) 451-457
  S   34 (1911) 49
MILLAIS, SIR JOHN EVERETT,
  zoology, 1829-1896,
  England
  S   6 (1897) 481
MILLARDET, ALEXIS, botany,
  1830-1902, France
  S   17 (1903) 37
MILLER, ALFRED BRASHEAR,

S 31 (1910) 341
S 39 (1914) 63
MITCHELL, WILLIAM, astron-
omy-mathematics, 1793-
1869, U.S.A.
A 97 (1869) 434
S 16 (1902) 958-959
MITCHELL-THOMSON, MITCHELL,
commerce, 1846-1918,
Scotland
E 40 (1919-1920) 8
MITSCHERLICH, EILHARD,
chemistry, 1794-1863,
Germany
A 86 (1863) 451
E 5 (1862-1866) 138
L 3 (1830-1837) 221
L 13 (1864) ix-xvi
MITSUKURI, KAKICHI, oceanog-
raphy-zoology, 1857-1909,
Japan
P 65 (1904) P 194
P 66 (1904-1905) P 24
P 75 (1909) P 615-618
S 30 (1909) 630-632
MITTAG-LEFFLER, MAGNUS GUSTAF,
mathematics, 1846-1927,
Sweden
L A119 (1928) P v-viii
N 55 (1897) P 320-321
N 120 (1927) 125, 626-628
S 43 (1916) 528
MIVART, ST. GEORGE JACKSON,
biology-zoology, 1827-1900,
England
A 159 (1900) 395
L 75 (1905) 95-100
N 61 (1900) 569-570
S 11 (1900) 556
M'KENDRICK, JOHN G., acoustics-
physiology,
E 21 (1895-1897) 520-521
M'LAREN, JOHN, law-mathematics,
1831-1910, Scotland
E 31 (1910-1911) 694-696
M'NAIR, JOHN,   ,
1801-1886, Scotland
E 14 (1886-1887) 138
M'NEILL, DUNCAN, LORD COLONSAY,
law, 1793-1874?, Scotland
E 8 (1872-1875) 445-453
MOBERG, JOHAN CHRISTIAN,
paleontology, 1854?-1915,
Sweden
A 191 (1916) 306
S 43 (1916) 274, 347

MOCHUS, . . ., science,
, Greece
N 77 (1908) 345
MÖBIUS, KARL AUGUST, zoology,
1825-1908, Germany
A 176 (1908) 100
N 78 (1908) 82-83
S 21 (1905) 398
S 27 (1908) 871
MÖBIUS, PAUL JULIUS, neurology-
psychiatry, 1853-1907,
Germany
S 25 (1907) 280, 916
MÖHL, HEINRICH, meteorology,
1832-1903, Germany
S 18 (1903) 767
MÖLLER, DIDRIK MAGNUS AXEL,
astronomy, 1830-1896,
Sweden
S 4 (1896) 793
MÖNNICH, PAUL LUDWIG FRIED-
RICH, meteorology, 1855-
1899, Germany
S 9 (1899) 158
MÖRICKE, WILHELM, geology,
1861-1897, Germany
S 6 (1897) 876
MOESTA, CARLOS GUILLELMO,
astronomy, 1825-1884,
Chile?
S1 4 (1884) 76
MOESTA, T.A.,
-1884,
S1 4 (1884) 76
MOGGRIDGE, JOHN TRAHERNE,
botany, 1842?-1874,
England
A 109 (1875) 69, 154
von MOHL, HUGO, botany,
1805-1872, Germany
A 103 (1872) 474
A 105 (1873) 393-395
E 8 (1872-1875) 14-15
L 23 (1875) i-vi
MOHN, HENRIK, meteorology,
1835-1916, Norway
A 193 (1917) 88
N 98 (1916) 211-212
S 41 (1915) 936
S 44 (1916) 493, 814
MOHR, KARL FRIEDRICH, chem-
istry, 1806-1879, Germany
N 20 (1879) 585
N 67 (1902) Supplement, 6
November, v-vi
N 71 (1904) 25-26

S   48 (1918) 415

MORETON, HENRY JOHN, Earl of
Ducie, geology, 1827-
, England
S   44 (1916) 52

MOREY, STEPHAN JULIUS,
zoology,   '
N   58 (1898) 429

MORGAN, AUGUSTUS DE--see DE
MORGAN

MORGAN, CONWY LLOYD, biology-
psychology, 1852-1936,
England
N   60 (1899) 32

MORGAN, LEWIS HENRY, anthro-
pology, 1818-1881, U.S.A.
A   123 (1882) 166
P   18 (1880-1881) P fr,
114-121
P   72 (1908) P 569-571
S   49 (1919) 163

MORGAN, WILLIAM, actuarial
statistics,   -1833,
L   3 (1830-1837) 226-227

MORICAND, ..., botany,
-1854, Switzerland
A   68 (1854) 429

MORICHINI, ..., physics,
-1837, Italy
L   4 (1837-1843) 18

MORIN, ARTHUR JULES, mathematics-physics, 1795-
1880, France
N   21 (1880) 349-350

MORIN, JEAN BAPTISTE, astrol-
ogy-medicine, 1583-1656,
France
Sl   2 (1883) 666

MORIS, GIUSEPPE, botany,
1796?-1869, Italy
A   99 (1870) 129

MORISON, GEORGE SHATTUCK,
engineering, 1842-1903,
U.S.A.
S   18 (1903) 61

MORLEY, EDWARD WILLIAMS,
chemistry-physics, 1838-
1923, U.S.A.
N   77 (1907) 110
S   26 (1907) 900-901

MORREN, C.F.D., botany,
1806?-1858, France
A   77 (1859) 443

MORREN, CHARLES JAMES EDWARD,
botany, 1833-1886, Belgium
A   133 (1887) 164

N   33 (1886) 447

MORRIESON, ROBERT, surgery,
1787-1864, Scotland
E   5 (1862-1866) 300-301

MORRIES-STIRLING, JOHN DAVY,
chemistry-metallurgy,
-1858,
E   4 (1857-1862) 112-114

MORRIS, EDWARD LYMAN, botany,
1870-1913, U.S.A.
S   38 (1913) 401, 476

MORRIS, JOHN, geology, 1810-
1886, England
N   2 (1870) 317-318
N   33 (1886) 248

MORRIS, JOHN GOTTLIEB, entomology, 1803-1895, U.S.A.
P   76 (1910) P 470-471

MORRIS, JOHN LEWIS, mechanics,
1842-1905, U.S.A.
S   22 (1905) 726

MORRISON, H.K., entomology,
-1885, U.S.A.
Sl   5 (1885) 532

MORRISON, SAMUEL LORD, en-
gineering, 1851?-1907,
England
S   25 (1907) 917

MORROW, G. E., agriculture,
1840?-1900, U.S.A.
S   11 (1900) 557

MORROW, PRINCE ALBERT, dermatology, 1846-1913, U.S.A.
S   37 (1913) 515

MORSE, EDWARD SYLVESTER,
anthropology-zoology, 1838-
1925, U.S.A.
P   13 (1878) P fr, 102-104
P   41 (1892) P 295
P   49 (1896) P 506
Sl   8 (1886) P 158
S   48 (1918) 66

MORSE, ELISHA WILSON, biology,
-1915, U.S.A.
S   41 (1915) 677

MORSE, SAMUEL FINLEY BREESE,
invention-telegraphy, 1791-
1872, U.S.A.
A   103 (1872) 399-400
N   5 (1872) 509
P   1 (1872) P fr, 115-116

MORSELLI, ENRICO AGOSTINO,
anthropology, 1852-1929,
Italy
P   52 (1897-1898) P 752-753

du MORTIER, BARTHELEMY CHARLES,

1796?-1878, Belgium
A 117 (1879) 179
de MORTILLET, LOUIS LAURENT
GABRIEL, anthropology,
1821-1898, France
N 58 (1898) 550
P 41 (1892) P 67
P 54 (1898-1899) P fp 433,
546-552
S 8 (1898) 509
MORTIMER, J. R., archeology,
1824?-1911, England
S 34 (1911) 376
MORTON, GEORGE HIGHFIELD,
geology, 1826-1900, England
S 11 (1900) 757
MORTON, HENRY, chemistry-
physics, 1836-1902, U.S.A.
A 163 (1902) 480
S 15 (1902) 758, 797, 858-
861
MORTON, JULIUS STERLING, agri-
culture, 1832-1902, U.S.A.
S 15 (1902) 718
MORTON, SAMUEL GEORGE, anthro-
pology-ethnology, 1799-
1851, U.S.A.
A 62 (1851) 144-146
A 63 (1852) 153-178
MOSELEY, HENRY, physics, 1801-
1872, England
A 103 (1872) 320
MOSELEY, HENRY GWYN JEFFREY,
physics, 1887-1915, England
A 190 (1915) 524
L A93 (1917) xxii-xxviii
N 96 (1915) 33-34
N 98 (1916) 279
MOSELEY, HENRY NOTTIDGE, biol-
ogy, 1844-1891, England
A 143 (1892) 80
N 37 (1887) 118
N 45 (1891) 79-80
MOSENTHAL, HENRY D., chemistry,
1850?-1912, England
S 37 (1913) 56
MOSES, ALFRED JOSEPH, mineral-
ogy, 1859-1920, U.S.A.
A 199 (1920) 389
MOSES, OTTO A., chemistry-
geology, 1846-1906, U.S.A.
S 23 (1906) 78
von MOSETIG-MOORHOF, ALBERT,
surgery,   -1907, Austria
S 25 (1907) 718
MOSSMAN, ROBERT C., meteorology,

E 38 (1917-1918) 233
MOSSO, ANGELO, physiology,
1846-1910, Italy
N 85 (1910) 174-175
S 32 (1910) 834
S 39 (1914) 782
MOTLEY, JOHN LOTHROP, diplomacy-
writer, 1814-1877, U.S.A.
E 9 (1875-1878) 508-511
Sl 13 (1889) 187
MOTORA, YUJIRO, psychology,
-1912, Japan
S 37 (1913) 145
MOTT, SIR FREDERICK WALKER,
physiology, 1853-1926,
England
L B100 (1926) P xxviii-xxx
N 54 (1896) 11
MOUAT, FREDERIC JOHN, medicine,
1816-1897, England
S 5 (1897) 223
MOUAT, SIR JAMES, surgery,
1815?-1899, England
S 9 (1899) 158
MOUCHEZ, ERNEST AMÉDÉE
BARTHÉLEMY, astronomy,
1821-1892, Spain
N 46 (1892) 253
MOUGEOT, J. B., botany, 1776?-
1858, France
A 77 (1859) 443
MOUQUIN-TANDON, C. HORACE
BENEDICT ALFRED, botany,
-1863, France
A 87 (1864) 288
MUDGE, B. F., geology,
-1879, U.S.A.
A 119 (1880) 82
MÜHLBERG, FRITZ, geology,
1840-1915, Switzerland
S 42 (1915) 157
von der MÜHLL, KARL, physics,
1841-1912, Switzerland
S 36 (1912) 14
MÜLLER, ...,
Austria
S 8 (1898) 667
MÜLLER, ...,
-1898, Austria
S 10 (1899) 782
von MÜLLER, ..., zoology,
-1915?, Germany
S 41 (1915) 500
MÜLLER, CARL, botany,   -1870,
Germany
A 103 (1872) 152

MÜLLER, EGON, physics, 1873-
1902, Germany
S 15 (1902) 758
MÜLLER, ERIK, anatomy, 1866-
, Sweden
S 44 (1916) 632
von MUELLER, FERDINAND, baron,
botany-physics, 1825-1896,
Germany
A 152 (1896) 464
L 63 (1898) xxxii-xxxvi
N 54 (1896) 596
S 4 (1896) 652-653
MÜLLER, F. A., zoology, 1816?-
1905, Austria
S 22 (1905) 868
MÜLLER, FRIEDRICH, ethnology,
1834-1898, Bohemia
S 7 (1898) 829
MULLER, HERMANN, botany-ento-
mology, 1829-1883, Germany
A 127 (1884) 243
N 28 (1883) 81, 462-463,
513-514
Sl 2 (1883) 484, P 487-488
MÜLLER, HUGO HEINRICH WILHELM,
chemistry, 1833-1915,
Germany
A 190 (1915) 96
L A95 (1919) P xii-xxv
N 95 (1915) 376-377
S 25 (1907) 917
S 41 (1915) 938
MÜLLER, JOHANN (ARGOMIENSIS),
lichenology, 1828?-1896,
Switzerland
A 151 (1896) 326
MÜLLER, JOHANN FRIEDRICH
THEODORE (FRITZ), zoology,
1821?-1897, Germany
N 56 (1897) 546-548
von MÜLLER, JOHANNES PETER,
physiology, 1801-1858,
Germany
A 76 (1858) 155
N 26 (1882) 408-409
P 72 (1908) P 512-533
P 73 (1908) P 287-288
S 4 (1896) 653
S 5 (1897) 653
S 10 (1899) 620-621
MÜLLER, KARL, biology, 1824?-
1905, Germany
S 22 (1905) 606
S 26 (1907) 61
MÜLLER, KARL, agriculture,

-1897, Germany
S 6 (1897) 805
MÜLLER, KARL, oceanography,
-1914, Germany
S 41 (1915) 129
MÜLLER, KARL ALEXANDER, agri-
culture, 1828-1906, Sweden
S 23 (1906) 478
MÜLLER, MAX, surgery, -1896,
Germany
S 4 (1896) 653
MÜLLER, SOPHUS OTTO, archeol-
ogy-biology, 1846-1934,
Sweden
P 47 (1895) P 12-15
P 68 (1906) P 94-96
MÜLLER, WILHELM, anatomy,
-1909, Germany
S 30 (1909) 82
von MÜLLER, WILHELM, technol-
ogy, -1899, Germany
S 9 (1899) 525
MÜNCH, . . ., physics, 1820?-
1895,
S 2 (1895) 340
MUENK, KARL, chemistry,
-1915, Germany
S 42 (1915) 336
MÜNSTERBERG, HUGO, psychology,
1863-1916, Germany
P 66 (1904-1905) P 26
S 44 (1916) 887
S 45 (1917) 81-82
MÜNTER, JULIUS, botany,
-1885, Germany
Sl 5 (1885) 264
MÜTTRICH, ANTON, physics,
1834?-1905, Germany
S 21 (1905) 158
MUHLENBERG, GOTTHILF HENRY
ERNEST, botany, 1753-1815,
U.S.A.
P 45 (1894) P fp 577,
689-698
MUIR, JOHN, biology-geology,
1838-1914, Scotland
A 189 (1915) 230
P 86 (1915) P 310
S 41 (1915) 353-354
S 45 (1917) 103-109
S 46 (1917) 261
MUIR, JOHN, orientalist,
1810-1882, Scotland
E 12 (1882-1884) 34-41

NEGRELLI, ALOIS, surveying,
, Germany
S 38 (1913) 401
NEGRI, CHRISTOPHER, geog-
raphy, 1810?-1896, Italy
S 3 (1896) 323
NEISSER, ALBERT LUDWIG
SIEGMUND, pathology, 1855-
1916, Germany
S 44 (1916) 198
NELATON, CHARLES, surgery,
-1911, France
S 34 (1911) 147
NELSON, EDWARD THOMSON, biol-
ogy, -1897, U.S.A.
S 5 (1897) 442
NELSON, HOWARD A., geology,
-1915, U.S.A.
S 42 (1915) 489
NELSON, JULIUS, biology, 1858-
1916, Denmark
S 43 (1916) 274
NELSON, THOMAS, publisher,
1822-1892, Scotland
E 19 (1891-1892) lviii-
lxii
E 20 (1892-1895) 9
von NENCKI, MARCELLUS, chem-
istry, 1847-1901, Poland
N 74 (1906) 173-174
S 14 (1901) 821, 889
NERNST, WALTHER HERMANN, chem-
istry, 1864-1941, Germany
N 90 (1913) 641-642
NERY DELGADO, J. F., geology,
1844?-1908, Portugal
S 28 (1908) 441
NESBIT, J. C., geology,
-1862,
A 86 (1863) 278
NESSLER, JULIUS, chemistry,
1827-1905, Germany
S 21 (1905) 758
NETTLESHIP, EDWARD, ophthal-
mology, 1845-1913, England
N 92 (1913) 297
NETTLETON, EDWIN S., agricul-
ture-engineering, 1831-
1901, U.S.A.
S 13 (1901) 717
NEUFELD, KARL ALBERT, nutri-
tion, 1866?-1914, Germany
S 39 (1914) 280
von NEUGEBAUER, F. L., gynecol-
ogy, -1916, Poland
S 43 (1916) 236

NEUHAUSS, RICHARD GUSTAV,
anthropology, 1855-1915,
Germany
S 41 (1915) 500
NEUMANN, FRANZ ERNST, mathe-
matics-physics, 1798-1895,
Germany
L 60 (1897) viii-xi
N 52 (1895) 176
N 53 (1895) 110
S 1 (1895) 668
S 8 (1898) 704
NEUMANN, KARL GOTTFRIED,
mathematics, 1832-1925,
Germany
S 15 (1902) 957
von NEUMAYER, GEORG BALTHASAR,
geography-meteorology, 1826-
1909, Germany
L A83 (1909-1910) xi-xiv
N 80 (1909) 402-403
S 24 (1906) 125
S 29 (1909) 931
NEUMAYR, MELCHIOR, paleontol-
ogy, 1845-1890, Austria
A 139 (1890) 326
von NEUSSER, EDMUND, medicine,
1852-1912, Austria
S 36 (1912) 211
NEVILL, GEOFFREY, conchology,
1843-1885, England
N 31 (1885) 435
Sl 5 (1885) 323
NEVILL, HUGH, zoology,
-1897,
S 5 (1897) 802
NEVILLE, FRANCIS HENRY, chem-
istry-physics, 1847?-1915,
N 56 (1897) 56
N 95 (1915) 432
S 42 (1915) 50-51, 119
NEWALL, ROBERT STIRLING, en-
gineering, 1812-1889,
England
L 46 (1890) xxxiii-xxxv
N 40 (1849) 13, 59
NEWBERRY, JOHN STRONG, geol-
ogy-medicine, 1822-1892,
U.S.A.
A 145 (1893) 79-80
A 146 (1893) 159
N 47 (1893) 276-277
P 9 (1876) P fp 280, 490-
492
S 10 (1898) 678-679
S 38 (1913) 607

PM III 8 (1836) 139-147,
  211-226
S 1 (1895) 141-157
S 2 (1895) 415-416
S 38 (1913) 46
S 50 (1919) 41-43
NEWTON, JOHN, engineering,
  1823-1895, U.S.A.
P 29 (1886-1887) P fp 721,
  834-840
S 1 (1895) 528
de NICÉVILLE, C. LIONEL A.,
  entomology,   -1901?,
S 15 (1902) 115-116
NICHÉLS, R., geology,
      -1917, France
S 46 (1917) 635
NICHOLAS, FRANCIS H., writer,
      -1904?, U.S.A.
S 21 (1905) 38
NICHOLS, EDWARD LEAMINGTON,
  physics, 1854-1937, England
P 70 (1907) P 98, 188
S 49 (1919) 211
S 50 (1919) 269-271
NICHOLS, ERNEST FOX, physics,
  1869-1924, U.S.A.
P 75 (1909) P 311
NICHOLS, FRANCIS,
      -1839, U.S.A.
A 38 (1839-1840) 193
NICHOLS, OTHNIEL FOSTER, en-
  gineering, 1845-1908,
  U.S.A.
S 27 (1908) 397
NICHOLSON, SIR CHARLES, medi-
  cine, 1808?-1903, Australia
S 18 (1903) 703
NICHOLSON, GEORGE, biology,
      -1908, England
S 28 (1908) 481
NICHOLSON, HENRY ALLEYNE,
  paleontology-zoology, 1844-
  1899, England
L 75 (1905) 35-38
N 56 (1897) 56-57
N 59 (1899) 298-299
S 9 (1899) 158
NICKLÉS, FRANÇOIS JOSEPH
  JÉRÔME, chemistry, 1820-
  1869, France
A 97 (1869) 434
NICOL, JAMES, geology-mineral-
  ogy, 1810-1879, Scotland
E 10 (1878-1880) 352-353
N 19 (1879) 590

S 25 (1907) 117-118
NICOL, WILLIAM, mineralogy-
  physics, c.1768-1851,
  Scotland
A 62 (1851) 446
N 73 (1906) 340
NICOLIS, ENRICO, geology,
      -1908, Italy
S 28 (1908) 441
NICOLLET, JOSEPH NICOLAS, ex-
  ploration-mathematics, 1786-
  1843, France
A 45 (1843) 404
NICOLSON, J. T., engineering,
  1860-1913, England
N 91 (1913) 351
NIEBUHR, BARTHOLD GEORG, geog-
  raphy-history, 1776-1831,
  Denmark
P 65 (1904) P 275
NIEMEYER, AUGUST HERMANN,
  theology-writer, 1754-1828,
  Germany
A 14 (1828) 381-382
NIEMILOWICZ, L., chemistry,
      -1904, Poland
S 20 (1904) 159
NIEPCE, JOSEPH NICEPHORE,
  photography-physics, 1765-
  1833, France
N 16 (1877) 142, 501
NIETZKI, RUDOLF HUGO, chemistry,
  1847-1917, Germany
S 49 (1919) 118
NIETZSCHE, FRIEDRICH WILHELM,
  philosophy, 1844-1900,
  Germany
S 12 (1900) 380
NIEUWLAND, PIETER, astronomy-
  mathematics, 1764-1794,
PM 1 (1798) 69-76
NIKITIN, SERGEI NIKOLAEVICH,
  geology, 1850-1909, Russia
A 179 (1910) 276
NILES, WILLIAM HARMON, geology,
  1838-1910, U.S.A.
P 55 (1899) P 460
S 32 (1910) 426
NILSON, LARS FREDERIK, chem-
  istry, 1840-1899, Sweden
S 9 (1899) 852
S 15 (1902) 423
NILSSON, ALBERT, forestry,
      -1906, Germany
S 23 (1906) 558-559
NILSSON, SVEN, zoology, 1787-

S   43 (1916) 530
OPPERT, JULIUS, archeology,
    1825-1905, Germany
    N   72 (1905) 432-433
von OPPOLZER, EGON, astronomy-
    mathematics, 1869-1907,
    Austria
    S   26 (1907) 61, 188
von OPPOLZER, THEODOR, astron-
    omy, 1841-1886, Austria
    N   35 (1887) 224-225
    P   27 (1885) 341
ORDRONAUX, JOHN, law-medicine,
    1830-1908, U.S.A.
    S   27 (1908) 198
ORDWAY, JOHN MORSE, metallurgy,
    1823-1909, U.S.A.
    S   30 (1909) 111
O'REILLY, ROBERT MAITLAND,
    medicine, 1845-1912, U.S.A.
    S   36 (1912) 669
ORIANI, BARNABA, astronomy,
    1752-1832, Italy
    A   25 (1833-1834) 186-187
    L   3 (1830-1837) 153
ORMEROD, ELEANOR ANNE, ento-
    mology, 1828-1901, England
    N   64 (1901) 330
    N   70 (1904) 219-220
    S   14 (1901) 158
ORMOND, ALEXANDER T., phi-
    losophy, 1848?-1915, U.S.A.
    S   42 (1915) 898
ORMOND, R. T., meteorology,
    -1914, Scotland
    S   39 (1914) 323
ORNIE, T., literature,
    -1832, Sweden
    A   23 (1832-1833) 370
ORPHANIDÈS, THÉODORE G.,
    botany, 1817?-1886, Greece
    A 133 (1887) 165
ORTON, EDWARD FRANCIS BAXTER,
    geology, 1829-1899, U.S.A.
    A 158 (1899) 400
    N   61 (1899-1900) 59
    P   56 (1899-1900) P fp 513,
        607-613
    S   10 (1899) P fp 265, 581
    S   11 (1900) 1-11
ORTON, JAMES, biology, 1830-
    1877, U.S.A.
    A 114 (1877) 512
    S   42 (1915) 50
ORTON, KENNEDY JOSEPH PREVITÉ,
    chemistry, 1872-1930,

England
    L A129 (1930) P xi-xiv
OSBORN, HENRY FAIRFIELD,
    paleontology-zoology, 1857-
    1935, U.S.A.
    N   70 (1904) 418
    P   66 (1904-1905) P 10
    S   46 (1917) 477
OSBORN, SHERARD, exploration,
    1822-1875, England
    A 110 (1875) 80
OSLER, ABRAHAM FOLLETT,
    meteorology, 1808-1903,
    England
    L   75 (1905) 328-334
    N   68 (1903) 448
    S   17 (1903) 837
OSLER, EDWARD, medicine,
    -1917, England
    S   46 (1917) 286
OSLER, SIR WILLIAM, medicine,
    1849-1919, Canada
    A 199 (1920) 156
    L B92 (1921) P xvii-xxiv
    N   58 (1898) 33
    P   67 (1905) P 569-571
    P   86 (1915) P 207-208
    S   20 (1904) 285
    S   50 (1919) 244-246
OSMOND, FLORIS, metallurgy,
    1849-1912, France
    N   89 (1912) 454-455
    S   36 (1912) 143
OSSIANNIKOV, PHILIP, anatomy,
    1827?-1906, Russia
    S   24 (1906) 96
OSSOVSKI, GODFRYD, geology,
    -1897, Russia
    S   5 (1897) 916
OSTENDORF, F., agriculture,
    -1915, Germany
    S   41 (1915) 678
von der OSTEN-SACKEN, CARL
    ROBERT ROMANOVICH, baron,
    biology-entomology, 1828-
    1906, Russia
    A 172 (1906) 194
    P   76 (1910) P 468-473
    S   23 (1906) 927
OSTWALD, CARL WILHELM WOLFGANG,
    chemistry, 1853-1932, Latvia
    A 155 (1898) 221-222
    A 167 (1904) 483
    N   64 (1901) P 428-430
    N   69 (1904) 387-388
    N   70 (1904) 422-423

PAGE, DAVID, geology, 1814-
1879, Scotland
N 19 (1879) 444
PAGET, SIR GEORGE EDWARD,
medicine, 1809-1892,
England
L 50 (1892) xiii
PAGET, SIR JAMES, medicine-
pathology, 1814-1899,
England
L 75 (1905) 136-140
N 61 (1900) 256
S 11 (1900) 39
PAGNOUL, CÉCILIEN AIMÉ JOSEPH,
agriculture, 1822-1912,
France
S 37 (1913) 16
PAINE, JOHN ALSOP, archeology-
botany, 1840-1912, U.S.A.
S 36 (1912) 238
PAINE, TIMOTHY O., egyptology,
-1895,
S 2 (1895) 849
PAINTER, JOSEPH H., botany,
-1908, U.S.A.
S 28 (1908) 921
PAITO, A. de CERQNEIRA, chem-
istry, -1896?,
S 3 (1896) 98
PALADINO, GIOVANNI, physiol-
ogy, 1842?-1917, Italy
S 45 (1917) 307
PALEY, F. A., classics,
-1889?, England
Sl 13 (1889) 381
PALGRAVE (COHEN), SIR FRANCIS,
history-literature, 1788-
1861, England
L 12 (1863) xiii-xx
PALGRAVE, SIR ROBERT H. INGLIS,
economics, 1826-1919,
England
S 44 (1916) 52
S 49 (1919) 191
PALISSY, BERNARD, chemistry,
c.1510-1589, France
N 93 (1914) 518
PALLADINO, EUSAPIA, extra-
sensory perception?,
, Italy
S 31 (1910) 776-780
PALLAS, PETER SIMON, geology,
1741-1811, Germany
S 6 (1897) 927
PALMER, MRS. ALICE FREEMAN,
education, 1855-1902, U.S.A.

S 16 (1902) 997
PALMER, ARTHUR WILLIAM, chem-
istry, 1861-1904, England
S 19 (1904) 276
PALMER, EDWARD, biology, 1821-
, England
P 78 (1899) P 341-354
PALMER, EDWARD HENRY, explora-
tion-linguistics, 1840-
1882, England
N 28 (1883) 292-293
PALMIERI, LUIGI, mathematics-
physics, 1807-1896, Italy
A 152 (1896) 398
S 4 (1896) 404
PAMPLIN, WILLIAM, botany,
1807?-1899, England
N 61 (1899-1900) 59
S 10 (1899) 863
PANCOAST, WILLIAM H., surgery,
-1897, U.S.A.
S 5 (1897) 103
PANTON, ARTHUR WILLIAM, mathe-
matics, 1846?-1906, Ireland
S 25 (1907) 78
PANUM, PETER LUDWIG, physiol-
ogy, 1820-1885, Denmark
Sl 6 (1885) 20
PAPE, CARL JOHANNES WILHELM
THEODOR, physics, 1836-
1906, Germany
S 23 (1906) 891
PAPIN, DENIS, invention-physics,
1647-1714?, France
E 2 (1844-1850) 211-214
N 21 (1880) 19
N 24 (1881) 377-379
N 25 (1881) 125-126
P 12 (1877-1878) P 25
PEPPENHEIM, ARTUR, morphology,
1870-1916, Germany
S 45 (1917) 236
PARACELSUS (PHILIPPUS AUREOLUS
PARACELSUS THEOPHRASTUS
BOMBAST von HOHENHEIM),
alchemy-medicine, 1493-1541,
Switzerland
N 50 (1894) 598-600
N 88 (1912) 473-474
PARÉ, AMBROISE, medicine-
surgery, 1510-1590, France
N 58 (1898) 49-50
S 12 (1900) 257
S 41 (1915) 846-848
PARK, ROSWELL, surgery, 1852-
1914, U.S.A.

N   43 (1891) P 481-485
N   47 (1892) 204-205
N   52 (1895) 550-551, 576
N   53 (1895) 110-111
N   55 (1896) 204, 275-276
N   56 (1897) 508-512
N   58 (1898) 290
N   64 (1901) 163
N   65 (1901) 97-99
N   70 (1904) 329
N   95 (1915) 228-229
P   20 (1881-1882) P fp 721,
    823-829
P   21 (1882) 667-679
P   25 (1884) 235-244
P   27 (1885) 86-96
P   28 (1885-1886) 289-295
P   66 (1904-1905) P 191-192
P   79 (1911) 1-19, P 518
P   85 (1914) P 519
S1   2 (1883) 414
S1   3 (1884) 546-549
S   2 (1895) 601-613, 620-
    621, 751, 804
S   3 (1896) 130, 185-189,
    510
S   4 (1896) 567
S   5 (1897) 56
S   6 (1897) 253
S   7 (1898) 836-837
S   14 (1901) 620
S   15 (1902) 422-423
S   16 (1902) 239, 517, 559
S   32 (1910) 505
S   33 (1911) 59
S   35 (1912) 941-943
S   36 (1912) 299
S   42 (1915) 920-921
PATERSON, ANDREW MELVILLE,
   anatomy, 1863?-1919, England
   S 49 (1919) 263, 328
PATIN, GUY, medicine, 1601-
   1672, France
   S   8 (1898) 367
PATON, DIARMID NOËL, physiol-
   ogy, 1850-1928, Scotland
   L B104 (1929) P ix-xii
PATRICK, DAVID, editor, 1849-
   1914, Scotland
   E 35 (1914-1915) 9-10
PATRICK, GEORGE EDWARD, chem-
   istry, 1851-1916, U.S.A.
   S 43 (1916) 639
PATTERSON, CARLILE POLLOCK,
   geodesy, 1816-1881, U.S.A.
   S 44 (1916) 47

PAUCHON, ALBERT, botany,
      -1904, France
   S 20 (1904) 774
PAUL, CARL MARIA, geology,
   1838-1900, Austria
   S 11 (1900) 476
PAULISON, JOHN PAUL, astron-
   omy,   -1895,
   S   1 (1895) 667
PAULMIER, FREDERICK CLARK,
   zoology, 1872?-1906, U.S.A.
   S 23 (1906) 556-557
PAULSEN, ADAM FREDERIK WIVET,
   meteorology, 1833-1907,
   Denmark
   N 75 (1907) 299
   S 25 (1907) 238, 674
PAULSEN, FRIEDRICH, philosophy,
   1846-1908, Germany
   S 28 (1908) 271
PAULY, AUGUST, zoology,
      -1914, Germany
   S 39 (1914) 421
PAUR, G., statistics,   -1914,
   Germany
   S 40 (1914) 812
PAVESI, PIETRO, zoology,
      -1907, Italy
   S 26 (1907) 846
PAVLOV, E. W., surgery,
      -1916, Russia
   S 43 (1916) 460, 682, 710
PAVLOV, IVAN PETROVICH, physiol-
   ogy, 1849-1936, Russia
   A 191 (1916) 382
   N 89 (1912) 534
   N 96 (1915) 374
   N 97 (1916) 9-11
   N 115 (1925) P 1-3
   S 43 (1916) 273, 460, 682,
   710
PAVLOV, LEV, medicine, 1847?-
   1906, Russia
   S 24 (1906) 789
PAVY, FREDERICK WILLIAM, medi-
   cine, 1829-1911, England
   N 87 (1911) 421-432
PAXTON, SIR JOSEPH, architec-
   ture-botany, 1801-1865,
   England
   A 90 (1865) 140
   A 91 (1866) 264
PAYER, JEAN BAPTISTE, botany,
   1818-1860, France
   A 81 (1861) 267-268, 462
von PAYER, JULIUS, exploration,

1842-1915, Bohemia
S 42 (1915) 335

PEABODY, GEORGE, philanthropy,
1795-1869, U.S.A.
A 98 (1869) 442-445

PEABODY, GEORGE LIVINGSTON,
medicine, 1850-1914, U.S.A.
S 40 (1914) 667

PEACH, BENJAMIN NEEVE, geology,
1842-1926, England
L B100 (1926) xi-xiii
N 46 (1892) 37

PEACH, CHARLES WILLIAM, zoolo-
gy, 1800-1886, England
E 8 (1872-1875) 509-512
N 33 (1886) 446-447
N 99 (1917) 221-222
Sl 7 (1886) 323

PEACOCK, GEORGE, mathematics,
1791-1858, England
N 99 (1917) 221-222
S 13 (1901) 516

PEAL, SAMUEL EDWARD, biology,
1834-1897,
N 56 (1897) 421

PEALE, ALBERT CHARLES, paleo-
botany, 1849-1913, U.S.A.
A 189 (1915) 230
S 40 (1914) 888

PEALE, CHARLES WILLSON, art-
paleontology, 1741-1827,
U.S.A.
P 75 (1906) 221-238
S 25 (1907) 297

PEALE, TITIAN RAMSAY, art-
biology, 1799-1885, U.S.A.
A 130 (1885) 168
P 75 (1906) 221-238
Sl 6 (1885) 20

PEARCE, JAMES ALFRED, administration, 1805-1862, U.S.A.
A 85 (1863) 155

PEARSON, GEORGE, chemistry-
medicine, 1751-1828, England
PM 15 (1803) P 274-277

PEARSON, HAROLD HENRY WELCH,
botany, 1870-1916, England
A 193 (1917) 88
L B89 (1917) 1x-lxvii
N 98 (1916) 211
S 44 (1916) 782

PEARSON, KARL, biology-mathe-
matics, 1857-1936, England
N 54 (1896) 11
N 59 (1898) 139

PEARSON, LEONARD, medicine-
zoology, 1868-1909, U.S.A.

S 30 (1909) 520
S 43 (1917) 924-925

PEARSON, WILLIAM, astronomy,
1767-1847, England
L 5 (1843-1850) 712

PEARY, ROBERT EDWIN, exploration, 1856-1920, U.S.A.
A 199 (1920) 226

PEASE, W. HARPER, zoology,
-1872, U.S.A.
A 103 (1872) 320

PEATE, JOHN, optics, 1820-1903,
Ireland
S 17 (1903) 559

PÉAU de ST. GILLES, LÉON,
chemistry, 1832-1863, France
A 86 (1863) 402

von PECHMANN, HANS, chemistry,
1850-1902, Germany
S 15 (1902) 838

PECHUEL-LÖSCHE, MORITZ EDUARD,
geography, 1840-1913,
Germany
S 38 (1913) 122

PECK, . . ., biology,   -1895,
S 1 (1895) 500

PECK, CHARLES HORTON, botany,
1833-1917, U.S.A.
S 40 (1914) 48
S 41 (1915) 202
S 46 (1917) 58

PECK, JAMES INGRAHAM, biology,
1863-1898, U.S.A.
S 8 (1898) 667-668, 744,
783

PECK, LOUIS W., physics, 1851?-
1898, U.S.A.
A 157 (1899) 248

PECK, WILLIAM GUY, mathematics,
1820-1892, U.S.A.
Sl 19 (1892) 102

PECKHAM, GEORGE WILLIAMS, en-
tomology, 1845-1914, U.S.A.
N 46 (1892) 611
S 39 (1914) 136

PECKHAM, STEPHEN FARNUM, chem-
istry, 1839-1918, U.S.A.
A 196 (1918) 620
S 21 (1905) 879-880
S 48 (1918) 67

PECLET, JEAN CLAUDE EUGÈNE,
physics, 1793-1857, France
A 75 (1858) 430-431

PEDDIE, WILLIAM, physics,
E 22 (1897-1899) 730-731

PEDERSEN, JAMES, zoology,
1811-1870, Norway

A   100 (1870) 436-437
PEDLER, SIR ALEXANDER, chem-
istry, 1850?-1918, England
A   196 (1918) 480
N   46 (1892) 37
S   47 (1918) 608
PEDROSO, . . ., geography,
-1910, Portugal
S   32 (1910) 405
PEEK, SIR CUTHBERT EDGAR, as-
tronomy-meteorology, 1855?-
1901, England
S   14 (1901) 158
PEEL, SIR ROBERT, administra-
tion, 1788-1850, England
L   5 (1843-1850) 1026
PEET, STEPHEN DENISON, anthro-
pology-editor, 1831-1914,
U.S.A.
P   41 (1892) P 305-307
S   40 (1914) 236
von PEETZ, HERMANN, geology,
-1908, Russia
S   28 (1908) 404
PEILE, JOHN, philology, 1838-
1910, England
N   84 (1910) 467, 496
PEIRCE, BENJAMIN, mathematics-
physics, 1809-1880, U.S.A.
A   120 (1880) 435-436
A   121 (1881) 337
A   122 (1881) 167-178
N   22 (1880) 607-608
P   18 (1880-1881) P fp 577,
691-695
S   5 (1897) 933
S   10 (1899) 632-634
PEIRCE, BENJAMIN OSGOOD,
mathematics-physics, 1854-
1914, U.S.A.
A   187 (1914) 208
P   84 (1914) P 412
S   37 (1913) 783
S   39 (1914) 135, 274-277
S   44 (1916) 46-47
PEIRCE, CHARLES SANTIAGO
SANDERS, physics-psychology,
1839-1914, U.S.A.
A   187 (1914) 566
S   39 (1914) 641
PEIRCE, JAMES MILLS PERKINS,
astronomy-mathematics,
1834-1906, U.S.A.
A   171 (1906) 408
S   23 (1906) 519, 637-638
S   24 (1906) 40-48

PELLAT, JOSEPH SOLANGE HENRI,
physics, 1850-1909, France
N   82 (1910) 287
PELLERIN, ARTHUR, botany,
-1900, France
S   12 (1900) 934
PELOUZE, THÉOPHILE JULES,
chemistry, 1807-1867, France
A   94 (1867) 137-138
PÉNAUD, ALPHONSE, aeronautics-
invention, 1850-1880, France
S   36 (1912) 336-337
PENCK, FRIEDRICH CARL ALBRECHT,
geology, 1858-1945, Germany
N   76 (1907) 605
PENFIELD, SAMUEL LEWIS,
mineralogy, 1856-1906,
U.S.A.
A   172 (1906) 264, P 353-
367
S   24 (1906) 221, 252-253
PENGELLY, WILLIAM, geology,
1812-1894, England
A   147 (1894) 484
L   59 (1896) xxxix-xli
N   49 (1894) 536-537
N   57 (1897) 4-6
P   55 (1899) P fr, 113-131
PENGER, CHRISTIAN, surgery,
1850?-1902, U.S.A.
S   15 (1902) 438
PENHALLOW, DAVID PEARCE,
botany, 1854-1910, U.S.A.
A   180 (1910) 431
N   85 (1910) 16
P   76 (1910) P 204
S   32 (1910) 626
PENIX, L., chemistry, 1862?-
1917, Italy
S   45 (1917) 429
PENNA, JOSÉ, medicine,   -1919,
Argentina
S   49 (1919) 539
PENNANT, THOMAS, biology,
1726-1798, Wales
A   37 (1839) 146-155
S   37 (1913) 404-405
PENNELL, H. L. L., exploration,
-1916, England
S   44 (1916) 17
PENNEY, FREDERICK, chemistry,
1817-1869, England
E   7 (1869-1872) 25-26
N   1 (1869) 138
PENNY, JOHN, medicine,   -1913,
Scotland

1714-1788, England
  S   12 (1900) 259-261
POTTER, . . ., geography,
      -1899, France
  S   9 (1899) 229
POUCHET, GEORGE, anthropology,
  1833?-1894,
  A   147 (1894) 484
POULTON, EDWARD BAGNALL, biol-
  ogy, 1856-1943, England
  N   94 (1914) 368
de POURTALES, LOUIS FRANÇOIS,
  zoology, 1823-1880, France
  A   120 (1880) 160, 253-255
  N   22 (1880) 322-323, 337,
      371-372
  P   18 (1880-1881) P fp 433,
      549-552
POWELL, BADEN, astronomy-
  mathematics, 1796-1860,
  England
  L   11 (1862) xxvi-xxix
POWELL, HUGH, microscopy-
  optics,   -1884?, England
  Sl   3 (1884) 210
POWELL, HUNTER H., medicine,
  S   44 (1916) 17
POWELL, JOHN WESLEY, ethnol-
  ogy-geology, 1834-1902,
  U.S.A.
  A   164 (1902) 377-382
  P   20 (1881-1882) P fp 289,
      390-397
  P   41 (1892) P 296-300
  S   16 (1902) fp 481, P 561-
      567, 782, 783-790
  S   20 (1904) 854
POWELL, SIR RICHARD DOUGLAS,
  medicine, 1842-1925, England
  N   76 (1907) 235
POWELL, WILLIAM BRAMWELL, edu-
  cation, 1836-1904, U.S.A.
  S   19 (1904) 318
POWER, SIR WILLIAM HENRY,
  medicine, 1842-1916, England
  L   B90 (1919) i-viii
  N   52 (1895) 33
  N   77 (1907) 111
  S   26 (1907) 902
  S   44 (1916) 270
POWERS, ABNER HOWARD, surgery,
  1856?-1916,
  S   43 (1916) 777
POWYS, THOMAS LITTLETON, Baron
  Lilford, biology, 1833-1896,
  N   63 (1901) 376-377

  N   67 (3 February 1903 Sup-
      plement) iii-iv
POYDESSAU, . . ., engineering,
      -1885, France
  Sl   5 (1885) 264
POYNTING, ARTHUR, engineering,
      -1916, England
  S   44 (1916) 306
POYNTING, JOHN HENRY, physics,
  1852-1914, England
  A   187 (1914) 486
  L   A92 (1916) P i-ix
  N   38 (1888) 12
  N   50 (1894) 542-543
  N   73 (1905) 131
  N   93 (1914) 138-140
  S   39 (1914) 530, 825
POZZI, SAMUEL JEAN, surgery,
  1846-1918, France
  S   48 (1918) 89
PRATT, ENOCH, philanthropy,
  1808-1896, U.S.A.
  S   4 (1896) 454
PRATT, W.,
  P   51 (1897) P 96
PREECE, SIR WILLIAM HENRY,
  electricity-physics, 1834-
  1913, Wales
  A   186 (1913) 659
  N   92 (1913) 322-324
  S   38 (1913) 700
PRENTISS, ALBERT NELSON,
  botany, 1836-1896, U.S.A.
  S   4 (1896) 267, 523-524
PRENTISS, CHARLES WILLIAM,
  anatomy, 1874-1915, U.S.A.
  S   42 (1915) 178-179
PRENTISS, DANIEL WEBSTER,
  ornithology,   -1899,
  U.S.A.
  S   11 (1900) 159
PRENTISS, ROBERT WOODWORTH,
  astronomy-mathematics,
  1857?-1913, U.S.A.
  S   37 (1913) 556
PRESCOTT, ALBERT BENJAMIN,
  chemistry, 1832-1905, U.S.A.
  P   66 (1804-1805) P 578-580
  S   21 (1905) 358, 601-603
PRESL, ..., botany,
      -1853?,
  A   66 (1853) 427
PRESTON, SAMUEL TOLVER, physics,
  1844-1917, England
  S   45 (1917) 499
PRESTON, THOMAS ARTHUR, biology,

PRINGLE, JAMES, commerce,
 1822-1886, Scotland
 E 14 (1886-1887) 166
PRINGLE, ROBERT, hygiene,
 -1899?, England
 S 9 (1899) 188
PRINGSHEIM, NATHANAEL, botany,
 1823-1894, Germany
 N 50 (1894) 580
 N 51 (1895) 399-402
PRINSEP, JAMES, chemistry-
 physics, 1799?-1840,
 L 4 (1837-1843) 259-260
PRITCHARD, CHARLES, astronomy,
 1808-1893, England
 L 54 (1894) iii-xii
 N 47 (1892) 110
 N 48 (1893) 130-131
 N 55 (1897) 601-602
PRITCHETT, CARR WALLER, astron-
 omy, 1823-1910, U.S.A.
 S 31 (1910) 454
PRITCHETT, HENRY SMITH, astron-
 omy, 1857-1939, U.S.A.
 P 57 (1900) P 283
 S 44 (1916) 49
PRITZEL, GEORGE AUGUSTUS,
 botany, 1815-1874, Germany
 A 109 (1875) 68
PROCTOR, HENRY RICHARDSON,
 chemistry, 1848-1927,
 England
 L A122 (1921) P i-vi
PROCTOR, RICHARD ANTHONY,
 astronomy, 1837-1888,
 England
 A 136 (1888) 304
 N 38 (1888) 499
 P 4 (1873-1874) P 486-491
 Sl 12 (1888) 143
de PRONY, GASPARD CLAIR
 FRANÇOIS MARIE, baron,
 mathematics-physics,
 1755-1839, France
 L 4 (1837-1843) 178-179
PROSSER, CHARLES SMITH, geol-
 ogy, 1860-1916, U.S.A.
 A 192 (1916) 372
 S 44 (1916) 421, 557-559
PROTONOTARI, GIUSEPPE,
 S 5 (1897) 270
PROUST, ACHILLE ADRIEN, hygiene,
 -1903, France
 S 19 (1904) 39
PROUT, HIRAM A., biology,
 -1862, U.S.A.

A 83 (1862) 453
von PROWAZEK, STANISLAUS JOSEF
 MATHIAS, zoology,   -1915?,
 Germany
 S 41 (1915) 500
PRUNIER, LOUIS LÉON ADOLPHE
 ADRIEN, pharmacology, 1841-
 1906, France
 S 24 (1906) 318
PRZHEVALSKY, NIKOLAY MIKHAILO-
 VICH, exploration, 1839-1888,
 Russia
 N 39 (1888) 31-34
 P 30 (1886-1887) P fp 289,
 402-408
PTOLEMY, CLAUDIUS, astronomy,
 fl. 140, Egypt
 N 50 (1894) 398-399
 N 53 (1896) 488-490
 N 97 (1916) 282-283, 341
 P 16 (1879-1880) P 484
 P 78 (1911) P 316-318
 S 24 (1906) 66
 S 47 (1916) 930-932
PUGH, EVAN, agriculture,
 1828-1864, U.S.A.
 A 88 (1864) 149, 301-302
PULLAR, FREDERICK,
 -1901, Scotland
 E 24 (1901-1903) 4-5
PULLAR, R. D., chemistry,
 1861?-1917, England
 S 46 (1917) 384
PULSIFER, WILLIAM HENRY, chem-
 istry, 1831?-1905, U.S.A.
 S 21 (1905) 758
PULTENY, RICHARD, biology-
 medicine, 1730-1801
 PM 12 (1802) P fr, P 289-
 296, 296-302
PUMPELLY, RAPHAEL, geology-
 mining, 1837-1923, U.S.A.
 A 197 (1919) 82
 S 49 (1919) 61-63
PURDIE, HENRY A., ornithology,
 -1911, U.S.A.
 S 49 (1919) 61-63
PURDIE, THOMAS, chemistry,
 1843-1916, Scotland
 A 193 (1917) 342
 L A101 (1922) P iv-x
 N 52 (1895) 33
 N 98 (1917) 391-392
PURDUE, ALBERT HOMER, geology,
 1861-1917, U.S.A.
 S 47 (1918) 67

N 65 (1902) P 587-590
S 20 (1904) 772-773
S 40 (1914) 929
QUOOS, FRIEDRICH, chemistry,
   -1915, Germany
   S 42 (1915) 898
RABAUD, ALFRED, geography,
   1828?-1886, France
   Sl 7 (1886) 416
RABENHORST, GOTTLIEB LUDWIG,
   mycology, 1807?-1881,
   Germany
   A 123 (1882) 333
   A 127 (1884) 243
RADAU, JEAN CHARLES RODOLPHE,
   astronomy-mathematics,
   1835-1911, Germany
   N 88 (1912) 354, 414
   S 35 (1912) 58
RADCLIFFE-GROTE, AUGUSTUS,
   entomology,   -1903,
   S 18 (1903) 446
RADDE, GUSTAV FERDINAND
   RICHARD, biology-zoology,
   1831-1903, Russia
   S 17 (1903) 559
RADELFINGER, FRANK GUSTAVE,
   mathematics, 1870-1904,
   U.S.A.
   S 20 (1904) 319
RADIGUET, ARTHUR, instrumen-
   tation,   -1906?, France
   S 23 (1906) 79
von RADINGER, JOHANN, engineer-
   ing, 1842-1901, Austria
   S 15 (1902) 595-596
RAE, JOHN, exploration-geog-
   raphy, 1813-1893, Scotland
   L 60 (1897) v-vii
   N 48 (1893) 321
   S 3 (1896) 131
RAFFARD, NICOLAS JULES, in-
   vention-physics, 1824-1898,
   France
   N 59 (1898-1899) 79
   S 8 (1898) 834
RAFFLES, SIR THOMAS STAMFORD,
   biology, 1781-1826, Jamaica
   P 50 (1896-1897) P 80-89
RAFFY, LOUIS, mathematics,
   1855-1910, France
   S 32 (1910) 109
RAFINESQUE (SCHMALTZ), CON-
   STANTINE SAMUEL, biology,
   1783-1840, Turkey
   A 40 (1840-1841) 221-241

A 42 (1841-1842) 280-291
A 149 (1895) 247-248
A 157 (1899) 473
P 29 (1866) 212-221
P 40 (1891-1892) P fp 721
S 1 (1895) 384-387
S 11 (1900) 449-451
S 12 (1900) 211-215
S 15 (1902) 713-714, 951
S 23 (1906) 785-786
RAID, ROBERT, geology,
   -1862,
   A 86 (1863) 278
RAIKES, . . ., medicine,
   -1908,
   S 27 (1908) 902-903
RAINES, GEORGE WASHINGTON,
   chemistry, 1817-1898, U.S.A.
   S 21 (1905) 878
RAJEWSKI, JOHANN, mathematics,
   -1907, Russia
   S 25 (1907) 398
RALEIGH, SAMUEL, commerce,
   -1882, Scotland
   E 12 (1882-1884) 29-31
RALPH, WILLIAM L., zoology,
   1850?-1907, U.S.A.
   S 26 (1907) 126
RAMANUJAN, SRINIVASA, mathe-
   matics, 1877-1920, India
   L A99 (1921) xiii-xxix
RAMBAUT, ARTHUR ALCOCK, astron-
   omy, 1859-1923, Ireland
   L A106 (1924) ix-xii
   N 62 (1900) 58
   N 112 (1923) 628-629
RAMBOUSEK, JOSEF, hygiene,
   1874?-1917, Germany
   S 46 (1917) 563, 635
DE la RAMÉE, PIERRE, logic-
   mathematics, 1515-1572,
   France
   P 44 (1893-1894) 109
RAMMELSBERG, CARL FRIEDRICH,
   chemistry-mineralogy, 1813-
   1899, Germany
   S 11 (1900) 198
RAMOND, . . ., biology,
      , France
   A 15 (1829) 177
   S 16 (1902) 399
RAMSAY, SIR ANDREW CROMBIE,
   geology, 1814-1891, Scotland
   A 143 (1892) 168
   N 45 (1891) 151-152
   N 51 (1895) 385-386

1815-1905, France
S 21 (1905) 600
RAVENEL, HENRY WILLIAM,
  botany, 1814-1887, U.S.A.
A 135 (1888) 263
N 35 (1887) 374
RAVENEL, ST. JULIEN, chemistry,
  1819-1882, U.S.A.
S 21 (1905) 878
RAVENSTEIN, ERNST GEORG,
  cartography, 1834-1913,
  Germany
S 37 (1913) 516, 705
RAVL-RUCKHARD, H., anatomy
    -1906, Germany
S 23 (1906) 199
RAWLINSON, SIR HENRY CRESWICKE,
  archeology, 1810-1895,
  England
L 58 (1895) xliv-xlvii
N 51 (1895) 536-547
S   1 (1895) 304
RAWLINSON, SIR ROBERT, en-
  gineering, 1810?-1898,
  England
N 58 (1898) 131
S   8 (1898) 102-103
RAWSON, SIR RAWSON WILLIAM,
  statistics, 1811?-1899,
  England
S 10 (1899) 863
RAY (WRAY), JOHN, biology-
  physics, 1627-1705, England
A 36 (1839) 223-230
N 78 (1908) 219, 294
S 26 (1907) 489-490
RAYET, GEORGES ANTOINE PONS,
  astronomy, 1839-1906,
  France
N 74 (1906) 382
S 24 (1906) 96, 287
RAYLEIGH, 3rd baron (lord)--
  see STRUTT, JOHN WILLIAM
RÁYMAN, BOHUSLAV, chemistry,
  1852-1910, Bohemia
S 32 (1910) 626
RAYMOND, FULGENCE, neurology,
  1844-1910, France
S 32 (1910) 506
RAYMOND, ROSSITER WORTHINGTON,
  engineering-mining, 1840-
  1918, U.S.A.
A 197 (1919) 148
S 49 (1919) 42
READE, THOMAS MELLARD, geology,

1832-1909, England
N 80 (1909) 404
S 29 (1909) 967
von REBEUR-PASCHWITZ, ERNST
  LUDWIG AUGUST, seismology,
  1861-1895, Germany
N 52 (1895) 599-600
S   2 (1895) 586
REBOUL, . . ., chemistry,
    -1903, France
S 17 (1903) 438
von RECKLINGHAUSEN, FRIEDRICH
  DANIEL, pathology, 1833-
  1910, Germany
S 32 (1910) 405
RECLUS, JEAN JACQUES ÉLISÉE,
  geography, 1830-1905,
  France
A 170 (1905) 412
P 44 (1893-1894) P fp 289,
    402-408
P 67 (1905) P 671-672
S 22 (1905) 95
RECLUS, PAUL, surgery, 1846?-
  1914, France
S 40 (1914) 205
RECORDE, ROBERT, mathematics,
  c.1510-1558, Wales
N 98 (1916) 172, 286
REDFERN, PETER, anatomy, 1821?-
  1912, Ireland
S 37 (1913) 96
REDFIELD, JOHN H., botany,
  1815?-1895, U.S.A.
A 149 (1895) 485
S   1 (1895) 470-471
S   3 (1896) 281
REDFIELD, WILLIAM C., meteorol-
  ogy, 1789-1857, U.S.A.
A 73 (1858) 292-293
A 74 (1857) P fr November
    (No. 72), P fp 305, 355-
    373
A 84 (1862) 442-443
P 49 (1896) P 504
P 50 (1896-1897) P fr,
    114-119
S 10 (1899) P fp 625, 627-
    628
REDFORD, FRANCIS, meteorology,
  1813-1885?, England
E 14 (1886-1887) 133-135
REDWOOD, SIR BOVERTON, chem-
  istry, 1846-1919, England
E 40 (1919-1920) 8-9

S   50 (1919) 208
REED, CHESTER A., ornithology,
   -1912,
   S   37 (1913) 16
REED, SIR EDWARD JAMES, en-
   gineering, 1830-1906,
   England
   N   75 (1906) 153-155
   S   24 (1906) 830
REED, EDWYN CARLOS, biology,
   -1911,
   S   33 (1911) 421
REED, MISS EVA M., botany,
   -1901, U.S.A.
   S   14 (1901) 158
REED, JOHN OREN, physics,
   1856-1916, U.S.A.
   S   16 (1902) 1039
   S   43 (1916) 131
   S   46 (1917) 207-208
REED, STEPHEN, geology, 1801?-
   1877, U.S.A.
   A   114 (1877) 168
REED, WALTER, medicine, 1851-
   1902, U.S.A.
   P   65 (1904) 262-268
   P   87 (1915) P 176
REED, WILLIAM HARLOW, geology-
   paleontology, 1848-1915,
   U.S.A.
   S   41 (1915) 722
REEKS, TRENHAM, mineralogy,
   -1879,
   N   20 (1879) 38-39
REES, GEORGE OWEN, medicine,
   -1889, England
   Sl   13 (1889) 480
REES, JOHN KROM, astronomy-
   geodesy, 1851-1907, U.S.A.
   A   173 (1907) 324
   S   25 (1907) 438, 475-477
REESS, MAXIMILLAN, botany,
   1845?-1901, Germany
   S   14 (1901) 622
REEVE, LOVELL AUGUSTUS, biol-
   ogy, 1810?-1865, U.S.A.
   A   91 (1886) 283
von REGEL, EDUARD, botany,
   1815?-1892, Germany
   N   46 (1892) 60-61
REGEL, CHRISTIAN FRIEDRICH
   (FRITZ) LEOPOLD, geography,
   1853-1915, Germany
   S   43 (1916) 131
RÉGIS, EMMANUEL, psychiatry,
   -1915, France

S   48 (1918) 137
REGNAULT, HENRI VICTOR, chem-
   istry-physics, 1810-1878,
   Germany
   A   115 (1878) 240
   E   10 (1878-1880) 5-6
   L   5 (1843-1850) 773-774
   L   6 (1850-1854) 298-300
   N   17 (1878) 263-264
   N   76 (1907) 493
   P   13 (1878) 20-25
REHNISCH, E., philosophy,
   1839?-1901, Germany
   S   14 (1901) 303
REICHENBACH, H. G. L., botany,
   1793?-1879, Germany
   A   119 (1880) 77
von REICHENBACK, GEORG, in-
   strumentation, 1772-1826,
   Germany
   A   15 (1829) 177
   N   91 (1913) 131-132
REICHENBACK, HEINRICH GUSTAV,
   botany, 1827?-1889, Germany
   N   40 (1889) 83-84
REID, CLEMENT, botany-geology,
   1853-1916,
   A   193 (1917) 174
   L   B90 (1919) P viii-x
   N   60 (1899) 32
   N   98 (1916) 312
   S   45 (1917) 14
REID, DANIEL BOSWELL, physics,
   -1863,
   E   5 (1862-1866) 133-136
REID, EDWARD WAYMOUTH, physiol-
   ogy,   ,
   N   58 (1898) 33
REID, JAMES DOUGLAS, telegraphy,
   1819?-1901, U.S.A.
   S   13 (1901) 755
REID, JOHN, pathology, 1809-
   1849, Scotland
   N   81 (1909) 163-165
REID, SIR WILLIAM, engineering-
   meteorology, 1791-1858,
   Scotland
   A   77 (1859) 153-155
REIL, JOHANN CHRISTIAN, anatomy,
   1759-1813, Germany
   S   16 (1902) 478
   S   42 (1915) 306
REINCKE, JOHANN JULIUS, sanita-
   tion,   -1906, Germany
   S   24 (1906) 789
REINGANUM, MAXIMILIAN, chemistry,

1876-1914, Germany
S 40 (1914) 632
REINWARDT, KASPAR GEORG,
botany, 1773-1854,
A 68 (1858) 133
REIS, PAUL, physics, 1828-1895,
Germany
S 3 (1896) 98
REIS, PHILIPP, physics, 1834-
1874, Germany
P 23 (1833) P fp 433, 540-
551
Sl 2 (1883) 472-477
Sl 5 (1885) 81
REISET, JULES, agronomy-chem-
istry, 1818-1896, France
S 3 (1896) 239
REISSEK, SIEGFRIED, botany,
-1871, Austria
A 103 (1872) 153
REMBOLD, OTTO, medicine,
1833?-1904, Austria
S 20 (1904) 509
REMINGTON, JOSEPH PRICE, chem-
istry-pharmacy, 1847-1918,
U.S.A.
S 47 (1918) 67-68
REMSEN, IRA, chemistry, 1846-
1927, U.S.A.
P 59 (1901) P fp 323, 317
P 82 (1913) P 619
S 21 (1905) 881
de REMUSAT, CHARLES, comte,
writer, 1797-1875, France
E 9 (1875-1878) 4-6
RÉMUSAT, JEAN PIERRE ABEL,
linguistics, 1788-1832,
France
A 23 (1832-1833) 371
REMY, JOSEPH, pisciculture,
1804?-1855?, France
A 69 (1855) 415-416
RENAN, JOSEPH ERNEST, archeol-
ogy, 1823-1892, France
P 42 (1892-1893) 288, P fp
721, 831-840
RENARD, ALPHONSE FRANÇOIS,
geology-mineralogy, 1842-
1903, Belgium
A 166 (1903) 268
S 18 (1903) 221
RENARD, LOUIS MARIE JOSEPH
CHARLES CLÉMENT, aeronautics,
1847-1905, France
S 21 (1905) 838
RENAULT, BERNARD, microbiology-

paleontology, 1836?-1904,
France
S 20 (1904) 855
S 21 (1905) 38
RENBAUGH, EMILE, biology,
-1896, Germany
S 4 (1896) 493
RENDEL, SIR ALEXANDER MEADOWS,
engineering, 1830?-1918,
England
S 47 (1918) 189
RENEVIER, EUGÈNE, geology,
-1906, Switzerland
S 23 (1906) 827, 891
RENNELL, JAMES, geography,
1742-1830, England
A 20 (1839) 304-305
L 3 (1830-1837) 7-8
N 52 (1895) 614-615
PM II 9 (1831) 39-40
S 2 (1895) 559-560
RENNIE, GEORGE, engineering,
1791-1866, England
L 16 (1868) xxxiii-xxxv
RENNIE, SIR JOHN, engineering,
1794-1884, England
L 23 (1875) x
RENOU, ÉMILIEN JEAN, meteorol-
ogy, 1815-1902, France
N 65 (1902) 590
S 15 (1902) 637
RENOUF, SIR PETER LE PAGE,
archeology, 1823?-1897,
England
S 6 (1897) 700
RENWICK, EDWARD SABINE, en-
gineering, 1823-1912, U.S.A.
S 35 (1912) 491
RENWICK, JAMES, physics, 1792-
1863, England
A 85 (1863) 306
RESAL, HENRI AMÉ, engineering,
1828-1896, France
S 4 (1896) 454
RESINELLI, G., obstetrics,
1865?-1915, Italy
S 41 (1915) 606
RESPIGHI, LORENZO, astronomy,
1824-1889, Italy
N 41 (1890) 254
Sl 15 (1890) 38
RETZIUS, ANDERS ADOLF, anatomy-
anthropology, 1796-1860,
Sweden
S 4 (1896) 753
RETZIUS, MAGNUS GUSTAF, anatomy,

1842-1919, Sweden
E   40 (1919-1920) 2
L   B91 (1920) P xxxvi-xxxviii
S   50 (1919) 206
REULEAUX, FRANZ, technology,
1829-1905, Germany
S   22 (1905) 381
REUSCH, HANS HENRIK, geology,
1852-1922, Norway
N   76 (1907) 605
REUTER, GEORGE FRANCIS, botany,
1817?-1872, Switzerland
A   105 (1873) 395
REUTER, ODO MORANNAL, zoology,
1850?-1913, Finland
S   38 (1913) 440
REVELY, . . ., architecture,
        -1799,
PM   4 (1799) 220-224
REX, GEORGE A., botany,
        -1895, U.S.A.
A   149 (1895) 328
REY, JEAN J., chemistry-physics,
1582?-1645, France
N   84 (1910) 527
P   44 (1893-1894) 247-255
REYER, EDUARD, geology, 1849-
1914, Germany
A   188 (1914) 370
S   40 (1914) 309
REYMOND, EMILE, surgery, 1865-
1914, France
S   40 (1914) 812
REYNMAN, L., meteorology, fl.
1520, Germany
Sl   23 (1896) 164
REYNOLDS, C. LESLIE, botany,
1858?-1913, U.S.A.
S   38 (1913) 300
REYNOLDS, ELMER ROBERT, arche-
ology, 1846-1907, U.S.A.
S   26 (1907) 423
REYNOLDS, JAMES EMERSON, chem-
istry, 1844-1920, Ireland
L   A97 (1920) iii-vi
REYNOLDS, JOSEPH JONES, army-
mechanics, 1822-1899, U.S.A.
S   9 (1899) 381
REYNOLDS, OSBORNE, physics,
1842-1912, Ireland
A   183 (1912) 516
L   A88 (1913) xv-xxi
N   62 (1900) 243-244
N   64 (1901) 549
N   88 (1912) 590-591
N   90 (1912) 20

S   35 (1912) 414
REYNOLDS, SIR RUSSELL, medi-
cine, 1828?-1896, England
S   3 (1896) 899
RHEES, WILLIAM JONES, bibliog-
raphy-statistics, 1830-1907,
U.S.A.
A   173 (1907) 324
RHYS, SIR JOHN, anthropology-
archeology, 1840-1915, Wales
A   191 (1916) 306
N   96 (1915) 484
RIBAN, ALEXANDRE JOSEPH, chem-
istry, 1838-1917, France
N   99 (1917) 247
S   45 (1917) 634
RICE, CHARLES, pharmacy, 1841-
1901, Germany
S   13 (1901) 837
RICE, JOHN MINOT, mathematics,
1833-1901, U.S.A.
S   13 (1901) 438
RICE, WILLIAM NORTH, geology,
1845-1938, U.S.A.
P   51 (1897) P 218
P   68 (1906) P 190
RICHARD, ACHILLE, botany, 1794-
1852, France
A   66 (1853) 427
A   67 (1854) 414
RICHARD, JULIUS WILHELM, mathe-
matics,   -1916, Germany
A   191 (1916) 472
RICHARDS, CHARLES BRINKERHOFF,
engineering, 1833-1919,
U.S.A.
A   197 (1919) 454
S   49 (1919) 446
RICHARDS, ELLEN HENRIETTA
SWALLOW (MRS. ROBERT H.),
chemistry, 1842-1911, U.S.A.
A   181 (1911) 468
S   33 (1911) 523, 686
S   35 (1912) 176-177
S   36 (1912) 677-678
RICHARDS, EUGENE LAMB, mathe-
matics, 1838-1912, U.S.A.
S   36 (1912) 211
RICHARDS, SIR GEORGE HENRY,
exploration, 1820-1896,
England
L   60 (1897) xxxii-xxxv
N   55 (1896-1897) 57
S   4 (1896) 793
RICHARDS, HERBERT MAULE, botany,
1871-1928, U.S.A.

P 74 (1909) P 206
RICHARDS, THEODORE WILLIAM,
 chemistry, 1868-1928,
 U.S.A.
 L A121 (1928) P xxix-xxxiv
 N 85 (1910) 144-145
 N 122 (1928) 28-29
RICHARDSON, SIR BENJAMIN WARD,
 medicine, 1828-1896, England
 L 75 (1905) 51-52
 N 55 (1896) 80
 N 57 (1898) 265-266
 S 4 (1896) 793
RICHARDSON, CLIFFORD, chem-
 istry, 1856-1932, U.S.A.
 P 70 (1907) P 183
RICHARDSON, J., geology,
 -1848, England
 A 56 (1848) 297
RICHARDSON, SIR JOHN, botany-
 exploration, 1787-1865,
 Scotland
 A 90 (1865) 140
 A 91 (1866) 265
 E 5 (1862-1866) 470-471
 L 15 (1867) xxxvii-xliii
RICHARDSON, MAURICE HOWE,
 surgery, 1851-1912, U.S.A.
 S 36 (1912) 211
RICHARDSON, THOMAS, chemistry,
 1816-1867, England?
 E 6 (1866-1869) 198-199
RICHE, ALFRED JEAN BAPTISTE
 LÉOPOLD, chemistry, 1829-
 1908, France
 S 27 (1908) 837
RICHER, JEAN FRANÇOIS, in-
 strumentation, 1743-   ,
 France
 PM 63 (1824) 252-259
RICHTER, AUGUST GOTTLOB, sur-
 gery, 1742-1812, Germany
 S 12 (1900) 258
RICHTER, EDUARD, geology,
 1847-1805, Austria
 S 21 (1905) 399
RICHTER, HEINRICH THEODOR,
 metallurgy, 1824-1898,
 Germany
 S 8 (1898) 629
RICHTER, JEREMIAS BENJAMIN,
 chemistry, 1762-1807,
 Germany
 PM III 21 (1842) 81-96
 S 12 (1900) 825-828

RICHTER, PAUL B., botany,
 1854?-1911, Germany
 S 34 (1911) 635
von RICHTHOFEN, FERDINAND PAUL
 WILHELM, baron, geology,
 1833-1905,
 A 170 (1905) 412
 L B79 (1907) xxxv-xl
 N 73 (1905) 8-9
 N 78 (1908) 194-195
 S 22 (1905) 476
RICKETTS, HOWARD TAYLOR,
 medicine, 1871-1910, U.S.A.
 S 32 (1905) 585, 834
RICKETTS, PIERRE de PEYSTER,
 chemistry-mineralogy,
 1848?-1918, U.S.A.
 A 197 (1919) 84
 S 48 (1918) 571
RICKMAN, JOHN,   , 1771-
 1840,
 L 4 (1837-1843) 261-262
RIDDELL, CHARLES JAMES BUCHANAN,
 magnetism, 1817-1903,
 England
 L 75 (1905) 302-304
RIDDELL, SIR JAMES MILES,
 1787?-1861, Scotland
 E 4 (1857-1862) 496-497
RIDDELL, JOHN LEONARD, medi-
 cine, 1807-1865, U.S.A.
 A 91 (1866) 141-143, 267
RIDDER, HERMANN, publishing,
 1851-1915, U.S.A.
 P 75 (1909) P 330
RIDGEWAY, WILLIAM, anthropology-
 archeology, 1853-1926,
 Ireland
 S 38 (1913) 189
RIDGWAY, AUDUBON WHELOCK,
 ornithology, 1877-1901,
 U.S.A.
 S 13 (1901) 599
RIEDER, ROBERT, pasha, surgery,
 1862?-1913, Germany
 S 38 (1913) 359
RIEHL, NICHOLAS, botany,
 c. 1808-1852, France
 P 74 (1909) P 129-130
RIEMANN, GEORG FRIEDRICH
 BERNHARD, mathematics-
 physics, 1826-1866,
 Germany
 L 16 (1868) lxix-lxx

England
L B95 (1924) P xliii-xlvii
N 96 (1915) 374
ROBB, JAMES, biology, 1815?-
1861, Scotland
A 82 (1861) 150, 304
ROBBINS, JAMES WATSON, biology,
1801-1879, U.S.A.
A 117 (1879) 180
A 119 (1880) 77
ROBERTS, CHARLES, surgery,
-1902, England
S 15 (1902) 198
ROBERTS, CHARLOTTE FICH,
chemistry, 1859-1917, U.S.A.
S 47 (1918) 140
ROBERTS, ISAAC, astronomy,
1829-1904, Wales
L 75 (1905) 356-363
N 42 (1890) 15
N 70 (1904) 302-303, 372
S 20 (1904) 159
ROBERTS, SIR OWEN, education,
1835-1915,
N 94 (1915) 537-538
ROBERTS, R.D., geology,
1851?-1911, England
S 34 (1911) 755-756
ROBERTS, SAMUEL, mathematics,
1827-1913, England
L A89 (1914) xx-xxi
S 38 (1913) 507
ROBERTS, SIR WILLIAM, medicine,
1830-1899, England
L 75 (1905) 68-71
S 9 (1899) 660-661
ROBERTS-AUSTEN, SIR WILLIAM
CHANDLER, metallurgy,
1843-1902, England
L 75 (1905) 192-198
N 67 (1902) 105-107
N 68 (1903) 447-448
N 93 (1914) 555
S 16 (1902) 557, 918, 974
ROBERTS-MARTYN, JOHN, engi-
neering, 1806-1878, Wales
E 10 (1878-1880) 26-31
ROBERTSON, A.C., army, 1816-
1884, Scotland
E 14 (1886-1887) 136-137
ROBERTSON, ARCHIBALD, medicine,
1789-1864, Scotland
E 5 (1862-1866) 305-306
L 14 (1865) xvii
ROBERTSON, DAVID, biology,
-1896, England
S 4 (1896) 874

ROBERTSON, ÉTIENNE GASPARD,
physics, 1763-1837, Belgium
N 28 (1883) 130
ROBERTSON, JAMES, theology,
1803-1860, Scotland
E 4 (1857-1862) 497-500
ROBERTSON, JOHN, mathematics,
1712-1776, England
S 32 (1910) 666-668
ROBERTSON, LESLIE S., engineer-
ing, 1863-1916, India
N 97 (1916) 324-325
ROBERTSON, ROBERT, mathematics,
1850-1917, Scotland
E 38 (1917-1918) 12
ROBERTSON, WILLIAM, medicine,
1818-1882, Scotland
E 12 (1882-1884) 22-24
ROBIN, CHARLES PHILIPPE, his-
tology, 1821-1885, France
N 33 (1885) 9
ROBINSON, BENJAMIN LINCOLN,
botany, 1864-1935, U.S.A.
P 66 (1904-1905) P 385
ROBINSON, CHARLES BUDD, botany,
1871-1913, Canada
A 187 (1914) 208
S 39 (1914) 20
ROBINSON, FRANKLIN CLEMENT,
chemistry, 1852-1910, U.S.A.
A 180 (1910) 96
S 31 (1910) 854
ROBINSON, JOHN, astronomy-
physics, 1739-1805,
PM 10 (1801) P fr, P 348-353
PM 13 (1802) 386-394
ROBINSON, SIR ROBERT SPENCER,
navy, 1809-1889, England
L 46 (1890) xl-xli
ROBINSON, THOMAS ROMNEY,
astronomy, 1792-1882, Ireland
N 25 (1882) 468-469
N 66 (1902) 478
ROBINSON, SIR JOHN, engineer-
ing-physics, 1778-1843,
E 2 (1844-1850) 68-79
ROCHE, ÉDOUARD ALBERT, astron-
omy, 1820-1883, France
N 28 (1883) 11-12
ROCK, MILES, astronomy, 1840-
1901, U.S.A.
S 13 (1901) 237, 278-279,
978-980
ROCKHILL, WILLIAM WOODVILLE,
exploration-geography,
1854-1914, U.S.A.
S 41 (1915) 61

ROLLAND, EUGÈNE, engineering,
1812-1885, France
Sl 5 (1885) 472
ROLLESTON, GEORGE, anthropology-
zoology, 1829-1881, England
A 129 (1885) 423
L 33 (1882) xxiv-xxvii
N 24 (1881) 192-193
Sl 5 (1885) 486-488
ROLLETT, ALEXANDER, physiology,
1834-1903, Austria
N 69 (1903) 86-87
S 18 (1903) 573
ROLLS, CHARLES STEWART,
aeronautics, 1877-1910,
Wales
N 84 (1910) 46
ROMANES, GEORGE JOHN, biology,
1848-1894, Canada
A 153 (1897) 358
L 57 (1895) vii-xiv
N 50 (1894) 108-109
N 53 (1896) 481-483
N 55 (1896) 124
S 3 (1896) 65, 492
S 4 (1896) 762-763
ROMINGER, CARL LUDWIG,
geology-paleontology,
1820-1907, Germany
S 25 (1907) 718
RONALDS, EDMUND, chemistry,
1819-1889, Scotland
E 17 (1889-1890) xxviii-xxix
RONALDS, SIR FRANCIS, electricity,
1788-1873, England
S 6 (1897) 58
ROOD, OGDEN NICHOLAS, physics,
1831-1902, U.S.A.
A 164 (1902) 470
A 165 (1903) 73-77
P 62 (1902-1903) P 284-286
S 16 (1902) 838, 881--884
ROOSEVELT, THEODORE, adminis-
tration-biology, 1858-1919,
U.S.A.
N 93 (1914) 79-80
ROOT, EDWIN W., chemistry,
1840?-1870, U.S.A.
A 101 (1871) 75
ROOT, ELIHU, mathematics-
physics, 1845-1880, U.S.A.
Sl 3 (1884) 467
ROOT, OREN, mathematics,
1838-1907, U.S.A.
S 26 (1907) 326
ROOZEBOOM, H.W. BAKHUIS--see
Bakhuis-Roozeboom

ROPER, CHARLES FRANCIS, inven-
tion, 1849?-1916, U.S.A.
S 44 (1916) 743
ROSA, DANIEL BENNETT ST. JOHN,
medicine, 1838-1908, U.S.A.
S 27 (1908) 435
S 36 (1912) 669
ROSATI, T., surgery, 1860-
1917, Italy
S 46 (1917) 260-261
ROSCOE, SIR HENRY ENFIELD,
chemistry, 1833-1915, England
A 191 (1916) 152
A 193 (1917) 80
L A93 (1917) P i-xxi
N 69 (1904) 613-614
N 74 (1906) 289-290
N 90 (1913) 520-521
N 92 (1913) 377-378
N 96 (1915) 459-461
N 98 (1916) 225
P 26 (1884-1885) P fp 289,
402-406
S 37 (1913) 143
S 38 (1913) 811
S 42 (1915) 932
ROSE, GUSTAV, chemistry-
mineralogy, 1798-1873,
Germany
A 106 (1873) 238-240
E 8 (1872-1875) 312-313
L 24 (1876) iii-v
N 8 (1873) 277-279
ROSE, HEINRICH, chemistry,
1795-1864, Germany
A 87 (1864) 304
A 88 (1864) 305-330
L 14 (1865) xix-xx
ROSEN, FRIEDRICH, Baron,
mineralogy, 1834?-1902,
S 15 (1902) 797
ROSENBERGER, ERNST, history-
physics, -1899, Germany
S 10 (1899) 620
ROSENBUSCH, KARL HEINRICH
FERDINAND, geology-mineralogy,
1836-1914, Germany
A 187 (1914) 288
S 24 (1906) 126
S 39 (1914) 249
ROSEMUND, MAX, topography,
1857?-1908, Switzerland
S 28 (1908) 370-371
ROSENTHAL, ISIDORE, physiology,
1836?-1915, Germany
S 41 (1915) 240
ROSING, ANTON, chemistry,

SAFFORD, TRUMAN HENRY, astron-
    omy, 1836-1901, U.S.A.
    S   13 (1901) 997
    S   14 (1901) 22
SAGE, HENRY WILLIAMS,
    philanthropy, 1814-1897,
    U.S.A.
    S   6 (1897) 481
SAGEMEHL, MAX, morphology,
        -1885, Netherlands
    Sl   6 (1885) 429
de la SAGRA, RAMON, botany,
    1798-1871, Spain
    A   103 (1872) 153
de SAINT-JOSEPH, ARTHUR, baron,
    entomology,   -1911, France
    S   34 (1911) 210
SAINT-VENANT, ADHÉMAR JEAN
    CLAUDE BARRÉ, comte de,
    physics, 1797-1886, France
    N   33 (1886) 319-321
    N   41 (1890) 458-459
SAINTE-CLAIRE DEVILLE, CHARLES
    JOSEPH, geology-mineralogy,
    1814-1876, Antilles
    A   112 (1876) 478
    N   14 (1876) 575-576
SAINTE-CLAIRE DEVILLE, HENRI
    ÉTIENNE, chemistry, 1818-
    1881, St. Thomas
    N   24 (1887) 219-221
    P   20 (1881-1882) P fp 433,
    543-547
SAKAKI, SINKU, psychiatry,
        -1897, Japan
    S   5 (1897) 728
SALINAS, ANTONIO, archeology,
    1841?-1914, Italy
    A   187 (1914) 486
SALISBURY, LORD--see
    Gascoyne-Cecil
SALISBURY, EDWARD ELBRIDGE,
    linguistics-orientalia,
    1814-1901, U.S.A.
    S   13 (1901) 279
SALMON, DANIEL ELMER,
    pathology, 1850-1914, U.S.A.
    S   49 (1914) 848
SALMON, GEORGE, mathematics,
    1819-1904, Ireland
    L   75 (1905) 347-355
    N   69 (1904) 324-326
    N   70 (1904) 372
    S   19 (1904) 199
    S   23 (1906) 198

SALMON, GEORGES, exploration,
        -1906, France
    S   24 (1906) 350
SALMON, PHILIPPE, anthropology,
        -1900, France
    S   11 (1900) 717
SALTER, SAMUEL JAMES AUGUSTUS,
    botany, 1825-1897, England
    L   61 (1897) iii-iv
de SALUZZO, ALEXANDER,
        -1851, Italy
    A   62 (1851) 446
SALVIN, OSBERT, ornithology,
    1835-1898, England
    L   64 (1899) xiii-xvii
    N   58 (1898) 129
    S   7 (1898) 858
SAMSON, GEORGE WHITEFIELD,
    education, 1819-1896,
    U.S.A.
    S   4 (1896) 224
SAMUELS, EDWARD AUGUSTUS,
    zoology, 1836-1908, U.S.A.
    S   28 (1908) 232
SAMUELSON, SIR BERNHARD,
    education-metallurgy, 1820-
    1905, England
    N   72 (1905) 60-61
    S   21 (1905) 870
SANARELLI, GIUSEPPE, bac-
    teriology, 1865-1940, Italy
    S   6 (1897) 405, 981-985
von SANBERGER, KARL LUDWIG
    FRIDOLIN, mineralogy, 1826-
    1898, Germany
    N   58 (1898) 16
    S   7 (1898) 634-635, 710
SANCHEZ, ALBERTO, astronomy,
        -1896,
    S   4 (1896) 939
SANCHEZ-TOLEDO, MIGUEL,
    physiology,   -1918, Cuba
    S   48 (1918) 317
SANDER, ENNO,
    P   52 (1897-1898) P 645
SANDERS, WILLIAM RUTHERFORD,
    medicine, 1828-1881,
    Scotland
    E   11 (1880-1882) 333-338
SANDERSON, GEORGE, mathematics,
    1733-1813,
    PM   16 (1893) P fr
SANDERSON, GORDON, archeology,
        -1915, England
    S   42 (1915), 794

medicine,   , France
S 9 (1899) 525
de SAUSSURE, HENRI, entomology-
zoology, 1829-1905, France
Sl 7 (1886) 119
S 21 (1905) 111, 274-275,
758
de SAUSSURE, HORACE BÉNÉDICT,
chemistry-physics, 1740-
1799, Switzerland
A 132 (1886) 246
PM 3 (1799) 332
PM 4 (1799) 96-102
SL 5 (1887) 512
de SAUSSURE, NICHOLAS THÉODORE,
biology-chemistry, 1767-
1845, Switzerland
A 5 (1822) 379
A 52 (1846) 145
L 5 (1843-1850) 583-586
PM III 28 (1846) 413-415
SAUVAGE, ALEXIS, invention,
1781-1858, France
A 76 (1858) 394-396
SAUVAGE, PIERRE LOUIS FRÉDÉRIC,
invention, 1785-1857,
France
A 76 (1858) 393-394
SAVART, FÉLIX, physics, 1791-
1841, France
L 4 (1837-1843) 341,
352-354
PM III 20 (1842) 259-261
SAVERY, THOMAS, engineering,
1650?-1715, England
P 12 (1877-1878) P 26
SAVORY, SIR WILLIAM SCOVELL,
surgery, 1826?-1895,
England
S 1 (1895) 364
SAWYER, HARRIS EASTMAN,
chemistry, 1868-1911, U.S.A.
S 34 (1911) 49
SAWYER, SIR JAMES, medicine,
1844?-1919, England
E 40 (1919-1920) 9
S 49 (1919) 213
SAXONY, ..., King of, botany,
-1854,
A 68 (1854) 429
SAY, THOMAS, zoology, 1787-
1834, U.S.A.
A 27 (1834-1835) 393
A 47 (1844) 10
A 53 (1847) 299

A 81 (1861) 155
P 21 (1882) P fp 577,
687-691
P 76 (1910) P 467-469
Sl 9 (1887) 10
SAYRE, LEWIS ALBERT, surgery,
1820-1900, U.S.A.
S 12 (1900) 492
SACCHI, ARCANGELO, mineralogy,
1810-1893, Italy
A 146 (1893) 484
SCAMMON, CHARLES M., zoology,
1825?-1911, U.S.A.
S 33 (1911) 887
SCANNELL, JAMES J., bacteriology,
-1915, U.S.A.
S 41 (1915) 322
SCARPA, ANTONIO, medicine-
surgery, 1746-1832, Italy
A 25 (1833-1834) 184
L 3 (1830-1837) 153-154
SCHACHT, GEORGE FREDERICK,
medicine, 1824?-1897,
S 5 (1897) 143
SCHACHT, HERMANN, botany, 1814?-
1864, Germany
A 91 (1866) 264
SCHÄFFER, KARL JULIUS TRAUGOTT
HERMANN, mathematics, 1824-
1900, Germany
S 11 (1900) 399
SCHALLBACH, K.,   , 1804- ,
Germany
S 21 (1905) 518
SCHANCK, JOHN STILLWELL, chem-
istry, 1817-1898, U.S.A.
S 8 (1898) 902
SCHAPER, ALFRED, embryology,
1863?-1905, Germany
S 22 (1905) 446
SCHAPIRA, HERMANN HIRSCH,
mathematics, 1840-1898,
Germany
S 7 (1898) 771
SCHAUDINN, FRITZ RICHARD,
zoology, 1871-1906, Germany
P 70 (1907) 274-278
S 24 (1906) 61, 154-155
SCHAUER, ..., botany,   -1849,
A 63 (1852) 45
SCHEELE, ADOLF, botany, 1807?-
1864, Germany
A 91 (1866) 264
SCHEELE (SCHEEL), KARL WILHELM,
chemistry, 1742-1786,

botany, 1780-1834, U.S.A.
P 44 (1893-1894) P fp 721,
833-840
SCHWEITZER, HUGO, chemistry,
1861-1917, Germany
S 47 (1918) 19
SCHWEITZER, JOHANN PAUL,
chemistry, 1840-1911,
Germany
S 34 (1911) 210
SCHWENDENER, SIMON, botany,
1829-1919, Switzerland
L B92 (1921) viii-x
P 50 (1896-1897) P 313
S 19 (1904) 438
S 39 (1914) 419
SCLATER, BERTRAM LUTLEY, ex-
ploration, 1866?-1897,
S 6 (1897) 252
SCLATER, PHILLIP LUTLEY,
zoology, 1829-1913, England
A 186 (1913) 576
L B87 (1914) iii-v
N 91 (1913) 455
S 4 (1896) 293-298
S 38 (1913) 83
SCORESBY, WILLIAM, exploration-
physics, 1789-1857, England
A 73 (1857) 448
A 76 (1858) 300-301
E 4 (1857-1862) 9-11
SCORESBY-JACKSON, ROBERT
EDWARD, medicine, 1833-
1867, England
E 6 (1866-1869) 197-198
SCOTT, ALEXANDER, chemistry,
1853-   , Scotland
N 58 (1898) 33
SCOTT, DUKINFIELD HENRY,
botany, 1854-1934, England
N 50 (1894) 56
SCOTT, HUGH,
1822-1877?, Scotland
E 10 (1878-1880) 13
SCOTT, JOHN HALLIDAY, anatomy,
1851-1914, Scotland
E 36 (1915-1916) 31
SCOTT, PETER ASTTE, explora-
tion, 1816?-1900,
S 11 (1900) 676
SCOTT, ROBERT HENRY, meteorol-
ogy, 1833-1916, Ireland
N 97 (1916) 365-366
S 44 (1916) 306, 357

SCOTT, RONALD FRASER, explora-
tion,   ,
S 39 (1914) 100-103
SCOTT, SIR WALTER, author,
1771-1832, Scotland
E 18 (1890-1891) 14-15
SCOTT, WILLIAM, horticulture,
1850?-1897, England
S 6 (1897) 660
SCOTT, WILLIAM BERRYMAN, geol-
ogy, 1858-1947, U.S.A.
P 66 (1904-1905) P 10
SCOTT, WILLIAM EARL DODGE,
ornithology, 1852?-1910,
U.S.A.
S 32 (1910) 303
SCOTT-MONCRIEFF, COLIN CAMPBELL,
engineering, 1837?-1916,
Scotland
S 43 (1916) 684
SCOUGAL, A. E., education,
1846-1916, Scotland
E 38 (1917-1918) 12
SCOVELL, MELVILLE AMASA, agri-
culture-chemistry, 1855-
1912, U.S.A.
S 36 (1912) 238
SCRIBA, JULIUS KARL, surgery,
1850?-1905,
S 21 (1905) 318
SCROPE, GEORGE JULIUS POULETT
(THOMSON), geology, 1797-
1876, England
A 111 (1876) 248
L 25 (1877) i-iv
N 13 (1876) 241-242
SCUDDER, SAMUEL HUBBARD, en-
tomology, 1837-1911, U.S.A.
A 181 (1911) 582
P 76 (1910) P 470-475
S 33 (1911) 809
S 34 (1911) 338-342
SEAMAN, WILLIAM HENRY, chem-
istry, 1837-1910, U.S.A.
S 31 (1910) 985
SEARLE, GEORGE MARY, astronomy-
mathematics, 1839-1918,
England
S 48 (1918) 66-67
SEATON, HENRY ELIASON, botany,
1869-1893, U.S.A.
A 145 (1893) 526-527
SEAVER, J. W., hygiene, 1855?-
1915, U.S.A.

S   34 (1911) 600
SERVICE, ROBERT, ornithology,
    -1911, Scotland
  S   33 (1911) 925
di SESSA, EMANUELE PATERNO,
    chemistry,   , Italy
  N   89 (1912) 534
SETON, ERNEST (EVAN) THOMPSON
(Orig. ERNEST SETON THOMPSON),
    biology, 1860-1946, England
  S   19 (1904) 623
SETTEGAST, HERMANN, agricul-
    ture, 1818?-1908, Germany
  S   15 (1902) 80
  S   28 (1908) 338
SEUBERT, MORITZ, botany, 1818?-
    1878, Germany
  A   117 (1879) 179
SEUILLART, ..., astronomy,
    -1898,
  N   58 (1898) 112
SEVERO, AUGUSTO, aeronautics,
    -1902, Brazil
  S   15 (1902) 838
SEVERSON, B. O., zoology,
    -1918, U.S.A.
  S   48 (1918) 644
SEVRET, PAUL, mathematics,
    1828?-1898, France
  S   8 (1898) 218
SEWARD, SIR ALBERT CHARLES,
    botany, 1863-1941, England
  N   58 (1898) 34
SEYBERT, ADAM, chemistry, 1773-
    1825, U.S.A.
  A   197 (1919) 383
SEYBERT, HENRY, mineralogy,
    -1833, France
  A   125 (1883) 320
SHABAD, I. A., pediatrics,
    1870?-1917, Russia
  S   45 (1917) 458
SHACKLETON, SIR ERNEST HENRY,
    exploration, 1874-1922,
    Ireland
  P   76 (1910) P 518
SHALER, NATHANIEL SOUTHGATE,
    geology, 1841-1906, U.S.A.
  A   171 (1906) 408, 480-481
  A   179 (1910) 90
  N   74 (1906) 226
  N   82 (1910) 274-275
  S   23 (1906) 599, 869-872,
    956

SHAND, JOHN, medicine, 1823?-
    1895, Scotland
  E   21 (1895-1897) 14
SHAPLEIGH, WALDRON, chemistry,
    1848-1901, U.S.A.
  S   14 (1901) 463
SHARIF, BAHADUR YUSUF, khan,
    geography,   -1906, Russia
  S   24 (1906) 415
SHARMAN, GEORGE, paleontology,
    1833?-1914, England
  S   39 (1914) 604
SHARP, BENJAMIN, zoology,
    1858-1915, U.S.A.
  A   189 (1915) 326
  S   41 (1915) 204
SHARP, DAVID, entomology, 1840-
    1922, England
  L   B95 (1924) xxxvi-xlii
  N   42 (1890) 16
SHARP, SAMUEL, geology, 1815-
    1882, England
  N   25 (1882) 319
SHARP, WILLIAM, biology, 1805?-
    1896, England
  S   3 (1896) 629
SHARPE (ELLIS), ALEXANDER JOHN,
    phonetics, 1814-1890,
    England
  Sl   16 (1890) 287
SHARPE, DANIEL, geology, 1806-
    1856, England
  A   72 (1856) 152
SHARPE, RICHARD BOWDLER, orni-
    thology, 1847-1909, England
  N   82 (1909) 253-254
  S   31 (1910) 65
SHARPEY, WILLIAM, medicine,
    1802-1880, Scotland
  E   11 (1880-1882) 110-116
  L   31 (1881) x-xix
  N   21 (1880) 567-568
SHARPEY-SCHAFER, SIR EDWARD
    ALBERT, physiology, 1850-
    1935, England
  N   67 (1902) 109
SHATTOCK, SAMUEL GEORGE,
    pathology, 1852-1924,
    England
  L   B96 (1924) xxx-xxxii
SHATTUCK, LYDIA W., botany,
    -1889, U.S.A.
  Sl   14 (1889) 402
SHATTUCK, SAMUEL WALKER,

mathematics, 1841-1915,
U.S.A.
S 41 (1915) 284
SHAW, CHARLES HUGH, botany,
1875-1910, U.S.A.
S 32 (1910) 239-240
S 33 (1911) 449-450
SHAW, EDWARD R., pedagogy,
1855-1903, U.S.A.
S 17 (1903) 318
SHAW, HENRY, botany, 1800-
1889, England
P 74 (1909) P 246-250
S1 14 (1889) 112, 148-149
SHAW, JOHN, architecture,
-1832,
L 3 (1830-1837) 149
SHAW, JOSEPH P., chemistry,
-1895, U.S.A.
S 2 (1895) 46
SHAW, SIR WILLIAM NAPIER,
meteorology, 1854-1945,
England
N 44 (1891) 16
SHEARMAN, EDWARD JAMES, medi-
cine, 1797-1878, Scotland
E 10 (1878-1880) 14-15
SHELDON, DAVID SYLVESTER,
biology,
P 51 (1897) P 86
SHELDON, J. R., agriculture,
1840?-1913, England
S 38 (1913) 359
SHELFORD, ROBERT WALTER
CAMPBELL, entomology, 1873?-
1912, England
S 36 (1912) 48
SHELLEY, GEORGE ERNEST, orni-
thology, -1910, England
S 32 (1910) 952
SHENSTONE, WILLIAM ASHWELL,
chemistry, 1850-1908,
England
L A82 (1909) xxii-xxiv
N 58 (1898) 34
N 77 (1908) 348-349
S 27 (1908) 435
SHEPARD, CHARLES UPHAM, JR.,
chemistry, 1842-1915, U.S.A.
S 21 (1905) 878
SHEPARD, CHARLES UPHAM, SR.,
mineralogy, 1804-1886,
U.S.A.
A 131 (1886) 482-483

P 47 (1895) P fp 433, 548-
553
S1 7 (1886) 504, 547
S 21 (1905) 878
SHEPARD, WILLIAM A., chemistry,
-1895, U.S.A.
S 1 (1895) 668
SHERMAN, FRANK ASBURY, mathe-
matics, 1841-1915, U.S.A.
S 41 (1915) 422
SHERRINGTON, SIR CHARLES SCOTT,
physiology, 1861-1952,
England
N 48 (1893) 10
SHIELDS, CHARLES WOODRUFF,
theology, 1825-1904, U.S.A.
S 20 (1904) 319
SHIMOSE, MASUCHIKA, chemistry,
1859?-1911, Japan
S 34 (1911) 343
SHIPLEY, SIR ARTHUR EVERETT,
sanitation-zoology, 1861-
1927, England
L B103 (1928) P i-viii
P 75 (1909) P 411
P 87 (1915) P 69
S 48 (1918) 433-434
SHIPMAN, JAMES P., geology,
1849?-1902, England
S 15 (1902) 158
SHORE, THOMAS WILLIAM, geology,
-1905, England
S 21 (1905) 237
SHORT, CHARLES WILKINS, botany,
1794-1863, U.S.A.
A 86 (1863) 130-132
A 87 (1864) 288
SHORT, SIDNEY HOWE, electricity,
1858-1902, U.S.A.
S 16 (1902) 716
SHRADY, GEORGE FREDERICK, medi-
cine, 1837-1907, U.S.A.
S 26 (1907) 806
SHUMARD, BENJAMIN FRANKLIN,
geology, 1820-1869, U.S.A.
A 98 (1869) 294-296
SHUTTLEWORTH, ROBERT JAMES,
botany-conchology, 1810-
1874, England
A 108 (1874) 155-156
SIBBALD, SIR ROBERT, biology,
c.1641-1712, Scotland
A 37 (1839) 138-142
SIBSON, FRANCIS, medicine,

entomology, -1899,
U.S.A.
S 10 (1899) 661-662
SNYDER, FRIEDRICH WILHELM,
botany, 1810?-1897, Germany
S 6 (1897) 990
SOANE, SIR JOHN, archeology,
1753?-1837, England
L 4 (1837-1843) 16-17
SÖMMERRING, ..., anatomy,
-1831, Germany
L 3 (1830-1837) 84
SOKOLOFF, ALEKSEI PETROVITSCH,
astronomy, 1854?-1910,
Russia
S 32 (1910) 151
SOKOLOV, NICOLAS, geology,
1856-1907, Russia
A 173 (1907) 324
SOLIGNAC, LOUIS, electricity,
-1902, France
S 16 (1902) 198
SOLLAS, WILLIAM JOHNSON,
biology-geology, 1849-1936,
England
N 94 (1914) 368
zu SOLMS-LAUBACH, HERMANN,
graf, botany, 1842-1915,
Germany
L B90 (1919) P xix-xxvi
N 81 (1909) 13
N 96 (1916) 541-542
S 43 (1916) 167
SOLOMON, ALFRED GORDON, chem-
istry, 1858?-1918, England
S 47 (1918) 587
SOLWYN, A. R. C., geology,
1824?-1902, Canada
S 16 (1902) 839
SOMERSET, EDWARD, Earl of
Worcester, engineering,
1601-1667, England
P 12 (1877-1878) P 22
SOMERVILLE, MRS. MARY FAIRFAX
GREIG, mathematics-physics,
1780-1872, Scotland
A 105 (1873) 241
N 7 (1872) 87
N 9 (1874) 417-418
P 25 (1884) P fr, 113-120
SOMERVILLE, MAXWELL, glyptol-
ogy, 1829-1904, U.S.A.
S 19 (1904) 773
von SOMMARUGA, ERWIN, chemistry,

1844?-1897, Austria
S 5 (1897) 916
SOMMER, FERDINAND, anatomy,
1828?-1902, Germany
S 16 (1902) 78
SONDER, OTTO WILHELM, biology,
1811?-1881, Germany
A 127 (1884) 243
SONDERICKER, JEROME, mathe-
matics-mechanics, 1859-1904,
U.S.A.
S 20 (1904) 159
SOOYSMITH, CHARLES, engineer-
ing, 1856-1916, U.S.A.
S 43 (1916) 815
SOPHIE CHARLOTTE, PRINCESS,
diplomacy, 1668-1705,
Germany
P 64 (1903-1904) P 418-421
SOPWITH, THOMAS, engineering,
1803-1879, England
N 44 (1891) 590
SORAUER, PAUL KARL MORITZ,
botany, 1839?-1916, Germany
S 43 (1916) 236
SORBY, HENRY CLIFTON, chemistry,
1826-1908, England
L B80 (1908) lvi-lxvi
N 77 (1908) 465-467
S 27 (1908) 518
SORET, CHARLES, physics, 1854-
1904, Switzerland
A 168 (1904) 96
N 70 (1904) 251-252
S 19 (1904) 743, 838
SOUILLART, CYRILLE JOSEPH,
astronomy, 1828-1898, France
N 58 (1898) 112
S 7 (1898) 799
S 8 (1898) 20
SOUTH, SIR JAMES, astronomy,
1785-1867, England
E 6 (1866-1869) 202-203
L 16 (1868) xliv-xlvii
SOUTHWELL, THOMAS, ornithology,
1830?-1909, U.S.A.
S 30 (1909) 437
SOUYET, M. P., chemistry,
1818?-1850, Belgium
A 60 (1850) 138
SOWERBY, JAMES de CARLE, art-
conchology, 1787-1871,
U.S.A.
A 102 (1871) 390

A 103 (1872) 153
SOWERBY, WILLIAM, botany,
    -1906, England
  S 23 (1906) 558
SPACH, EDOUARD, botany, 1801?-
  1879, France
  A 119 (1880) 77
SPAGNOLETTI, C. E. P., en-
  gineering, 1832?-1905,
  England
  S 42 (1915) 157
SPALDING, DOUGLAS A., psychol-
  ogy, c.1840-1877, England
  N 17 (1877) 35-36
SPALDING, VOLNEY MORGAN,
  botany, 1839-1918, U.S.A.
  S 44 (1916) 914-915
  S 48 (1918) 543-544
SPANGLER, HENRY WILSON, en-
  gineering, 1858-1912, U.S.A.
  S 35 (1912) 487-488
SPANUTIUS, FREDERICK WILLIAM,
  chemistry, 1868?-1915,
  U.S.A.
  S 42 (1915) 50
SPARKS, E. J., medicine,
    -1880,
  N 22 (1880) 591
SPEKE, JOHN HANNING, explora-
  tion, 1827-1864, England
  A 88 (1864) 449
SPENCE, DAVID WENDELL, en-
  gineering,   -1917, U.S.A.
  S 46 (1917) 111
SPENCE, JAMES, surgery, 1812-
  1882, Scotland
  E 12 (1882-1884) 31-32
SPENCE, WILLIAM, entomology,
  1783-1860, England
  L 11 (1862) xxx-xxxi
SPENCER, CHARLES A., optics,
  U.S.A.
  A 55 (1848) 237-240
  A 63 (1852) 31-32
SPENCER, HERBERT, philosophy,
  1820-1903, England
  A 167 (1904) 96
  A 177 (1909) 99
  N 69 (1903) 155-156
  N 70 (1904) 265-266
  N 79 (1908) 122-125
  N 99 (1917) 163
  P 8 (1875-1876) P 620-626
  P 50 (1896-1897) 433-454

P 55 (1899) P fp 433, 542-
  552
P 64 (1903-1904) P 194
P 73 (1908) P 283-285
P 74 (1909) 5-18
S 18 (1903) 799, 838
S 19 (1904) 873-879
S 24 (1906) 505-506
S 28 (1908) 760-763
S 43 (1916) 462-464
SPENCER, SIR WALTER BALDWIN,
  anthropology-biology, 1860-
  1929, England
  L B106 (1930) P vi-x
  N 62 (1900) 59
SPERRY, FRANCIS LOUIS, mineral-
  ogy,   -1906, U.S.A.
  S 23 (1906) 891
SPEZIA, GIORGIO, geology,
  1842-1911, Italy
  A 183 (1912) 72
  S 34 (1911) 912
SPIRGALIS, JOHANN JULIUS
  HERMANN, pharmacy, 1822-1899,
  Germany
  S 10 (1899) 863
SPÖRER, GUSTAV FRIEDRICH
  WILHELM, astronomy, 1822-
  1895, Germany
  N 52 (1895) 417-418
  S 2 (1895) 163
SPOTTISWOODE, WILLIAM, mathe-
  matics-physics, 1825-1883,
  England
  A 126 (1883) 160
  L 38 (1885) xxxiv-xxxix
  N 26 (1882) 583
  N 27 (1882) 134, P 597-601
  N 28 (1883) 205, 217-218,
    246-247
  N 29 (1883) 136
  P 14 (1878-1879) P fr,
    105-106
  Sl 2 (1883) 27-28, 116, 385
SPRAGUE, JOSEPH WHITE, philan-
  thropy,   -1900?, U.S.A.
  S 13 (1901) 117-118
SPRATT, THOMAS ABEL BREMAGE,
  geology, 1811-1888, England
  L 43 (1888) xi-xii
SPRENGEL, CHRISTIAN KONRAD,
  botany, 1750-1816, Germany
  N 28 (1883) 513
  N 29 (1883) 29, 171-172

N 29 (1884) 334-335, 406,
572-573
N 30 (1884) 240-241
SPRENGEL, HERMANN JOHANN
PHILIPP, chemistry-physics,
1834-1906, Germany
N 74 (1906) 356-357
S 23 (1906) 198
S 24 (1906) 354
SPRENGEL, O. K., medicine,
1853?-1915, England
S 41 (1915) 284, 322
SPRING, ANTON FRANCIS, botany,
1813?-1872, Belgium
A 105 (1873) 393
SPRING, WALTHER VICTOR, chem-
istry, 1848-1911, Belgium
N 87 (1911) 252-253
S 34 (1911) 147
SPRUCE, RICHARD, botany, 1817-
1893, England
N 49 (1894) 317-319
SPURZHEIM, JOHANN KASPAR
(CHRISTOPH), phrenology,
1776-1832, Germany
A 23 (1832-1833) 356-370
SQUIBB, EDWARD ROBINSON, chem-
istry-pharmacy, 1819-1900,
U.S.A.
S 21 (1905) 877
SSETSCHENOFF, IVAN MICHAELO-
VITCH, physiology, 1829-
1905, Russia
N 73 (1905) 133
STACY, ORVILLE BRIGGS, mathe-
matics, 1832?-1912, U.S.A.
S 36 (1912) 79
STADLER, ERNST, philology,
1833-1914, Germany
S 40 (1914) 741
von STAHL, HERMANN BERNHARD
LUDWIG, mathematics, 1843-
1909, Germany
S 29 (1909) 893
STAINTON, HENRY TIBBATS, en-
tomology, 1822-1892, England
L 52 (1893) ix-xii
STALKER, MILLIKEN, zoology,
1842?-1909, U.S.A.
S 30 (1909) 237
STALKER, WILFRED, ornithology,
1879?-1910, England
S 31 (1910) 342
STALLO, JOHN BERNARD, chemistry-

physics, 1823-1900, Germany
P 34 (1888-1889) P fp 433,
548-555
S 11 (1900) 238
STANCULEANU, G., ophthalmology,
-1917, Roumania
S 46 (1917) 261
STANFORD, EDWARD, geography,
-1917, England
S 49 (1917) 135
STANFORD, JANE LATHROP, edu-
cation-philanthropy, 1825-
1905, U.S.A.
P 75 (1909) 157-173
STANGE, ALEXANDER, astronomy,
1818-1876, England
N 13 (1876) 408-409
STANGE, HERBERT, chemistry,
-1914, Germany
S 41 (1915) 129
STANGER, ..., geology,
1812-1854, England
A 70 (1855) 392
STANLEY, ANTHONY D.,
mathematics, 1810-1853,
U.S.A.
A 65 (1853) 464
STANLEY, ARTHUR PENRHYN,
history, 1815-1881, England
L 33 (1882) xx-xxii
STANLEY, EDWARD, theology,
1779-1849,
L 5 (1843-1850) 880-887
STANLEY, EDWARD, surgery,
1793-1862, England
L 12 (1863) lxiii-lxiv
STANELY, SIR HENRY MORTON
(John Rowlands), exploration,
1841-1904, Wales
N 70 (1904) 35
Sl 6 (1885) P 177-180
Sl 15 (1890) 309
S 19 (1904) 807
S 31 (1910) 196-197
STANLEY, WILLIAM, engineering,
1858-1916, U.S.A.
S 43 (1916) 710
STANLEY, WILLIAM FORD ROBINSON,
instrumentation-invention,
1829-1909,
N 86 (1911) 277
S 30 (1909) 306
STANTON, JONATHAN YOUNG,
ornithology, 1834-1918,

astronomy-mathematics,
1832-1920, U.S.A.
A   200 (1920) 398
STODDARD, JOHN TAPPAN, chem-
istry, 1852-1919, U.S.A.
S   50 (1919) 564
STOEBER, . . ., medicine,
      -1897,
S   6 (1897) 628
STÖCKHARDT, ERNST, agricul-
ture,   -1898, Germany
S   7 (1898) 596
STÖCKHARDT, JULIUS ADOLPH,
chemistry, 1809-1886,
England
P   19 (1881) P fp 145, 261-
264
Sl   7 (1886) 568
STÖHR, . . ., anatomy, 1849?-
1911, Germany
S   34 (1911) 838
von STOFFELA, RICHARD, medi-
cine,   -1912, Austria
S   35 (1912) 449
STOHMAN, FRIEDRICH CARL ADOLF,
chemistry, 1832-1897,
Germany
S   6 (1897) 805
STOKES, ARTHUR HENRY, mining,
      -1910, England
S   32 (1910) 626
STOKES, SIR GEORGE GABRIEL,
mathematics-physics, 1819-
1903, Ireland
A   165 (1903) 242
A   171 (1906) 174
A   174 (1907) 81-82
E   23 (1899-1901) 4-5
L   6 (1850-1854) 243
L   75 (1905) P 199-216
N   12 (1875) P 201-203
N   29 (1883-1884) 145-146,
545-546
N   32 (1885) 361-362
N   36 (1887) 98-99
N   37 (1887) 49-50, 76-77,
103-104
N   60 (1899) 109-110, 125-
129
N   66 (1902) 49-50
N   67 (1903) 337-338, 345-
346, P Supplement 5
March, cliii
N   68 (1903) 447
N   70 (1904) 247, 373-374,
503-504

N   72 (1905) 555-556
N   76 (1907) 218-219
P   7 (1875) P 742-745
P   56 (1899-1900) P 23
P   62 (1901-1902) P 477-478
P   65 (1904) 509-513
Sl   3 (1884) 204-205
S   5 (1897) 579-580
S   9 (1899) 872
S   17 (1903) 277-278
S   27 (1908) 180-182
STOKES, SIR JOHN, engineering,
1825?-1902, England
S   16 (1902) 959
STOKES, MISS MARGARET, archeol-
ogy,   -1900, Ireland
S   12 (1900) 573
STOKES, WILLIAM, medicine,
1804-1878, Ireland
N   58 (1898) 245
STOKES, SIR WILLIAM, surgery,
1839-1900, Ireland
S   12 (1900) 348
STOKVIS, BAREND JOSEPH, pathol-
ogy-pharmacology, 1834-1902,
Netherlands
S   16 (1902) 683
STOLETOW, ALEXANDER
GRIGORIEVITCH, physics,
1839-1896, Russia
S   4 (1896) 140, 393
STOLICZKA, FERDINAND, paleon-
tology, 1838-1874, Czecho-
slovakia
N   10 (1874) 185-186
N   34 (1886) 574-575
STOLL, . . ., botany, 1813?-
1897,
S   6 (1897) 628
STOLPE, HJALMAR, ethnology,
      -1905, Sweden
S   21 (1905) 478
STOLZ, JOSEPH ALEXIS, medicine,
1803-1896, France
S   3 (1896) 899
STOLZ, OTTO, mathematics, 1842-
1905, Austria
S   23 (1906) 39
STONE, EDWARD JAMES, astronomy,
1831-1897, England
L   62 (1898) x-xxiii
N   56 (1897) 57-58
S   5 (1897) 839
STONE, GEORGE HAPGOOD, geology,
1841-1917, U.S.A.
A   194 (1917) 86

STONE, SIR JOHN BENJAMIN,
photography, 1838?-1914,
England
S 40 (1914) 446
STONE, ROYCE, engineering,
1836?-1905, U.S.A.
S 22 (1905) 221
STONEY, BINDON BLOOD, engineer-
ing, 1828-1909, Ireland
L A85 (1911) viii-x
N 80 (1909) 315
S 29 (1909) 893
STONEY, GEORGE JOHNSTONE,
mathematics-astrophysics,
1826-1911, Ireland
L A86 (1911-1912) P xx-
xxxv
N 87 (1911) 50-51
P 79 (1911) P 207
S 34 (1911) 49
STOPES, HENRY, archaeology,
-1903?,
S 17 (1903) 119
STORCH, K. S., chemistry,
1852?-1907, Austria
S 26 (1907) 326
STORER, FRANCIS HUMPHREYS,
chemistry, 1832-1914, U.S.A.
A 188 (1914) 370
S 40 (1914) 205
S 41 (1915) 85-86
STORY-MASKELYNE, MERVYN
HERBERT NEVIL, mineralogy,
1823-1911, England
A 182 (1911) 84
L A86 (1911-1912) xlvii-lv
N 86 (1911) 452-453
S 33 (1911) 889
STOTT, HENRY GORDON, engineer-
ing, 1866-1917, Scotland
S 45 (1917) 412
STOW, GEORGE WILLIAM, ethnol-
ogy, 1822-1882, England
N 78 (1908) 150
STOWE, HARRIETT ELIZABETH
BEECHER, author, 1811-1896,
U.S.A.
Sl 14 (1889) 3-8
STOWELL, WILLIAM, exploration,
-1919?, U.S.A.
S 50 (1919) 565
STOŽIR, IVAN, meteorology,
-1908, Hungary
S 27 (1908) 436
STRACHEY, SIR RICHARD, geol-
ogy-meteorology, 1817-1908,

England
L A81 (1908) lxxxiv-xciii
N 57 (1897) P 109-110
N 77 (1908) 395-397
N 78 (1908) 425
P 72 (1908) 382-383
S 27 (1908) 397
S 28 (1908) 458-460
STRAHAN, SIR AUBREY, geology,
1852-1928, England
L B103 (1928) P xvi-xx
P 65 (1904) P 566-568
STRASBURGER, EDUARD ADOLF,
botany, 1844-1912, Poland
A 184 (1912) 228
N 77 (1908) P 321-322
N 89 (1912) 379-380
S 35 (1912) 924
STRATFORD, WILLIAM, biology,
1844-1908, U.S.A.
S 27 (1908) 234-235
STRATHCONA--see SMITH, SIR D. A.
STRATTON, JAMES T., geography,
1830-1903, U.S.A.
S 17 (1903) 797
STRAUB, MANUEL, ophthalmology,
1859?-1916, Netherlands
S 43 (1916) 777
STRAUGHN, M. N., chemistry,
-1919, U.S.A.
S 49 (1919) 213
STRAUSS, ISIDORE, pathology,
1845?-1897, France
S 4 (1896) 941
S 5 (1897) 181
STREBEL, HERMANN, malacology,
1833?-1914, Germany
S 40 (1914) 812
STRECKER, ADOLPH FRIEDRICH
LUDWIG, chemistry, 1822-
1871, Germany
A 103 (1872) 320
STRECKER, HERMAN, lepidoptery,
1836-1901, U.S.A.
P 76 (1910) P 470-472
S 14 (1901) 941
STRENG, JOHANN AUGUST, mineral-
ogy, 1830-1897, Germany
S 5 (1897) 223
STRICKER, SALOMON, pathology,
1834-1898, Hungary
S 7 (1898) 633-634
STRICKLAND, HUGH EDWIN, geol-
ogy, 1811-1853, England
A 66 (1853) 447-450
L 6 (1850-1854) 359

STRINGHAM, WASHINGTON IRVING,
mathematics, 1847-1909,
U.S.A.
S 30 (1909) 520
von STROMBECK, AUGUST, geology,
1808-1900, Germany
S 12 (1900) 348
STRONG, MOSES, geology,
-1877, U.S.A.
A 114 (1877) 336
STRONG, THEODORE, mathematics,
1790-1869, U.S.A.
A 97 (1869) 293
STRÜMPELL, LUDWIG, philosophy,
1812?-1899, Germany
S 9 (1899) 789
STRUTHERS, SIR JOHN, anatomy,
1823-1899, England
E 23 (1899-1901) 10-11
N 59 (1899) 468-469
S 9 (1899) 421
STRUTT, JOHN WILLIAM, 3rd
Baron Rayleigh, physics,
1842-1909, England
A 198 (1919) 249-250
E 40 (1919-1920) 2
L A98 (1920-1921) P i-1
N 43 (1890) 43-45
N 61 (1900) 588
N 68 (1903) 289-290
N 70 (1904) P 361-363
N 78 (1908) 12-13
N 92 (1913) 227-228
N 94 (1914) 368
N 118 (18 December 1926
Supplement) P 47-49
P 25 (1884) P fp 721, 840-
842
P 67 (1905) P 90-93
P 78 (1911) P 517-519
Sl 4 (1884) P 161-163
S 11 (1900) 580-585
S 50 (1919) 37
STRUTT, WILLIAM, invention,
-1831,
L 3 (1830-1837) 84
von STRUVE, FRIEDRICH GEORG
WILHELM, astronomy, 1793-
1864, Germany
A 89 (1865) 114
A 90 (1865) 145-160
E 5 (1862-1866) 468-469
L 3 (1830-1837) 221
L 14 (1864) xx-xxii
S 10 (1899) 962-963
STRUVE, HEINRICH WILHELM,

chemistry, 1822-1908,
Estonia
S 28 (1908) 143
von STRUVE, OTTO WILHELM,
astronomy, 1819-1905, Russia
A 169 (1905) 473
L A78 (1907) liv-lix
N 72 (1905) 61
P 17 (1880) P fp 145,
263-264
S 21 (1905) 798
STUART, AMBROSE PASCAL SEVIBON,
chemistry, 1820-1899, U.S.A.
S 10 (1899) 423
STUART, CHARLES, biology,
-1902, England
S 15 (1902) 396
STUART, SIR THOMAS PETER
ANDERSON, physiology, 1856?-
1920,
A 199 (1920) 390
STUBENRAUCH, ARNOLD VALENTINE,
pomology, 1871-1917, U.S.A.
S 45 (1917) 235-236
STUCKENBERG, ALEXANDER ANTONO-
VICH, geology, 1844-1905,
Russia
S 21 (1905) 999
STUDER, BERNHARD, geology,
1794-1887, Switzerland
N 36 (1887) 87
STUDNICKA, FRANZ JOSEF, mathe-
matics, 1836-1903, Germany
S 17 (1903) 598
STUIVAERT, CHARLES E., astron-
omy, 1851?-1908, Belgium
S 28 (1908) 921
STUMPE, OSCAR, astronomy,
1862-1897, Germany
N 57 (1898) 299-300
S 7 (1898) 168
STUMPF, R., pathology,
-1914, Germany
S 40 (1914) 812
STUR, DIONYS RUDOLF JOSEF,
paleontology, 1827-1893,
Austria
A 147 (1894) 80
STURGE, WILLIAM ALLEN, ethnol-
ogy, -1919, England
S 49 (1919) 446
STURGEON, WILLIAM, electricity,
1783-1850, England
A 61 (1851) 444-446
Sl 16 (1890) 199-202
STYFFE, KNUT, technology,

TARUFFI, CESARE, pathology,
1821-1902, Italy
S 16 (1902) 318
TASCHENBERG, ERNST LUDWIG,
entomology, 1819?-1898,
N 57 (1897-1898) 300-301
S 7 (1898) 129
TASSIN, WIRT, chemistry, 1869-
1915, U.S.A.
A 190 (1915) 670
S 42 (1915) 688
TATE, ALEXANDER NORMAN, chem-
istry, 1837-1892, England
N 46 (1892) 298
TATE, RALPH, geology,   -1901,
S 14 (1901) 821
TATUM, SLEDGE, geology,
-1916, U.S.A.
S 43 (1916) 166
TAUSCH, EDWIN, psychology,
-1912, Germany
S 37 (1913) 179-180
TAVEL, ERNST, bacteriology-
surgery, 1858-1912,
Switzerland
S 37 (1913) 145
TAWNEY, EDWARD B., geology,
1841-1882, England
N 27 (1883) 295-296
TAYLOR, ALFRED, geology, 1743-
1884, England
A 129 (1885) 268
TAYLOR, CANNON ISAAC, archeol-
ogy, 1829?-1901,
S 14 (1901) 742
TAYLOR, CHARLES, mathematics,
1840-1908, England
S 28 (1908) 338
TAYLOR, EDWARD BURNETT, anthro-
pology, 1832-1917, England
N 98 (1917) 373-374
TAYLOR, EDWARD RANDOLPH, chem-
istry, 1844-1917, U.S.A.
S 46 (1917) 58-59
TAYLOR, FREDERICK WINSLOW, en-
gineering, 1856-1915, U.S.A.
S 41 (1915) 460
TAYLOR, GEORGE WILLIAM, zoolo-
gy,   -1912, Canada
S 36 (1912) 343
TAYLOR, H. A., telegraphy,
1841-1915?, England
S 43 (1916) 131
TAYLOR, HENRY MARTYN, mathe-
matics, 1842-1927, England
L A117 (1928) P xxix-xxxi

N 58 (1898) 34
TAYLOR, HERBERT DOUGLAS, medi-
cine, 1888?-1918, U.S.A.
S 48 (1918) 392, 411
TAYLOR, JOHN, mining, 1779-
1863, England
L 13 (1864) v-vi
TAYLOR, RICHARD COWLING, geol-
ogy, 1789-1851, England
A 63 (1852) 144-147
TAYLOR, MISS ROSE M., botany,
-1918, U.S.A.
S 38 (1918) 616
TAYLOR, SIR WILLIAM, medicine,
-1917, England
S 45 (1917) 458
TAYLOR, WILLIAM J., chemistry,
1833?-1864, U.S.A.
A 87 (1864) 447
TCHEBYCHEF (CHEBYSHEV), PAFNUTI
LVOVICH, mathematics, 1821-
1894, Russia
N 52 (1895) 345
S 1 (1895) 129-131
TCHERNYCHEFF, THEODOSIE, geol-
ogy, 1857?-1914, Russia
A 187 (1914) 288
S 39 (1914) 137
TEALE, THOMAS PRIDGIN, medi-
cine, 1831-1923, England
L B96 (1924) P xxi-xxv
N 38 (1888) 12
TEALL, JETHRO JUSTINIAN HARRIS,
geology, 1849-1924,
England
L B97 (1925) xv-xvii
N 42 (1890) 16
N 114 (1924) 95
TEBBUTT, JOHN, astronomy,
1834-1917?, Australia
S 38 (1913) 225
S 45 (1917) 184
TEGETMEIER, WILLIAM BERNHARD,
zoology, 1816-1912, England
N 97 (1916) 399
S 37 (1913) 16
TEGMEYER, JOHN H., engineering,
1821?-1901, U.S.A.
S 14 (1901) 77
TEICHMANN, . . ., engineering,
1839?-1900, Germany
S 11 (1900) 596
TEICHMANN, LUDWIG, anatomy,
-1895, Poland
S 3 (1896) 66
TEISSERENC de BORT, PHILIPPE

L B106 (1930) xxiii-xxix
N 70 (1904) 419
THOBURN, WILBUR WILSON, bio-
mechanics,   -1899, U.S.A.
S 9 (1899) 301
THOLLEN, . . ., geology,
-1897,
S 5 (1897) 652
THOMAS, BENJAMIN FRANKLIN,
physics, 1850-1911, U.S.A.
S 34 (1911) 74
S 35 (1912) 647
THOMAS, CYRUS, archeology-
ethnology, 1825-1910, U.S.A.
S 32 (1910) 53
THOMAS, EDWARD, astronomy,
-1832, U.S.A.
A 22 (1832) 380
THOMAS, HONORATUS LEIGH,
surgery, 1769?-1846,
L 5 (1843-1850) 640-641
THOMAS, MASON BLANCHARD,
botany, 1866-1912, U.S.A.
S 35 (1912) 414
THOMAS, MICHAEL ROGERS OLDFIELD,
anthropology, 1858-1929,
L B106 (1930) P i-v
N 64 (1901) 37-38
THOMAS, PHILLIPPE ÉTIENNE,
geology, 1843-1910, France
S 31 (1910) 411
THOMAS, SIDNEY GILCHRIST, in-
vention-metallurgy, 1850-
1885, England
Sl 5 (1885) 221
THOMAS, WILLIAM D., psychology,
-1901, U.S.A.
S 13 (1901) 877
THOME, MRS. FRANCES, astronomy,
-1916,
S 43 (1916) 710
THOME, JOHN MACON, astronomy,
1843-1908, U.S.A.
S 28 (1908) 752
THOMPSON, ALMON HARRIS, geog-
raphy, 1839-1906, U.S.A.
S 24 (1906) 190
THOMPSON, BENJAMIN, Count
Rumford, physics, 1743-1814,
U.S.A.
A 19 (1830-1831) 28-46
A 33 (1837-1838) 21-30
A 102 (1871) 230-231
A 103 (1872) 237-238
N 9 (1873) 117-119
N 11 (1875) 203-206

P 9 (1876) P 231-238
P 73 (1908) P 32-51
Sl 2 (1883) 147
S 9 (1899) 838-839, 883
S 21 (1905) 874
THOMPSON, MRS. ELIZABETH, phi-
lanthropy,   -1899, U.S.A.
S 10 (1899) 126
THOMPSON, E. S.--see SETON,
E. T.
THOMPSON, F. F., philanthropy,
-1899, U.S.A.
S 9 (1899) 598
THOMPSON, SIR HENRY, surgery,
1820-1904, England
S 16 (1902) 437
S 19 (1904) 712
THOMPSON, SIR HENRY, physiol-
ogy,   -1918, Ireland
S 48 (1918) 617
THOMPSON, ISAAC COOKE, zoology,
-1903,
N 69 (1903) 60-61
THOMPSON, JAMES MAURICE, en-
gineering-geology, 1844-
1901, U.S.A.
S 13 (1901) 397
THOMPSON, JOHN TATHAM, ophthal-
mology,   -1911, England
S 33 (1911) 767
THOMPSON, JOSEPH, exploration,
1858-1895,
S 2 (1895) 233
THOMPSON, SETON, biology,
S 19 (1904) 623
THOMPSON, SILVANUS PHILLIPS,
physics, 1851-1916, England
A 192 (1916) 90
L 94 (1918) P xvi-xix
N 44 (1891) 16
N 97 (1916) 325, 343-344,
442
S 43 (1916) 924
S 44 (1916) 849
THOMPSON, THEOPHILUS, medicine,
1807-1860, England
L 11 (1862) xxxi-xxxii
THOMPSON, THOMAS PERONNET,
mathematics, 1783-1869,
England
L 18 (1870) xi-xvi
THOMPSON, WILLIAM, zoology,
1805?-1852, Ireland
A 63 (1852) 443
THOMPSON, ZADOK, biology-
geography, 1796-1856, U.S.A.

A   200 (1920) 474
TÖRÖK, AUREL, anthropology,
      -1912, Hungary
   S   36 (1912) 431
TOKASKY, A. A., physiology,
      -1901, Russia
   S   14 (1901) 1022
von TOLL, EDUARD, baron, ex-
   ploration, 1858-   ,
   Russia
   S   20 (1904) 123
   S   38 (1913) 439-440
TOLLES, ROBERT BRUCE, optics,
   1822-1883, U.S.A.
   S1 2 (1883) 726
   S   35 (1912) 444-446
TOLMIE, W. F., ethnology,
      -1886, Scotland
   A   133 (1887) 244-245
   A   135 (1888) 260
   S1 8 (1886) 628
TOMBO, RUDOLF, JR., philology,
      -1914, U.S.A.
   S   39 (1914) 784
TOME, JACOB, philanthropy,
   1810-1898, U.S.A.
   S   7 (1898) 421
TOMES, SIR CHARLES SISSMORE,
   odontology, 1846-1928,
   England
   L   B104 (1929) P xiii-xix
TOMES, SIR JOHN, histology,
   1815-1895, England
   L   59 (1896) xiii-xiv
   N   52 (1895) 396
   S   2 (1895) 188
TOMLINSON, CHARLES, biology-
   geology, 1808-1897, England
   N   55 (1896-1897) 371
   S   5 (1897) 340
TOMMASINI, J. S., botany,
      -1879, Italy
   A   127 (1884) 242
TOMUSOARY, EDMUND,
      -1884, Romania
   S1 5 (1885) 62
TOMSA, . . ., physiology,
      -1895, Czechoslovakia
   S   1 (1895) 556
TONE, FRANK JEROME, chemistry,
   1868-   , U.S.A.
   S   21 (1905) 882
TOOKE, WILLIAM, administration,
   1777-1863, Russia
   L   13 (1864) vi-vii
TOOKER, WILLIAM WALLACE,

archeology-ethnology, 1848-
   1917, U.S.A.
   S   46 (1917) 135
TOPINARD, PAUL, anthropology,
   1830-1912, France
   P   41 (1892) P 68-69
   S   35 (1912) 58
TOPLEY, WILLIAM, geology, 1841-
   1894, England
   A   148 (1894) 514
   L   59 (1896) lxix-lxxi
   N   38 (1888) 12
   N   50 (1894) 579-580
TORREY, BRADFORD, biology-
   ornithology, 1843-1912,
   U.S.A.
   S   36 (1912) 669
TORREY, HENRY AUGUSTUS, chem-
   istry, 1871-1910, U.S.A.
   S   31 (1910) 499
   S   32 (1910) 50-51
TORREY, JOHN, botany-chemistry,
   1796-1873, U.S.A.
   A   105 (1873) 324, 397,
      411-421
   A   107 (1874) 239
   P   3 (1873) P 632-638
   P   70 (1907) P 297-299
   S   10 (1899) 635-637
   S   12 (1900) 161-162
TORRIE, THOMAS JAMESON, geol-
   ogy-mineralogy,   -1858,
   E   4 (1857-1862) 112
TOSCANI, DAVID, medicine,
      -1898, Italy
   S   8 (1898) 509
TOSH, JAMES RAMSEY, zoology,
   1872-1917, Scotland
   E   39 (1918-1919) 15-16
   S   46 (1917) 337
TOURNIER, ALFRED, botany,
      -1915?, France
   S   41 (1915) 240
TOWNSEND, DAVID, botany, 1777?-
   1858, England
   A   77 (1859) 443
TOWNSEND, FITZHUGH, engineer-
   ing, 1872?-1906, U.S.A.
   S   24 (1906) 830
TOWNSEND, SIR JOHN SEALY EDWARD,
   physics, 1868-1927, Ireland
   N   94 (1914) 368
TOWNSEND, RICHARD, mathematics,
      -1884?, Ireland
   S1 5 (1885) 62
TOWNSHEND, NORTON STRANGE,

1841-1907, Germany
N 76 (1907) 446-447
VOGEL, HERMANN WILHELM,
photography, 1834-1898,
Germany
N 59 (1898) 204-205
S 9 (1899) 78
VOGEL, KARL HERMANN, astro-
physics, 1842-1907, Germany
S 26 (1907) 326
VOGEL, PETER, mathematics,
1857?-1915, Germany
S 42 (1915) 898
VOGLER, G. H. OTTO, biology,
1822?-1897,
S 6 (1897) 805
VOGT, KARL CHRISTOPH, zoology,
1817-1895, Germany
A 149 (1895) 485
N 52 (1895) 34, 108-110
N 54 (1896) 386-388
P 52 (1897-1898) P fr,
116-122
S 2 (1895) 187
S 4 (1896) 168, 947-954
VOIGT, WOLDEMAR, physics,
1850-1919, Germany
L A99 (1912) **xxix-xxx**
von VOIT, KARL, biology-
physiology, 1831-1908,
Germany
S 27 (1908) 315-316
VOLHARD, JACOB, chemistry,
1834-1910, Germany
S 31 (1910) 295
VOLK, ERNEST, archeology-
geology, 1845-1919, U.S.A.
S 50 (1919) 451-453
VOLKENHAUER, AUGUST, geology,
-1915, Germany
S 41 (1915) 606
de VOLNEY, CONSTANTIN FRANÇOIS
de CHASSEBOEUF, comte,
geography, 1757-1820, France
A 2 (1820) 345
S 8 (1898) 704
VOLPICELLI, PAOLO, physics,
1804-1879, Italy
A 118 (1879) 80
N 20 (1879) 126
VOLTA, ALESSANDRO GIUSEPPE
ANTONIO ANASTASIO, conti,
physics, 1745-1827, Italy
A 15 (1829) 67-76, 177
N 60 (1899) 181-182, 440
P 41 (1892) P fr, 117-122

S 10 (1899) 94-95
de VOLTAIRE (AROUET), FRANCOIS
MARIE, philosophy, 1694-1778,
France
A 118 (1879) 333
VOLTERRA, VITO, mathematics,
1860-1940, Italy
N 70 (1904) 418-419
VOLZ, WILHELM THEODOR AUGUST
HERMANN, biology, 1870-1907,
Germany
S 25 (1907) 917
VORONINE, ..., botany, 1828?-
1903, Russia
S 17 (1903) 559
VOSMAER, G. C. J., morphology,
1854?-1916, Netherlands
S 44 (1916) 672
VOSS, AUREL EDMUND, mathemat-
ics, 1845-1931, Germany
S 44 (1916) 705
VOUSAKIS, CONSTANTINE, physiol-
ogy,   -1899, Greece
S 9 (1899) 229
VULPIAN, EDME FÉLIX ALFRED,
medicine, 1826-1887, France
P 34 (1888-1889) P fp 145,
262-266
WAAGE, PETER, chemistry, 1833-
1900, Norway
S 11 (1900) 277
WAAGEN, WILHELM HEINRICH,
geology, 1841-1900, Austria
A 159 (1900) 395
WACHSMUTH, CHARLES, paleontol-
ogy, 1829-1896, Germany
A 151 (1896) 250
WADE, JOHN, chemistry, 1864?-
1912, England
S 36 (1912) 399
WAGENER, N., zoology, 1830?-
1907, Russia
S 25 (1907) 758
WAGER, HAROLD, botany, 1862-
1929, England
L B106 (1930) P xix-xxii
WAGNER, CLINTON, medicine,
1840?-1914?, U.S.A.
S 41 (1915) 129
von WAGNER, JOHANN RUDOLF,
chemistry, 1822-1880,
Germany
N 23 (1880) 11-12
WAGNER, RUDOLF, physiology,
1805-1864, Germany
A 88 (1864) 149

WAGHER, WILLIAM, biology,
S 11 (1900) 449-451
WAHL, WILLIAM HENRY, chemistry-
technology, 1848-1909,
U.S.A.
S 29 (1909) 542
WAHLENBERG, . . ., botany,
1781?-1851,
A 63 (1852) 45
WAHLFORSS, HENRIK ALFRED,
chemistry, 1839-1899,
Germany
S 9 (1899) 661
WAIT, LUCIEN AUGUSTUS, mathe-
matics, 1846-1913, U.S.A.
S 38 (1913) 507
WAITZ, GEORG, history, 1813-
1886, Germany
Sl 7 (1886) 504
WAITZ, KARL, astronomy-physics,
1853-1911, Germany
S 34 (1911) 485
WAKE, CHARLES STANILAND, eth-
nology, 1835-1910, England
S 32 (1910) 14
WAKEHAM, WILLIAM, ichthyology,
-1915, Canada
S 41 (1915) 859
WAKLEY, THOMAS, medicine,
1851?-1909, England
S 29 (1909) 542
de WALCKENAER, CHARLES
ATHANASIUS, baron, entomol-
ogy-geography, 1771-1852,
France
A 64 (1852) 449, 450
WALCOTT, CHARLES DOOLITTLE,
geology-paleontology, 1850-
1927, U.S.A.
P 52 (1897-1898) P fp 433,
547-553
P 70 (1907) 285-286, P 479
WALCOTT, HELENE B. (MRS. C. D.),
geology, -1911, U.S.A.
S 34 (1911) 109-110
WALCOTT, HENRY PICKERING,
medicine, 1838-1932, U.S.A.
S 39 (1914) 779-780
WALDEN, PAUL, chemistry, 1863-
1957, Russia
P 82 (1913) P 551-555
von WALDENHOFEN, ADELBERT,
physics, 1828?-1914, Austria
S 39 (1914) 503
von WALDEYER, HEINRICH WILHELM
GOTTFRIED, anatomy, 1836-1921,

Germany
P 66 (1904-1905) P 6
S 24 (1906) 573
S 34 (1911) 708
S 44 (1916) 632, 848
WALDHEIM, G. F. FISCHER von--
see Fischer von Waldheim
WALDIE, DAVID, medicine, 1815-
, Scotland
S 42 (1915) 118
WALKER, FRANCIS, entomology,
-1874?,
A 109 (1875) 76
WALKER, FRANCIS AMASA, eco-
nomics, 1840-1897, U.S.A.
A 153 (1897) 164
P 57 (1900) P 278
S 5 (1897) 102-103
S 7 (1898) 60
WALKER, GEORGE WALKER, physics,
1874-1921, England
L A102 (1923) xxii-xxvi
WALKER, JAMES, engineering,
1781-1862, Scotland
E 5 (1862-1866) 29-30
L 12 (1863) lxiv-lxvi
WALKER, SIR JAMES, chemistry,
1863-1935, Scotland
N 62 (1900) 59
WALKER, JAMES THOMAS, geog-
raphy, 1826-1896, India
L 59 (1896) xliii
N 53 (1896) 373, 469-470
WALKER, JOHN JAMES, mathemat-
ics, 1825-1900, England
L 75 (1905) 93-94
WALKER, SEARS COOK, astronomy-
mathematics, 1805-1853,
U.S.A.
A 65 (1853) 293-295
P 46 (1894-1895) P fr,
116-121
WALKER, WILLIAM JOHNSON,
surgery, 1790-1865, U.S.A.
A 89 (1865) 374
WALKER-ARNOTT, GEORGE A.,
botany, 1799-1868, Scotland
A 96 (1868) 273
A 97 (1869) 140-141
WALLACE, ALFRED RUSSEL, biol-
ogy, 1823-1913, England
A 186 (1913) 659
E 35 (1914-1915) 1-2
L B95 (1924) P i-xxxv
N 43 (1890) 136
N 48 (1893) 10

S 22 (1905) 203
S 34 (1911) 312-316
WEBSTER, FRANCIS MARION, en-
tomology, 1849-1916, U.S.A.
S 43 (1916) 64, 162-164
WEBSTER, FREDERICK S.,
P 59 (1901) P 12
WEBSTER, HARRISON EDWIN,
biology-geology, 1841?-1906,
U.S.A.
S 23 (1906) 989
WEBSTER, NATHAN BURNHAM, edu-
cation, 1821-1900, U.S.A.
S 13 (1901) 78
WEDDELL, HUGH ALGERNON, botany,
1819-1877, England
A 115 (1878) 225
WEDDERBURN, ERNEST MACLAGAN,
limnology-physics,
E 31 (1910-1911) 705
WEDDING, GUSTAV FRIEDRICH
HERMANN, mining, 1834-1908,
Germany
S 27 (1908) 966
WEDEKIND, LUDWIG, mathematics,
1839?-1908, Germany
S 27 (1908) 518
WEEDON, WILLIAM STONE, chem-
istry, 1877-1912, U.S.A.
S 36 (1912) 273
WEEKS, JOSEPH D., economics,
1840-1896?, U.S.A.
S 5 (1897) 270
WEEREN, JULIUS, metallurgy,
1832?-1915, Germany
S 41 (1915) 204
WEIBRECHT, CARL, technology,
-1904, Germany
S 20 (1904) 62
WEIDEL, HUGO, chemistry, 1849-
1899, Austria
S 10 (1899) 63
WEIERSTRASS, KARL THEODOR
WILHELM, mathematics, 1815-
1897, Germany
N 53 (1895) 113
N 55 (1897) 443
N 57 (1897) 107
S 5 (1897) 472
WEIGERT, CARL, histology-pathol-
ogy, 1845-1904, Germany
S 20 (1904) 287
WEIL, RICHARD, medicine-
pathology, 1876-1916, U.S.A.
S 46 (1917) 538, 557-558
WEINGARTEN, JULIUS, mathematics,

1836-1910, Germany
S 32 (1910) 109
WEINLECHNER, JOSEF, surgery,
1830?-1906, Austria
S 24 (1906) 574
WEINSTEIN, JOSEPH, chemistry,
1862?-1917, U.S.A.
S 46 (1917) 14
WEISMANN, AUGUST FRIEDRICH
LEOPOLD, biology-embryology,
1834-1914, Germany
A 188 (1914) 573
E 36 (1915-1916) 27
L B89 (1917) xxvii-xxxiv
N 79 (1908) 136-137
N 87 (1911) P 182-183
N 94 (1914) 342-343
P 87 (1915) P 103
S 18 (1903) 191
S 19 (1904) 317
S 39 (1914) 204
S 40 (1914) 739
S 41 (1915) 917-923
WEISS, EDMUND, astronomy,
1837-1917, Austria
S 26 (1907) 390
S 49 (1919) 539
WEISS, ERNST CHRISTIAN,
paleontology, 1832-1890,
Germany
Sl 16 (1890) 202
WEISS, WILHELM, mathematics,
1859-1904, Germany
S 20 (1904) 95
WEISSENBORN, BERNHARD, zoology,
-1889, Germany
Sl 13 (1889) 501
WEITZENBÖCK, RICHARD, chem-
istry, 1885-1915, Germany
S 41 (1915) 386
WELCH, WILLIAM HENRY, pathol-
ogy, 1850-1934, U.S.A.
P 68 (1906) P 98
P 74 (1909) P 101
S 46 (1917) 240-241
WELCKER, HERMAN, anatomy,
1822-1897, Germany
S 6 (1897) 591
WELD, CHARLES G., philanthropy,
-1911, U.S.A.
S 34 (1911) 12
WELDON, WALTER, chemistry,
1832-1885, England
L 46 (1890) xix-xxiv
WELDON, WALTER FRANK RAPHAEL,
morphology, 1860-1906,

England
L B80 (1908) xxv-xli
N 42 (1890) 16
N 73 (1906) 611-612
S 23 (1906) 718
WELLINGTON, ARTHUR MELLEN,
engineering, 1847-1895,
U.S.A.
S 1 (1895) 614
WELLMAN, SAMUEL THOMAS, en-
gineering, 1847-1919, U.S.A.
S 50 (1919) 249
WELLS, CHARLES F., explora-
tion, -1897,
S 5 (1897) 917
WELLS, DAVID AMES, economics,
1828-1898, U.S.A.
P 32 (1887-1888) P fp 721,
832-840
S 8 (1898) 667
WELLS, F. J., agriculture,
-1904, U.S.A.
S 19 (1904) 743
WELLS, HORACE, anesthesia-
dentistry, 1815-1848,
U.S.A.
A 110 (1875) 76
WELLSTEAD, ..., army,
-1842,
L 4 (1837-1843) 419
WELSCH, ROBERT F., ichthyol-
ogy, -1895?,
S 3 (1896) 66
WELSH, JOHN, astronomy, 1824-
1859, Scotland
L 10 (1860) xxxiv-xxxviii
WELWITSCH, FRIEDRICH MARTIN
JOSEPH, botany, 1807-1872,
Austria
A 105 (1873) 396-397
WELWOOD, ALEXANDER MACONOCHIE,
Lord Meadowbank, law, 1777-
1861, Scotland
E 5 (1862-1866) 28-29
WENDELL, OLIVER CLINTON, as-
tronomy, 1845-1912, U.S.A.
S 36 (1912) 914
WENDEROTH, G. W. F., botany,
1774?-1861, Germany
A 83 (1862) 428
WENZEL, ERNST, anatomy, 1840?-
1896, Germany
S 4 (1896) 793
WENZELL, WILLIAM THEODORE,
chemistry, 1829-1913, U.S.A.
S 38 (1913) 623

WERNER, ABRAHAM GOTTLOB, geol-
ogy, 1750-1817, Germany
A 118 (1879) 335
PM 50 (1817) 182-189
Sl 24 (1894) 19-20
S 6 (1897) 928
WERNLE, C. HENRY, instrumen-
tation, 1831?-1902, U.S.A.
S 15 (1902) 878
WESBROOK, FRANK FAIRCHILD,
pathology, 1868-1918, U.S.A.
S 48 (1918) 442
WESSEL, CASPAR, mathematics,
1745-1818, Norway
S 6 (1897) 297-307
WEST, GEORGE STEPHEN, botany,
1876?-1919, England
S 50 (1919) 249
WEST, WILLIAM, biology, 1875?-
1901, U.S.A.
S 14 (1901) 660
WEST, WILLIAM, botany, 1846?-
1914, England
S 39 (1914) 867
WESTERGAARD, REGINALD L. A. E.,
mycology, -1920, Denmark
E 40 (1919-1920) 194-195
WESTERMAYER, MAX, botany,
-1903, Switzerland
S 17 (1903) 916
WESTHOFF, FRITZ, zoology,
1856?-1896, Germany
S 4 (1896) 941
WESTINGHOUSE, GEORGE, engineer-
ing, 1846-1914, U.S.A.
S 39 (1914) 421, 599-601
WESTON, EDWARD, electricity,
1850-1936, England
S 41 (1915) 484-492
WESTON, STEPHEN,
-1830,
L 3 (1830-1837) 10
WETHERILL, CHARLES MAYER,
chemistry, 1825-1871,
U.S.A.
A 101 (1871) 310, 478-479
WETZEL, LEWIS, exploration,
1764-1808, U.S.A.
A 31 (1837) 14-18
WEYENBERGH, H., zoology,
-1885, Netherlands
Sl 6 (1885) 20
WEYER, GEORGE DANIEL EDUARD,
astronomy-mathematics,
1818-1896, Germany
S 5 (1897) 181

WOLFF, KASPAR FRIEDRICH,
   anatomy-physiology, 1733-
   1794, Germany
   P 67 (1905) 106-111
WOLFFHÜGEL, G., hygiene,
        -1899, Germany
   S 9 (1899) 301
WOLKENHAUER, AUGUST, geog-
   raphy,   -1915, Germany
   S 41 (1915) 678
WOLLASTON, C. J., telegraphy,
   1820?-1915?,
   S 43 (1916) 18
WOLLASTON, WILLIAM HYDE,
   chemistry-physics, 1766-
   1828, England
   A   3 (1821) 373
   A 16 (1829) 216
   A 17 (1829-1830) 159-160,
      361-364
   A 20 (1839) 20-21
   L   3 (1830-1837) 220-221
   N 26 (1882) 572
   N 94 (1914) 308
   PM II 7 (1830) 34-35,
      228-229
WOLLEY, JOHN, JR., zoology,
   1823?-1859,
   N 67 (1903) 219-220
WOOD, ALEXANDER, law, 1788-
   1864, Scotland
   E   5 (1862-1866) 309
WOOD, ALPHONSO, botany,
   1810?-1881, U.S.A.
   A 123 (1882) 333
   A 127 (1884) 242
WOOD, ANDREW, medicine,
   1810-1881, Scotland
   E 11 (1880-1882) 338-342
WOOD, DE VOLSON, engineering,
   1832-1897, U.S.A.
   S   6 (1897) 28
WOOD, EDWARD STICKNEY, chem-
   istry, 1846-1905, U.S.A.
   S 22 (1905) 95
WOOD, HUDSON A., mathematics,
   1841?-1903, U.S.A.
   S 18 (1903) 477
WOOD, JOHN CLAIRE, zoology,
   1871?-1916, U.S.A.
   S 44 (1919) 564
WOOD, JOHN GEORGE, biology,
   1827-1884, England
   Sl 13 (1889) 288
WOOD, JOHN MEDLEY, botany,
   1852?-1915, England

N 96 (1915) 174-175
   S 42 (1915) 641
WOOD, JOHN TURTLE, archeology,
   1820-1890, England
   P   7 (1875) P 223-228
WOOD, NICHOLAS, engineering,
   1795-1865, England
   L 16 (1868) lxi-lxiii
WOOD, ROBERT WILLIAMS, physics,
   1868-1955, U.S.A.
   S 39 (1914) 25-27
WOOD, SEARLES VALENTINE, JR.,
   paleontology, 1829?-1884,
   England
   A 129 (1885) 348
   N 31 (1885) 318-319
WOOD, SEARLES VALENTINE, SR.,
   paleontology, 1798-1880,
   England
   N 23 (1880) 40-41
WOODBRIDGE, LUTHER DANA,
   anatomy, 1850-1899, U.S.A.
   S 10 (1899) 702
WOODBRIDGE, WILLIAM CHANNING,
   education, 1794-1845, U.S.A.
   A 51 (1846) 152
WOODBURY, CHARLES JEPTHA HILL,
   engineering, 1851-1916,
   U.S.A.
   S 43 (1916) 460
WOODCROFT, BENNET, technology,
   1803-1879, England
   L 29 (1879) xxxii-xxxiv
WOODFORD, STEWART LYNDON,
   diplomacy, 1835-1913, U.S.A.
   P 75 (1909) P 330
WOODHOUSE, E. J., botany,
        -1918, England
   S 47 (1918) 237
WOODHOUSE, JAMES, chemistry,
   1770-1809, U.S.A.
   A 196 (1914) 541-542
   A 197 (1919) 383
WOODHOUSE, SAMUEL W., biology,
   1820-1904, U.S.A.
   S 20 (1904) 694-695
WOODMAN, HENRY J., biology,
        -1903, U.S.A.
   S 17 (1903) 916
WOODROW, JAMES, science,
   1828-1907, U.S.A.
   S 25 (1907) 158
WOODRUFF, CHARLES EDWARD,
   anthropology-surgery, 1860-
   1915, U.S.A.
   S 41 (1915) 937-938

WOODWARD, AMOS E., geology,
-1891, U.S.A.
Sl 18 (1891) 199
WOODWARD, ANTHONY, geology,
-1915, U.S.A.
S 41 (1915) 240
WOODWARD, SIR ARTHUR SMITH,
geology-paleontology,
1864-1944, England
N 64 (1901) 38
N 100 (1917) 277
P 66 (1904-1905) P 10
P 75 (1909) P 411
WOODWARD, CALVIN MILTON,
mathematics, 1837-1915,
U.S.A.
P 64 (1903-1904) P 378
S 39 (1914) 496-498
WOODWARD, HENRY, geology, 1832-
1921, England
L B98 (1925) P xxiii-xxv
WOODWARD, HORACE BOLINGBROKE,
geology, 1848-1914, England
A 187 (1914) 366
L B91 (1920) xxxi-xxxii
N 54 (1896) 12
N 92 (1914) 692
S 39 (1914) 355
WOODWARD, JULIUS HAYDEN,
ophthalmology, 1858-1916,
U.S.A.
S 44 (1916) 53
WOODWARD, MARTIN FOUNTAIN,
zoology, 1865-1901,
England
N 64 (1901) 578-579
S 14 (1901) 581
WOODWARD, ROBERT SIMPSON,
physics, 1849-1924, U.S.A.
P 57 (1900) P fp 339,
442-443
WOODWARD, SAMUEL PICKWORTH,
biology-geology, 1821-1865,
England
A 90 (1865) 288
WOODWORTH, ROBERT SESSIONS,
psychology, 1869-1962,
U.S.A.
P 74 (1909) P 207
WOODWORTH, WILLIAM McMICHAEL,
zoology, 1864-1912, U.S.A.
A 184 (1912) 228
WOOLF, SOLOMON, geometry,
1841?-1911, U.S.A.
S 33 (1911) 889
WOOLSEY, THEODORE DWIGHT,

education, 1801-1889, U.S.A.
Sl 14 (1889) 9
WOOSNAM, R. B., zoology,
-1915, England
S 42 (1915) 119
WORMLEY, THEODORE GEORGE,
chemistry, 1826-1897, U.S.A.
P 49 (1896) P 460
S 5 (1897) 56
WORMS de ROMILLY, . . .,
physics,   -1903, France
S 17 (1903) 878
WORSAAE, JENS JACOB ASMUSSEN,
archeology, 1821-1885,
Denmark
P 47 (1895) P 12-15
WORTHEN, AMOS HENRY, geology,
1813-1888, U.S.A.
A 136 (1888) 80, 161-162
Sl 11 (1888) 240
WORTHEN, GEORGE CARLTON,
botany, 1871?-1919, U.S.A.
A 197 (1919) 454
S 49 (1919) 398
WORTHINGTON, ARTHUR MASON,
physics, 1852-1916, England
A 193 (1917) 174
N 48 (1893) 10
N 98 (1916) 293-294
S 45 (1917) 14
von WRANGELL, FERDINAND, baron,
ethnology-exploration,
1796-1870, Russia
Sl 6 (1885) 417-418
WRANGHAM, FRANCIS,
L 5 (1843-1850) 489
WRAY, . . ., medicine,
-1908,
S 27 (1908) 902-903
WREN, SIR CHRISTOPHER, archi-
tecture-physics, 1632-1723,
England
N 25 (1882) 505
WRIGHT, ALBERT ALLEN, geology,
1846-1905,
S 21 (1905) 600
WRIGHT, SIR ALMROTH EDWARD,
bacteriology, 1861-1947,
England
N 100 (1917) 277
WRIGHT, ARTHUR WILLIAMS,
physics, 1836-1915, U.S.A.
A 191 (1916) 152, 361-366
S 42 (1915) 932
S 43 (1916) 270-272, 650
WRIGHT, CARROLL DAVIDSON,

Inserts from Page 12

CORRELATION TABLES

A — AMERICAN JOURNAL OF SCIENCE

(First Series)				(Second Series)			
1	1819	26	1834	51	1846	76	1858
2	1820	27	1834-35	52	1846	77	1859
3	1821	28	1835	53	1847	78	1859
4	1822	29	1835-36	54	1847	79	1860
5	1822	30	1836	55	1848	80	1860
6	1823	31	1837	56	1848	81	1861
7	1824	32	1837	57	1849	82	1861
8	1824	33	1837-38	58	1849	83	1862
9	1825	34	1838	59	1850	84	1862
10	1826	35	1838	60	1850	85	1863
11	1826	36	1839	61	1851	86	1863
12	1827	37	1839	62	1851	87	1864
13	1828	38	1839-40	63	1852	88	1864
14	1828	39	1840	64	1852	89	1865
15	1829	40	1840-41	65	1853	90	1865
16	1829	41	1841	66	1853	91	1866
17	1829-30	42	1841-42	67	1854	92	1866
18	1830	43	1842	68	1854	93	1867
19	1830-31	44	1842-43	69	1855	94	1867
20	1831	45	1843	70	1855	95	1868
21	1831-32	46	1844	71	1856	96	1868
22	1832	47	1844	72	1856	97	1869
23	1832-33	48	1845	73	1857	98	1869
24	1833	49	1845	74	1857	99	1870
25	1833-34	50	Index 1-50	75	1858	100	1870

(Third Series)				(Fourth Series)			
101	1871	126	1883	151	1896	176	1908
102	1871	127	1884	152	1896	177	1909
103	1872	128	1884	153	1897	178	1909
104	1872	129	1885	154	1897	179	1910
105	1873	130	1885	155	1898	180	1910
106	1873	131	1886	156	1898	181	1911
107	1874	132	1886	157	1899	182	1911
108	1874	133	1887	158	1899	183	1912
109	1875	134	1887	159	1900	184	1912
110	1875	135	1888	160	1900	185	1913
111	1876	136	1888	161	1901	186	1913
112	1876	137	1889	162	1901	187	1914
113	1877	138	1889	163	1902	188	1914
114	1877	139	1890	164	1902	189	1915
115	1878	140	1890	165	1903	190	1915
116	1878	141	1891	166	1903	191	1916
117	1879	142	1891	167	1904	192	1916
118	1879	143	1892	168	1904	193	1917
119	1880	144	1892	169	1905	194	1917
120	1880	145	1893	170	1905	195	1918
121	1881	146	1893	171	1906	196	1918
122	1881	147	1894	172	1906	197	1919
123	1882	148	1894	173	1907	198	1919
124	1882	149	1895	174	1907	199	1920
125	1883	150	1895	175	1908	200	1920

E — PROCEEDINGS OF THE EDINBURGH ROYAL SOCIETY

1	1832–1844	11	1880–1882	21	1895–1897	31	1910–1911
2	1844–1850	12	1882–1884	22	1897–1899	32	1911–1912
3	1850–1857	13	1884–1886	23	1899–1901	33	1912–1913
4	1857–1862	14	1886–1887	24	1901–1903	34	1913–1914
5	1862–1866	15	1887–1888	25	1903–1905	35	1914–1915
6	1866–1869	16	1888–1889	26	1905–1906	36	1915–1916
7	1869–1872	17	1889–1890	27	1906–1907	37	1916–1917
8	1872–1875	18	1890–1891	28	1907–1908	38	1917–1918
9	1875–1878	19	1891–1892	29	1908–1909	39	1918–1919
10	1878–1880	20	1892–1895	30	1909–1910	40	1919–1920

L — PROCEEDINGS OF THE ROYAL SOCIETY (of London)

1	1800–1814	44	1888	B81	1909	A103	1923
2	1815–1830	45	1888–1889	A82	1909	B103	1928
3	1830–1837	46	1889	B82	1909–1910	A104	1923
4	1837–1843	47	1889–1890	A83	1909–1910	B104	1928–1929
5	1843–1850	48	1890	B83	1910–1911	A105	1924
6	1850–1854	49	1890–1891	A84	1910–1911	B105	1929–1930
7	1854–1855	50	1891–1892	B84	1911–1912	A106	1924
8	1856–1857	51	1892	A85	1911	B106	1930
9	1857–1859	52	1892–1893	B85	1912	A107	1925
10	1859–1860	53	1893	A86	1911–1912	B107	1930–1931
11	1860–1862	54	1893	B86	1912–1913	A108	1925
12	1862–1863	55	1894	A87	1912	B108	1931
13	1863–1864	56	1894	B87	1913–1914	A109	1925
14	1865	57	1894–1895	A88	1913	B109	1931–1932
15	1866–1867	58	1895	B88	1914–1915	A110	1926
16	1867–1868	59	1895–1896	A89	1913–1914	B110	1932
17	1868–1869	60	1896–1897	B89	1915–1917	A111	1926
18	1869–1870	61	1897	A90	1914	B111	1932
19	1870–1871	62	1897–1898	B90	1917–1919	A112	1926
20	1871–1872	63	1898	A91	1914–1915	B112	1932–1933
21	1872–1873	64	1898–1899	B91	1919–1920	A113	1926–1927
22	1873–1874	65	1899	A92	1915–1916	A114	1927
23	1874–1875	66	1899–1900	B92	1921–1922	A115	1927
24	1875–1876	67	1900	A93	1916–1917	A116	1927
25	1876–1877	68	1901	B93	1922	A117	1927–1928
26	1877	69	1901–1902	A94	1917–1918	A118	1928
27	1878	70	1901–1902	B94	1922–1923	A119	1928
28	1878–1879	71	1901–1903	A95	1918–1919	A120	1928
29	1879	72	1903–1904	B95	1923–1924	A121	1928
30	1879–1880	73	1904	A96	1919–1920	A122	1929
31	1880–1881	74	1904–1905	B96	1924	A123	1929
32	1881	75	1905	A97	1920	A124	1929
33	1881–1882	A76	1905	B97	1924–1925	A125	1929
34	1882–1883	B76	1905	A98	1920–1921	A126	1929–1930
35	1883	A77	1906	B98	1925	A127	1930
36	1883–1884	B77	1905–1906	A99	1921	A128	1930
37	1884	A78	1906–1907	B99	1925–1926	A129	1930
38	1884–1885	B78	1906	A100	1921–1922	A130	1930–1931
39	1885	A79	1907	B100	1926	A131	1931
40	1886	B79	1907	A101	1922	A132	1931
41	1886	A80	1907–1908	B101	1927	A133	1931
42	1887	B80	1908	A102	1922–1923	A134	1931–1932
43	1887–1888	A81	1908	B102	1927–1928		

N — NATURE

1	1869-1870	26	1882	51	1894-1895	76	1907
2	1870	27	1882-1883	52	1895	77	1907-1908
3	1870-1871	28	1883	53	1895-1896	78	1908
4	1871	29	1883-1884	54	1896	79	1908-1909
5	1871-1872	30	1884	55	1896-1897	80	1909
6	1872	31	1884-1885	56	1897	81	1909
7	1872-1873	32	1885	57	1897-1898	82	1909-1910
8	1873	33	1885-1886	58	1898	83	1910
9	1873-1874	34	1886	59	1898-1899	84	1910
10	1874	35	1886-1887	60	1899	85	1910-1911
11	1874-1875	36	1887	61	1899-1900	86	1911
12	1875	37	1887-1888	62	1900	87	1911
13	1875-1876	38	1888	63	1900-1901	88	1911-1912
14	1876	39	1888-1889	64	1901	89	1912
15	1876-1877	40	1889	65	1901-1902	90	1912-1913
16	1877	41	1889-1890	66	1902	91	1913
16	1877-1878	42	1890	67	1902-1903	92	1913-1914
18	1878	43	1890-1891	68	1903	93	1914
19	1878-1879	44	1891	69	1903-1904	94	1914-1915
20	1879	45	1891-1892	70	1904	95	1915
21	1879-1880	46	1892	71	1904-1905	96	1915-1916
22	1880	47	1892-1893	72	1905	97	1916
23	1880-1881	48	1893	73	1905-1906	98	1916-1917
24	1881	49	1893-1894	74	1906	99	1917
25	1881-1882	50	1894	75	1906-1907	100	1917-1918

P -- POPULAR SCIENCE MONTHLY

1	1872	23	1883	45	1894	67	1905
2	1872-1873	24	1883-1884	46	1894-1895	68	1906
3	1873	25	1884	47	1895	69	1906
4	1873-1874	26	1884-1885	48	1895-1896	70	1907
5	1874	27	1885	49	1896	71	1907
6	1874-1875	28	1885-1886	50	1896-1897	72	1908
7	1875	29	1886	51	1897	73	1908
8	1875-1876	30	1886-1887	52	1897-1898	74	1909
9	1876	31	1887	53	1898	75	1909
10	1876-1877	32	1887-1888	54	1898-1899	76	1910
11	1877	33	1888	55	1899	77	1910
12	1877-1878	34	1888-1889	56	1899-1900	78	1911
13	1878	35	1889	57	1900	79	1911
14	1878-1879	36	1889-1890	58	1900-1901	80	1912
15	1879	37	1890	59	1901	81	1912
16	1879-1880	38	1890-1891	60	1901-1902	82	1913
17	1880	39	1891	61	1902	83	1913
18	1880-1881	40	1891-1892	62	1902-1903	84	1914
19	1881	41	1892	63	1903	85	1914
20	1881-1882	42	1892-1893	64	1903-1904	86	1915
21	1882	43	1893	65	1904	87	1915
22	1882-1883	44	1893-1894	66	1904-1905		

PM — PHILOSOPHICAL MAGAZINE

Vol	Year	Vol	Year	Vol	Year	Vol	Year	Vol	Year
1	1798	25	1806	67-68	1826	30-31	1847	39-40	1870
2	1798-1799	26	1806	Ser. II		32-33	1848	41-42	1871
3	1799	27	1807	1-2	1827	34-35	1849	43-44	1872
4	1799	28	1807	3-4	1828	36-37	1850	45-46	1873
5	1799-1800	29	1807-08	5-6	1829	Ser. IV		47-48	1874
6	1800	30	1808	7-8	1830	1-2	1851	49-50	1875
7	1800	31-32	1808	9-10	1831	3-4	1852	Ser. V	
8	1800-1801	33-34	1809	11-12	1832	5-6	1853	1-2	1876
9	1801	35-36	1810	Ser. III		7-8	1854	3-4	1877
10	1801	37-38	1811	1	1832	9-10	1855	5-6	1878
11	1801	39-40	1812	2-3	1833	11-12	1856	7-8	1879
12	1802	41-42	1813	4-5	1834	13-14	1857	9-10	1880
13	1802	43-44	1814	6-7	1835	15-16	1858	11-12	1881
14	1802	45-46	1815	8-9	1836	17-18	1859	13-14	1882
15	1803	47-48	1816	10-11	1837	19-20	1860	15-16	1883
16	1803	49-50	1817	12-13	1838	21-22	1861	17-18	1884
17	1803	51-52	1818	14-15	1839	23-24	1862	19-20	1885
18	1804	53-54	1819	16-17	1840	25-26	1863	21-22	1886
19	1804	55-56	1820	18-19	1841	27-28	1864	23-24	1887
20	1804	57-58	1821	20-21	1842	29-30	1865	25-26	1888
21	1805	59-60	1822	22-23	1843	31-32	1866	27-28	1889
22	1805	61-62	1823	24-25	1844	33-34	1867	29-30	1890
23	1805	63-64	1824	26-27	1845	35-36	1868	31-32	1891
24	1806	65-66	11825	28-29	1846	37-38	1869	33-34	1892
								35-36	1893
								37-38	1894

S1 — SCIENCE (First Series)

Vol	Year	Vol	Year	Vol	Year	Vol	Year	Vol	Year
1	1883	6	1885	11	1888	16	1890	21	1893
2	1883	7	1886	12	1888	17	1891	22	1893
3	1884	8	1886	13	1889	18	1891	23	1894
4	1884	9	1887	14	1889	19	1892	24	1894
5	1885	10	1887	15	1890	20	1892		

S — SCIENCE (New Series)

Vol	Year	Vol	Year	Vol	Year	Vol	Year	Vol	Year
1-2	1895	11-12	1900	21-22	1905	31-32	1910	41-42	1915
3-4	1896	13-14	1901	23-24	1906	33-34	1911	43-44	1916
5-6	1897	15-16	1902	25-26	1907	35-36	1912	45-46	1917
7-8	1898	17-18	1903	27-28	1908	37-38	1913	47-48	1918
9-10	1899	19-20	1904	29-30	1909	39-40	1914	49-50	1919